Sir John Tenniel: Alice's White Knight

Publications by Rodney Engen

Walter Crane as a Book Illustrator (Academy Editions, London/St Martin's Press, New York)
Kate Greenaway (for Collectors) (Academy Editions, London/Harmony Books, New York)
Victorian Engravings (St. Martin's Press, New York)
Randolph Caldecott – Lord of the Nursery (Oresko Books, London)
Dictionary of Victorian Engravers (Chadwyck-Healey, Cambridge)
Dictionary of Victorian Wood Engravers (Chadwyck-Healey, Cambridge)
Kate Greenaway: A Biography (Macdonald, London/Schocken Books, New York)
Richard Doyle (Catalpa Press, Stroud, Gloucestershire)
Laurence Housman (Catalpa Press, Stroud, Gloucestershire)
A Country Paradise: Helen Allingham's Countryside (forthcoming)
Black Beauty (Signet/Mentor Classic new edition)

In addition Rodney Engen has written for magazines and journals including issues of *Apollo*, *Country Life*, *Connoisseur*, *Antiquarian Book Review Monthly*, *Washington Post*, *American Book Collector*, *Country Living*, *Times Literary Supplement*, *Antique Collector*.

Rare Tenniel oil self-portrait, dated 1882 (Aberdeen Art Gallery)

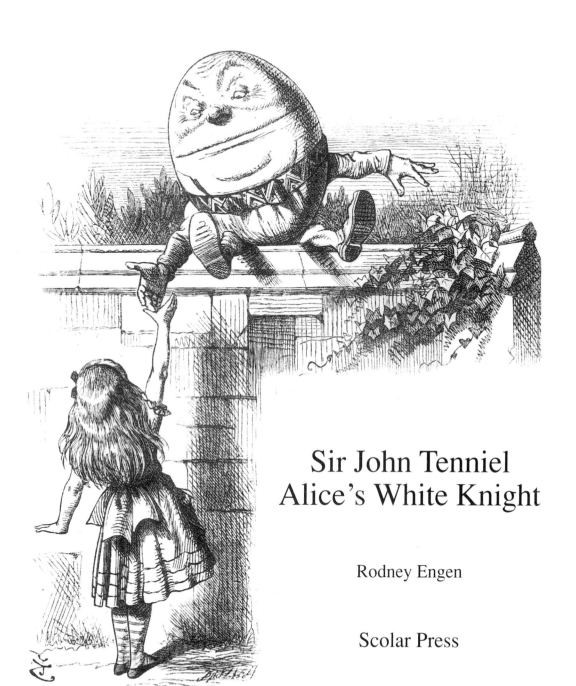

Sir John Tenniel
Alice's White Knight

Rodney Engen

Scolar Press

Published by
SCOLAR PRESS
Gower House
Croft Road
Aldershot
Hants GU11 3HR
England

Gower Publishing Company
Old Post Road
Brookfield
Vermont 05036
USA

British Library Cataloguing in Publication Data
Engen, Rodney K.
John Tenniel : Alice's White Knight.
1. England. Drawings. Tenniel, John
I. Title
I. Title
741.942

Library of Congress Cataloging-in-Publication Data
Engen, Rodney K.
    Sir John Tenniel : Alice's White Knight/Rodney Engen.
        p.   cm.
    Includes bibliographical references and index.
    ISBN 0-85967-872-5
    1. Tenniel, John, Sir, 1820–1914—Criticism and interpretation.
    I. Title
    N6797.T44E64 1991
    741.6'092—dc20   91-8130
                        CIP
    ISBN 0 85967 872 5

Printed in Great Britain at the University Press, Cambridge

Contents

Acknowledgements

The author would like to thank the following individuals and institutions for their invaluable help in the preparation of this book over the last three years: Ian Hodgkins and Catalpa Press who originally proposed the idea; Michael Wright of *Country Life,* Alice-Munro-Faure and Simon Taylor of Sotheby's (London) for photographs, Michael Heseltine of Sotheby's for advice and valuable research material; John Wilson for manuscripts; Chris Beetles for illustrations; Lady Elton and Adam Langlands of Christie's for photographs; the staffs of the British Library, Victoria and Albert Museum Library and Print Room, British Museum Print Room, Tate Gallery, City Art Gallery of Aberdeen, National Portrait Gallery, as well as my word processor operator Bob Keen, photographer Graham Bush and Thomas Schuster. In the States I was greatly assisted by Sarah Phelps Smith and Karen Peltz of the Boston Museum of Fine Arts; Sara Hodson and Robert Wark at the Huntington Art Gallery; Kenneth A. Lohf of the Columbia University Library, the staffs of the Pierpoint Morgan Library, New York Public Library Berg Collection and Print Room; Harvard University Library; and the special interest and assistance given by Justin Schiller in New York.

RKE

Tailpiece for *Punch*

1889

Sir John Tenniel. Pen and ink self portrait, 1889 (National Portrait Gallery)

1 On The Edge of Respectability 1820–1846

Sir John Tenniel, illustrator of the Alice books and the most famous *Punch* cartoonist of his day, was an elusive, enigmatic and thoroughly private figure. Throughout his ninety-three years he preferred a routine, dignified life out of the public eye; it gave him a better chance to view objectively the sweeping social and political changes which he experienced during his long lifetime. These he recorded with sure, even, seemingly effortless line – the essence of how he saw the world about him. His critics and admirers thought him the supreme representative and prophet of "higher" artistic principles. His dogged belief in "High Art" – inspired by the classics and religious themes – coloured his earliest attempts to create an artistic name for himself. While other artist colleagues bowed to fashion and sought fame, Tenniel remained quietly working away on his book illustrations and *Punch* drawings, and lived the exemplary life of the self-effacing gentleman, content to remain firmly out of the limelight. It was this enigmatic principle which dominated his long productive life.

Tenniel, the supreme Victorian, appropriately, was born during the final year of the Regency, grew up inspired by the hopefulness and prosperity of the young Queen Victoria's reign, endured and watched over the trials of her empire as well as the war and political battles of her long rule which he drew with such skill; and when the Queen died, Tenniel retired from duty the same year. He died himself on the eve of the greatest upheaval of all – the First World War – which he anticipated in his last *Punch* cartoon. Such breadth of experience through almost a century of change inevitably coloured and directed his life and his work; but in a most unexpected way. It forced him inward, deeper into the very private world which only he knew, and which he jealously guarded from intrusion. To the outside world, with its sweeping changes and turmoil, he was a supremely devoted artist, working to create drawings of unmistakable events in a hard classical style which had been long out of fashion. He seemed unaffected by competition or change; his life and career was that of the supreme gentlemanly outsider, living on the edge of respectability.

It was to some extent an inherited characteristic, for the Tenniel family were aliens to England. Their French Huguenot ancestry went back before the eighteenth century, when they had emigrated to Liverpool and endured life as strangers in a strange land, cleverly adopting English customs and occupations as befit the current fashions to help them prosper. This sense of independence was soon passed on to one of the Tenniel sons, John Baptist, John Tenniel's father. Born in 1793 he quickly mastered the tenets of respectability so vital in England, and coupled with them a desire to prosper in his own independent way. It does not seem surprising then, it was these qualities which he eventually passed on to his sons. At the age of twenty-seven he left Liverpool with his young wife Eliza Maria, for an uncertain future in Regency London.

John Baptist's talents fortunately suited the times. He developed his skills as a sportsman into a prosperous business which catered to the rising leisured class of Regency bucks and the volatile world of polite society. Indeed, the capital had recently been engulfed by an outrageous new king and his court, who helped to give London the reputation of the most opulent and extravagant city in the world. Society was filled with bored young bachelors in search of amusement, as well as in need of those gentlemanly skills necessary to maintain their position in high society. They sought inspiration from the past, were lured by the historical romances of Sir Walter Scott (recently created baronet), while their ladies dreamed of Byronic heroes. In such a climate John Baptist Tenniel emerged a successful instructor in arms of the Angelo School. Aspiring young gentlemen came to him for instruction in swordsmanship, fencing, boxing and rowing, and stayed on to learn the latest dances essential for social success in the ballroom. It was the age of Almack's, the Assembly Rooms in King Street, St James's, where the *beau monde* collected like shameless disciples in an exclusive temple. There novices nervously edged near the battery of formidable dowager patronesses whose smiles consigned the aspiring to happiness or despair. It was a world of supreme social presences where to see and be seen were paramount. As a result, the dances Tenniel taught his pupils were merely polite alternatives to the remorseless gossiping generally done on such occasions. One of the most popular new dances at the time was "the seductive waltz . . . the voluptuous waltz" (according to Byron) which some believed more graceful than the country dances, while others dismissed it as merely an excuse for "squeezing and hugging". The waltz, though, was part of Tenniel's training and on his own admission he taught it and those sports suitable for gentlemen "with unparalleled assiduity".

With the accession of Queen Victoria, the Victorian age brought new hopefulness and strong moral overtones to the education of the young. John Baptist Tenniel typically adopted his teaching methods accordingly. In his twenty-two page treatise "On the Importance of Including Personal Education in a Scheme of General Education", which he published privately in 1845, he set out those high-minded Victorian virtues on which he now ran his school. In turn he taught these to his own children. He presented his own invention, a tension exercise pole, the "Systolic and Diastolic Exercising Staff" (a forerunner of today's popular Bullworker) which, when engraved as the frontispiece to his booklet, was intended to be the key to his theories. It suited his new personal approach: "We mean the new fashion of exercising our youth in the manner which is to supersede dancing, fencing, boxing, rowing and cricket, and the natural impulse of youth to activity".[1]

His success as an instructor influenced the lives and early attitudes of the six children he and Eliza eventually reared in London. Each showed strong purposefulness in whatever they chose to do, tempered by the courtesy and parental respect they had been taught to be cardinal virtues. Of the three Tenniel sons for example, the eldest, Reginald, accepted his father's domineering influence and eventually followed in his footsteps, carried on his theories and became a dancing instructor. Another son, Adolphus, tried but eventually failed to find fulfilment under his father's dominant shadow, and he eventually left London for the independent life of a farmer. The third son, the artist John Junior, was far more responsive to his father's instruction, and while less athletic than was hoped, he accepted his father's theories and developed a much-admired soldierly bearing and courteous appreciation of the benefits of healthy sport and exercise. This he maintained throughout his long life, mastering fencing, dancing and especially rowing and riding – his two favourite pastimes. But he too maintained an independent streak, which for him took the more antisocial form of intense study and private sketching – activities which were so very alien to his father's hail-and-hearty attitude to life. As for the three Tenniel daughters, the essential tenet of respectability ruled their futures: one chose a suitable marriage with a solicitor, another married the son of the famous artist John Martin – both thoroughly admirable matches. In addition the third daughter, Victoire, re-mained a devoted spinster housekeeper and paragon of virtue and strength to her family.

John Tenniel Junior was born on 28 February 1820, the year his parents left Liverpool for London. They had settled in the then rural district of Bayswater, at 22 Gloucester Place, New Road, where there was space enough for John Senior to pursue his athletic training and for his sons to learn to ride, row and fence at

THE BABES IN THE WOOD.

Tenniel's boyhood fencing lessons inspired his *Punch* work – *Punch*, 20 December, 1890

John Martin by Charles Muss

an early age.[2] When young John was old enough, he was sent to a local private school, as befitted the respectable standards set by his father. One can imagine his father's disappointment, however, when his favourite son began to show disturbing signs of introversion; his daily fencing and riding lessons alternated with hours spent alone silently sketching, free from "healthier" disturbances. This early need for solitude and privacy was to follow John throughout his working life. A dutiful son, he recognized from his father's pupils the standards of gentlemanly behaviour expected of a young man about to be launched into the polite world of the drawing room, yet he never felt comfortable in such a world. If given the chance he preferred his own company or at best small groups of artist friends, and shunned the formalities of society for his own carefully devised social routine. He had an endearing wit, a dry, intellectual sense of humour which he fed on great doses of classical and theatrical literature. He especially loved Shakespeare and could quote whole passages from his plays, sometimes twisting the lines into puns or comic *double-entendres*. The theatre appealed to him from an early age; the spectacle of elaborate costumes, historical settings and exaggerated acting was to haunt him all his life: in fact his earliest attempts to draw were inspired by the theatre, in which he brought together the stilted sophistication of the drawing room with the farcical qualities he would later master so well in his *Punch* cartoons.

He was attracted to religious themes as well, largely through his associations with the popular biblical painter John Martin. The Martins were in fact firm family friends, and the great painter was one of young John's earliest and most impressive mentors. He would never forget the early glimpses he received into a successful artist's life, and he often visited Martin's crowded, fascinating studio. Here were the famous massive biblical canvases, more recently the engravings and the "Last Judgement" series which were some of the earliest book illustrations young Tenniel studied closely. Moreover, his mentor possessed that admirable independent attitude toward his profession which Tenniel would share and later try to emulate. While Martin's vast canvases like "Belshazzar's Feast" commanded substantial sums (it sold for 200 guineas in 1821), serious critics (including John Ruskin) dismissed his success and popularity. And yet Martin was proud of his good fortune; according to one influential admirer he was "the most justly celebrated artist whose wonderful conceptions are the finest productions of modern art".[3] A man just four years older than Tenniel's father, he too had left home in the provinces for opportunities in London, had prospered there and raised a large family which he loved to share with his distinguished friends and houseguests. The elder Tenniel children were occasionally invited to delightful social evenings, where they might meet some of the period's most distinguished political, literary, artistic or scientific figures. On one occasion, for example, the Irish poet Tom Hood sang one of his Irish melodies, "placing himself at the piano forte, with a fascinating smile and glance at L.E.L [unidentified], Caroline Norton, Isabella Martin (the painter's daughter), and the lovely sister of John Tenniel".[4]

Of the three Martin sons, Alfred, Charles and Leopold, it was Leopold who became John's closest friend at this time. He was an endearing fellow, whose godfather and namesake was his father's prestigious patron, Prince Leopold of Saxe-Coburg. He nurtured artistic ambitions of a similar nature to his new friend's and the two young men were often seen sketching together; their artistic experiments soon influenced the other two Martin brothers, who would later try their hands at drawing for *Punch* (presumably under Tenniel's tutorage). It was John's beautiful sister though who eventually bridged the gap between the two families when she agreed to marry Leopold, thus joining the Tenniels and the Martins by marriage.

At the moment John and Leopold were content to pursue their ambitions to become famous artists. They took sketchbooks to London's Townley Gallery, where they drew classical statues; later they read and copied from illustrated books of costumes and armour in the Reading and Print Rooms of the British Museum. For Tenniel this was inspired work. Here he learned to love detail, to make meticulous mental notes and sketches of costumes, to study the differences in native dress in such faraway lands as the South Sea Islands, or such ancient sources as medieval manuscripts which he copied under the friendly guidance of Sir Frederick Madden, Keeper of Manuscripts at the Museum. It was during these painstaking sessions sketching from old documents and books that Tenniel became impatient, disillusioned with his work. He was happy, he discovered, only when he could draw from memory what he had previously studied so carefully in the museum. Fortunately he was blessed with a photographic memory – a mixed blessing which would undermine his early training and seriously restrict his artistic ambitions.

No doubt influenced by the current taste for massive canvases of exalted scenes from the past, as well as his mentor John Martin's success, Tenniel decided he too would train to become a historical painter. The most successful

John Martin's *Paradise Lost*, 1827, inspired young Tenniel

history painters, it seems, had studied at the Royal Academy Schools; those giants like Benjamin West; Benjamin Haydon, the high priest of "High Art"; Daniel Maclise and William Dyce – all favourites with Tenniel. Their canvases sought to glorify the past by using scenes from historic battles, the Bible, or even incidents from Walter Scott for their inspiration. Such work was most often filled with masses of figures and required a thorough knowledge of human anatomy as well as historic costumes and uniforms. This knowledge, according to contemporary thought, could only be gained from a thorough study of classical casts and sculpture, and the Royal Academy Schools were the most prestigious venue for such study. There prevailed impenetrable doctrines, unchanged since the rise of

Tenniel's costume study of the George II (1751) period

Sir Joshua Reynolds's dictum, "an implicit obedience to the rules of art", which continued to dominate the school. So it was that Tenniel attempted to join the Academy Schools. By then the Academy had moved from Somerset House on the Thames to the new National Gallery building in Trafalgar Square. Here he applied for admission and became a probationer, which meant he had to endure a long period of copying from classical sculpture in the British Museum to provide the necessary admission portfolio – "at least six accurately finished drawings of groups of figures from the antique . . . accompanied by other drawings as large as nature of a hand and foot". The work required discipline and patience, for drawing sessions were entirely unsupervised. According to the Art Union at the time, this was "not only imprudent but positively dangerous...the idleness, the irrevocable waste of time, the fatal acquirement of a vicious or incorrect style of drawing is perfect ruin in after life".[5] Tenniel though, was encouraged by his struggling colleagues, especially two determined fellow probationers J.C. Hook, who later succeeded well enough to be elected RA for his landscape paintings, and Henry Le Jeune, the future ARA and noted genre painter. They joined with Tenniel, persevered and won through the first round of obstacles set by the Academy Schools admission committee, each obtaining a place there. There were, though, serious grounds for misgivings, especially by Tenniel, who agreed with another fellow student about their preliminary training so far:

Leopold Martin, pencil portrait by Tenniel, 1837 (Sotheby's)

> The British Museum, where I had commenced the special study of the human figure, was in many respects not the best drawing school for a tyro. The Pheidian marbles realise one type of perfect human form, but the mutilations they have suffered make few of instructive value for the copying of a novice who has not a connected knowledge of human proportions.[6]

Once they had been admitted to the school, new discouraging obstacles reenforced Tenniel's doubts. He learned that a student was expected to spend a further year in the Antique School, copying those classical casts and sculptures which he had just spent so much time mastering. Then, when one reached the coveted Painting School, all teaching was by means of copying from a selection of paintings, a practice continued until 1847, and even then the use of brush and paint was resisted for as long as possible. The Life Class was intended to give a student a thorough knowledge of anatomy before paint was applied, but here a stream of constantly changing senior academicians and accomplished visitors (including Maclise, Mulready, Stanfield, Landseer and Turner) drifted in and out; they were changed each year to provide only brief, fragmentary and often – to the chagrin of the students – contradictory tuition. Moreover, the new school premises were cramped and awkward; the Life Class was placed in the "pepper box" – an octagonal dome-covered room at the top of the east wing – while the annual Academy summer exhibition cleared the students from their usual gallery work spaces.

Despite these obstacles Tenniel continued to nurture his artistic ambitions. He began to experiment with paint and at sixteen he produced an acceptable equestrian picture, "The Stirrup Cup", which was not only his first work accepted for exhibition – at the prestigious Society of British Artists where John Martin had launched some of his best work – but also found a buyer. It hung alongside his fellow Academy student Richard Dadd's painting, "Head of a Man", and caught the eye of the visiting Irish actor Tyrone Power, who bought Tenniel's picture, and who three years later purchased Dadd's "Don Quixote", for he was a keen admirer of new painting talent. This proved a considerable morale boost for young Tenniel, and he began to wonder whether he might continue his studies away from the rigours of art school.

By this time Tenniel was proud of his independence and openly disagreed with the school's teaching methods. "I never learned drawing," he proudly recalled years later and continued in a defiant tone: "Except in so far as attending a school and being allowed to teach myself . . . . I attended the Royal Academy Schools after becoming a probationer, soon left in utter disgust of there being no teaching. I had a great idea of High Art!"[7] It was this "high" ideal, inspired by his history painter mentors, which spurred him on to return to his own independent studies at the British Museum, where he concentrated upon books of costume and military engravings. At the Tower of London he developed a life-long interest and expertise in armour, in later years owning a collection of arms and armour on which he could speak with authority. He became obsessed with the past, especially medieval and Tudor details, which gradually extended into later periods, as his colleague the medieval-revival painter Henry Stacy Marks recalled:

> With fourteenth-century hood and liripipe (long tail on the hood), Elizabethan doublet and hose, the wig and jack-boots of Queen-Anne's time, and all the manifold changes that dress has undergone in this country from the earliest to the latest times, he is perfectly acquainted . . . He revives the sports of hunting and hawking, tilting at the ring or quintain (sandbag on a pole), and the joust and tournament, where the "queen of beauty and love" sits smiling amid the clash of arms and the fanfare of trumpets, ready to reward the victim with a laurel wreath.[8]

Tenniel's student companions encouraged his private studies. He had recently befriended Thomas Harrington Wilson, an aspiring landscape and genre painter who accompanied him to the National Gallery to make sketches of historical

Tenniel sketchbook studies of exotic costumes and animals (Huntington Art Gallery)

detail for his own paintings. Wilson concentrated upon faces and figure poses as well as costumes, and in later years he became a famous theatrical portraitist. Tenniel concentrated upon accuracy in whatever subjects he chose. A sketchbook from this period, which still survives, hints at the diversity of the subjects he chose: apart from a page of aboriginal costume sketches native to Borneo, and a rather plaintive looking chimpanzee, he drew Zulu and other African tribal costumes and an Indian dancer, as well as items borrowed directly from nature. There are some especially fine pencil sketches of the beach at Shanklin, Isle of Wight, notably a collection of wickerwork crab traps on the sand, their stone weights and twisted ropes carefully pencilled in. Tenniel clearly accepted the necessity and value of such nature study, despite his outspoken claim that he drew best only from memory.[9]

In the age of Turner, Landseer, Etty and Mulready, when classical subjects vied with romantic landscapes of sublime effects, the young aspiring painters wisely sought more manageable subjects on which to launch their careers, and Tenniel was no exception. A popular painting theme among new Academy exhibitors was a narrative; a scene from a popular drama or novel like those in Sir Walter Scott's picaresque works, filled with stirring characters which appealed to many a budding history painter. Tenniel was especially fond of Scott and, fresh from his early exhibition success at Suffolk Street, he began to paint a series of scenes from his favourite, *The Fortunes of Nigel*. According to Scott's publisher, this was "a brilliant account of London in the days of James VI of Scotland and Ist King of England. Some of the character studies, such as that of the King, are among the best of the Waverley novels." Tenniel's paintings of it were successful enough to launch his debut at the Royal Academy, where they appeared regularly from 1837 to 1843. The first was "Captain Peppercull interceding for Nigel with Duke Hildebrand", which was chosen to hang in the

Tenniel study of military costume, from the British Museum (Sotheby's)

Crab traps – Shanklin beach, Isle of Wight, by Tenniel (Huntington Art Gallery)

first summer exhibition in the Academy's new building. The competition for wall space that year was staggering, as an apologetic note in the catalogue explained: "It may be proper to observe that, in consequence of the great number of works sent for exhibition this year, it has been found impossible to assign places to many of those which had been accepted." Tenniel's Nigel series brought together in strong, clear outline the elements of costume study and illustrative detail which had preoccupied him for so long. On the other hand it was a bid for popular acceptance, for those familiar with the story (and there were many) found some of their favourite characters brought to life in his paintings. They renewed impressions gained while reading the struggles of the unfortunate Nigel Oliphant, Lord Glenvarloch, as he battled for his ancestral estate. He duelled with the wicked Lord Dalgarno, escaped to Alsatia where he fell in love with Margaret Ramsay, a clockmaker's daughter, who pleaded his case before the King, then married Nigel and eventually helped him to recover his estate. For other paintings in the series, Tenniel chose the more eccentric characters like Captain Culpepper, the goodly messenger, or the inimitable, po-faced Dame Ursula Suddlechop, milliner and secret agent who dominates part of the story. Tenniel later painted her as a shuffling, matronly landlady administering to the bemused and despondent Nigel in "Doleful Dumps".

Tenniel continued to exhibit successfully at the Royal Academy, and had one picture accepted annually for the next seven years (see Appendix III for a complete list). The competition was keen, however. In 1843 his enchanting "Willie Courted Jenny" was chosen for exhibition as just one of 1,500 entries

"Doleful Dumps", watercolour by Tenniel, 1888, based upon Scott's *Fortunes of Nigel*: "Jim Vin threw himself into Dame Ursley's great leather chair and declared himself the most miserable dog within the sound of Bow Bells".

selected that year. It was a measure of his determination to succeed that he achieved slow but steady progress, and this in the face of a disastrous personal calamity which would have broken a less determined young artist.

The disaster occurred in 1840, when Tenniel was twenty. One day he joined his father for their ritual daily fencing match, and during the struggle his father's protective button fell off the tip of his foil, and the sharp blade flicked across his son's right eye, blinding it. Despite the seriousness of this accident, Tenniel kept his terrible injury a secret from his father, whom he was certain would have been crushed by guilt. Tenniel in fact never seems to have shown the slightest hint of resentment or anger at such a seemingly serious setback to his artistic career. "He regarded it merely as an annoying, though not very important, accident", a close friend later recalled. "Being satisfied that the Almighty had only given us *two* eyes as a measure of precaution, to provide against such vexatious accidents as he had experienced, he went on working as if nothing had happened." Some later critics attributed the distortion in his drawings to his disability; but Tenniel remained determined to ignore it as much as possible. In the end "it only made him more careful".[10]

John Tenniel at 24, pencil portrait by G.I.R., 1844 (National Portrait Gallery)

An early portrait of Tenniel by "G.I.R", dated 1844, tactfully avoided his blinded eye with a profile view from the left. It clearly showed the glint of his remaining good eye, the high, prominent forehead and upright posture of a sturdy, determined individual, with only a light upturn of the mouth to suggest his carefully cultivated sense of humour. Indeed, the few friends he accepted into his confidence at this early stage in his career admired him not only for his artistic skills, but for his love of comedy, his quick wit and fund of clever word games. He had begun to collect favourite verses, which he called "bout-rimes", and from 1840 he copied the best into a book which he illustrated with slight, comic sketches of round-faced medieval knights in full armour, or sailors with doughy-looking faces and clown-like poses. Here were the early seeds of his later comic *Punch* drawings, set down at his leisure, whenever he found a passage in a verse story which appealed. The stories were strong on adventure, predictably filled with valiant crusaders and their forlorn maidens. In "A Pleasant Poem of ye Portleye Paladin and his pensive Page" he also wrote the following verse around a drawing of a rotund knight on horseback with his poor, threadbare page alongside:

> The Boy was young, but sorrow deep and care
> Had bade each thought of joy and hope depart
> And through his bristled features soft and rare
> Was traced stern disappointments bitter smarting.

Tenniel was also attracted to those popular exotic gift-book themes of romances set in Spain or some more remote country which formed the basis of so many engravings and verses at the time. He chose the verse romance of the ill-fated Widdicombe and Susan, as well as the familiar chivalric themes of knights returning from battle to their fair maidens. In "Lord Tremain", he experimented with illustration and the text in a composition for a page, taken from the scene of the noble lord's triumphant return home:

> Blow a long blast for Lord Tremain!
> He's been and won the fight again
> His blows were loud
> And well he doubl'd the dastard crowd.

Here Tenniel incorporated handwritten text within an elaborate herald's banner which he decorated with surrounding roundels to tell of the brave knight's conquests. It was an indication, even at this early stage, of his skills as an illustrator, as were the clever swashbuckling characters he stretched across two pages of "A Son of yr Sea Serpent" by "Julia". Its eight verses were joined by a fearsome sea serpent writhing through the lines and terminating in a fearful beheading.[11]

This playful, comic side to Tenniel's character was generally reserved for private moments with his few friends; to the world he was still an aspiring, serious-minded painter with "high ideals". He was a frequent and much welcomed guest of the Barretts, a jovial family with a talented son, Thomas, who became Tenniel's close friend. The Barretts were pleasantly receptive to Tenniel's flashes of wit; they encouraged and entertained him with the struggling young artist Charles Keene, over casual, relaxed dinners which stretched into entertaining evenings filled with jokes and puns. Mr Barrett was a meek, mild-mannered "Mr Caudle-type" husband; a tall, very thin figure who signed himself "5-12ths". This was in contrast to his jovial, outspoken and plump wife's "nobler proportions"; a woman he claimed to be "unquestionably his 'better half'". They would join the three young artists after dinner when, seated in the lamplight, they would discuss the latest additions to the composite book of illustrated parodies, *The Book of Beauty*, which they composed together. It was a project which mercilessly parodied those popular gift-books filled with romantic verses and grey steel-engravings of Shakespearean themes, or portraits of perfect feminine beauty like *The Book of British Beauty* or *The Keepsake*, which graced the tables of many middle-class drawing rooms. In their uninspired blandness and unashamed inferiority they seemed to the critical young men the perfect subject for ridicule. Indeed, they produced striking full-page designs on that proven formula: Charles Keene chose comic versions of the signs of the Zodiac; Tenniel, with his wide knowledge of literature, chose favourite quotations from Shakespeare and dramatic scenes from history and the opera, as well as his favourite poems, to transform into his own brand of witty parody; all drawn in bright coloured chalk. One later critic praised Tenniel's contributions for "the humour being infused into them being equal to anything he afterwards produced in *Punch*".[12] While this is perhaps too sweeping a claim, his chalk drawings do prefigure some of his best *Punch* cartoons as well as his Alice illustrations. For example, he chose themes from Hamlet to transform the ghostly figure of Hamlet's father, in long white beard stalking the battlements alongside his rather foolish-looking son, into a moonlight farce: "Thus twice before, and jump at this dead hour/ With martial stalk hath he gone by our watch." (Act I, scene 1) In a second drawing, he chose the final banquet scene when the King promises to drink to Hamlet's health and victory with a poisoned cup:

The King shall drink to Hamlet's better breath
And in the cup an union shall be throw,
Richer than that which four successive kings
In Denmark's crown have worn: give me the cups,
And let the kettle to the trumpet speak,
The trumpet to the cannoner without,
The cannons to the heavens, the heaven to earth,
"Now the King drinks to Hamlet" (Act V, scene 2)

Scene from *King John*, black, chalk sketch by Tenniel 5½ x 8¼" (Christie's)

Here Tenniel interpreted the lines literally, and devised a striking Carrollian

Tenniel's chalk drawing to the *Book of Beauty* "And let the kettle to the trumpet speak . . ." 6¹/₄ x 9¹/₄" (Victoria and Albert Museum)

fantasy in which the kettle and trumpet, dressed as courtiers in raven-emblazoned tunics, speak to a worried cannoneer of the disasters to come.[13] Although the entire project was meant only for private amusement between friends, the book was eventually exhibited and many of the drawings broken up and sold, despite Tenniel's and Keene's misgivings. Thinking "very little of them as art", Tenniel was especially surprised "that in their rubbed condition they should attract any notice whatever".[14]

Apart from his annual Royal Academy entries Tenniel had some sixteen works accepted at the Society of British Artists over the years, although he understood that acceptance there lacked the prestige he sought to launch his painting career. The Suffolk Street gallery had, after all, been founded by a rebel group of artists in 1824 and remained a secondary venue despite its Royal charter in 1847, and the impressive exhibitions held in its elegant Nash-designed premises off Pall Mall. He also accepted the serious deficiency in his anatomical studies now that he had left the Academy Schools. He half-heartedly began to attend Dr Roger's lectures on anatomy, but they too failed to inspire. He still preferred his own approach and continued to have some success with this rebellious attitude. Like many of his art-student colleagues, he sought exposure for his work in an era when discontented painters banded together to help promote themselves and teach each other necessary skills. His contemporaries, the celebrated "Mal-contents" – composed of Richard Dadd, William Powell Frith and Augustus Egg – were a successful example, who met and worked together on subjects set by them (usually literary themes from Shakespeare or Byron), to prepare their entries for major London exhibitions. This was in the face of what they regarded as an unfair monopoly by academicians, but what some regarded cynically as an attempt to "get their innings before their time".[15]

Tenniel joined one of these groups in the mid-1840s. It was called the "Artist's Society or Clipstone Street Life Academy" – a misnomer since no-one actually taught there. Instead, in its ramshackle premises just off Fitzroy Street, north of Oxford Street, professional artists and aspiring painters gathered to draw from a live model (alternate weeks nude or costumed) which was selected and posed by the members themselves. Similarly the school itself was managed by a committee of its members. Here, free from the rules that stifled, Tenniel worked as he pleased, although the facilities and premises themselves were far from Royal Academy standards, set as the school was all on one floor in a makeshift series of large sheds in a stonemason's yard. Eventually a library of art books and wardrobe of period costumes was acquired and loaned out to members "under certain regulations". On Friday evenings the Sketch Club held its regular meetings, with a fixed set given for two hours, followed by a critique. Here for the first time Tenniel was allowed to work alongside professionals as well as struggling artist illustrators like himself. It exposed him to men who sought the necessary skills for his future life as an illustrator draughtsman. Indeed, the Clipstone's members were some of the period's most promising artists and engravers of the illustrated book; men like the Dalziel brothers (destined to become Tenniel's future engravers), and their fellow engraver J.R. Clayton.

Of the aspiring illustrators at the Clipstone, his most trusted and closest colleague was the eccentric bohemian Charles Keene, who lived the true romantic artist's life in lonely disordered squalor. Having given up promising law studies and a career in architecture to train as a wood-engraver and draughtsman on wood, he now attended the Clipstone to perfect his woodblock drawings. Tenniel would learn much about the private nature of the illustrator's life from this one unique friend. Keene was a courteous yet uninhibited man, famous for his eccentric habits. His studio was filled with flint tools, books, prints, armour and musical instruments which he collected; a dusty and inaccessible place in the squalid back-streets off the Strand, which Tenniel often visited and where he acquired his own collector's fever. Just three years Tenniel's junior, Keene lived a relatively uneventful life punctuated by essential visits from his friends, who provided him with most of his ideas to meet the soul-destroying daily deadlines, drawing for papers like the *Illustrated London News*. His real comfort was a plaintive love of music, especially the baleful cry of his beloved bagpipes which he would take into the country to "torture". Essentially hermetic by nature, Keene, like Tenniel, avoided society and preferred the routine life of his own making. This made him one of Tenniel's most devoted friends and a kindred spirit: "His ways were always so simple and retiring, his life so entirely uneventful, so far as I know it", Tenniel marvelled years later. Obviously still impressed by Keene's admirable self-effacing habits, he added, "and he was, moreover, so reserved in all matters concerning himself, especially in connection with his art".[16]

Tenniel greatly admired this retiring, seemingly ineffectual friend. Yet on the other hand his own character revealed flashes of daring and a willingness to express himself publicly. It was a curious dichotomy in this most private of men. He admired actors for their ability to express themselves, especially when placed

Charles Keene in his studio by W. Corbould (National Portrait Gallery)

outside the standard conventions. This one tenet had fired his love for the theatre. For example, he followed the fate of the period's greatest Shakespearean actor, now turned theatre-manager, William Charles Macready. Once famed for his Shakespearean revivals which had brought ovations but little financial success to Covent Garden, by late August 1843 he prepared to tour America to try his luck in the New World in the successful footsteps of his beloved Dickens. It was then that Macready received one of his devoted fans, the aspiring artist John Tenniel, who made enough of an impression to merit inclusion in Macready's diary: "August 22 1843, A Mr. Tenniel called to see me", he noted before he set off to dine with Mrs Caroline Norton, Lord Melbourne and the Sheridans.[17]

At this time, Albert, the Prince Consort, helped to bring a distinct Germanic influence to the arts in England, especially in the popular fields of decoration and illustration. Young craftsmen, designers and illustrators now looked to Germany for fresh influences, and the inspiration they found there took the form of a crisp, hard-edged classicism, heavy woodcut medievalism and a religious preoccupation best seen in the works of the Nazarenes. The new mentor to a generation of illustrators was undoubtedly Adolph Menzel, whose recent triumph, a set of wood engravings to Kugler's *History of Frederick the Great*, 1840 (English edition 1843), helped to change the face of English illustration. Artists like Tenniel and his generation looked to the Germans for models. When Charles Keene discovered Menzel's distinctive medievalism he changed his own sketchy, loose approach so successfully that he was later compared favourably with the German. Tenniel too found strength in the Germanic sense of history; that unashamed borrowing from the past which he had always admired. It was a lesson he learned well and, coupled with the Germanic sense of assured ornate design, it would serve him for the remainder of his career.

In the face of such foreign competition, worried English critics and government officials looked for their own distinct national style to combat the Germans. Tenniel's first book illustration commission was done in this spirit, for Samuel Carter Hall's verse anthology *The Book of British Ballads* was intended to rival the very best German (and French) illustrators. Hall gathered together a promising battery of twenty-seven artists and wood-engravers, not all of them well-known names, but those he thought most capable of producing a national style for his patriotic publication, issued in two parts in 1842 and 1844. The unashamed unevenness of styles was intended to emphasize the diversity of English talent, although a third of the book's illustrations were done by John Franklin, Hall's "sheet anchor", and recently successful illustrator of that other nationalistic enterprise, the Eglinton Tournament. The younger generation was represented by Tenniel, who was joined by his fellow Academy student Richard Dadd and his innovative circle of draughtsmen, E.M. Ward, Thomas Joy, William Powell Frith, and William Bell Scott, as well as the more established wood draughtsmen like John Gilbert, Kenny Meadows and Alfred Crowquill. Their drawings were interpreted by a rising generation of reproductive black-line wood-engravers like James Linton, Edmund Evans, George Dalziel, W.T. Green and John Bastin. Each contributor was carefully selected by Hall, who explained in his preface how they "apply the great and admitted capabilities of British Art, as to prove that the embellished volumes of Germany and France were not of unapproachable excellence, in reference either to design or execution". In a double-edged compliment, he dedicated the book to "Louis (Ludwig), King of Bavaria", that famous patron of those German artists who now seemed such a threat to their English counterparts.

Eccentric and single-minded as Hall undoubtedly was, he and his team of artists and engravers compiled what is today generally recognized as a pioneering volume. It set standards and the vogue for heavily illustrated poetic anthologies of the type Tenniel was to spend a good part of his spare time illustrating over the next few years. Indeed, this first commission gave Tenniel the confidence to consider working as a professional illustrator. His part in the project began when he was summoned with his fellow artists in the spring of 1842 to "The Rosary", Hall's Brompton cottage. There they were given coffee and biscuits (Hall was a devout teetotaller) and waited to receive their illustration assignments and the wood blocks from Hall himself. Hall was, as always, a thorough if not obsessive editor who jealously supervised each step in his book's production. His little soirées, as he loved to regard these editorial meetings, began when he read out each ballad to the assembled artists before allocating them for illustration. "They were brilliant evenings when so many young artists – all of rare promise – assembled at The Rosary", he recalled. Not every guest shared his enthusiasm, however. The rebellious Kenny Meadows and William Powell Frith, for example,

HEARKEN to me, gentlemen,
Come and you shall heare ;
Ile tell you of two of the boldest
brethren
That ever borne y-were.

The tone of them was Adler younge,
The tother was King Estmere ;
They were as bolde men in their deeds,
As any were farr and neare.

"King Estmere" from S.C. Hall's *Book of British Ballads, 1842* waited impatiently until they could escape the pious atmosphere of The Rosary for the more congenial atmosphere of their favourite local pub. There they drank into the small hours "with the rueful consequence for Meadows who arrived home with the milk, which 'pretty well settled' his wife's query about the time".[18]

To the novice like Tenniel, Hall's doctrinaire manner must have seemed occasionally trying, but then he was a difficult character to understand. Dickens had immortalized him, much to his chagrin, as the architect and arch-hypocrite Peckersniff in *Martin Chuzzlewit*; Ford Madox Brown called him "Shirt-collar Hall" because he was so "starchy". Yet his industry and dedication were models of Victorian virtue: he not only wrote numerous books on subjects as far-ranging as art, temperance and spiritualism, but he edited the *Art Journal*, filling it with exemplary engravings that boosted its circulation, while his wife accepted his influence over her own prolific literary career – she wrote and compiled some 250 books.

For his newest project Hall gave his artists a choice of three ornate decorative borders within which they were to work. Tenniel provided ten drawings on the blocks given to him by Hall to fit these restrictions and although he had never before drawn on wood, he managed skilfully. He was allotted the appropriate medieval tale of knights and a royal wedding of King Estmere set in Moorish Spain, which echoed his favourite Widdicombe *bouts-rimes* romance. He drew the King and his Spanish bride in clear, even Germanic-style line and took special care with the battle scene and the final equestrian composition, the processional of the King and his bride surrounded by the loyal knights which were to become a familiar Tenniel theme and were reused in compositions several times. Significantly, it was Tenniel's ten drawings, and those delicate fairy roundels by his colleague Richard Dadd, which attract the only favourable critical notices the book receives today; a curious fact considering the importance of the project as a whole.

About the time Tenniel was engaged on *The Book of British Ballads* illustrations, the government announced its own initiative to promote a truly national school of art. It took the form of a series of ill-fated public competitions for fresco designs (cartoons) to decorate the new Houses of Parliament. The plan was a noble one, inspired, ironically, by German models. It would, in time, help change the path of Tenniel's career. The first competition ended in a much-heralded exhibition of the winning cartoons in July 1843, when all 140 competitors assembled their chalk or charcoal designs based upon inspiring scenes from British history, the works of Spenser, Shakespeare or Milton, to the general enthusiasm of the public who paid an admission fee and flocked to study them. Yet only two of the winning designs were eventually completed in fresco. The competition marked the beginning of a long and frustrating series of similar contests organized by the Royal Fine Arts Commission with Prince Albert as its chairman. Fresco had been adopted on the advice of that German master of the medium, Cornelius, and his champion, the Prince Consort. They had persuaded the committee of fresco's suitability for so monumental a decorative scheme. At first the round of competitions and exhibitions caught the nationalistic public mood and the crowds flocked to Westminster Hall to see examples of great British artists' work. *Punch*, on the other hand, found the entire enterprise a farce in the present terrible "Hungry Forties", "The poor ask for bread, and the philanthropy of the State accords – an exhibition.".

Two further competitions and exhibitions were held in 1844. Then in the following year more specific subjects were announced for the prestigious House of Lords competition. Only six allegorical themes were to be considered, composed of allegorical designs representative of the spirits of religion, chivalry and justice. It was this new competition which Tenniel, with his love of allegory and medievalism, chose to enter. He decided upon the Spirit of Justice for his theme and worked hard on the rigorous and demanding entry requirements to meet the June 1845 deadline. The committee prescribed not only a full-sized cartoon to fit an arch (16' x 9'3"), but also a coloured sketch and, most difficult of all, a specimen fresco to indicate a candidate had mastered this most difficult of mediums. It was a daunting and expensive business and critics were quick to point out the prohibitive costs to new artists at a time of national economic depression. On the other hand, the rewards were tantalizing: three premiums of £200 each. No doubt inspired by his own burning belief that he "had a great idea of High Art" – for this was indeed High Art, to have one's design immortalized in the nation's parliament – Tenniel suffered the expense and the frustrations and entered the competition. As he discovered later, he was in inspired company, for many of the country's most successful history painters, like his mentors Maclise and Dyce, had entered the competition as well, and it was their work against which Tenniel's was to be judged.

Unfortunately the deadline for entries passed without Tenniel's submission. He had never worked in fresco before, and like most of his colleagues he found the medium daunting. He wisely chose to complete his coloured sketch first, with the cartoon and fresco sample to follow. It was a shrewd decision for, in the words of a contemporary, fresco painting demanded considerable patience which even the professional would find trying:

> In executing paintings in fresco the necessary preparations are the sketch, the cartoon in full size cut in suitable pieces, – the (powdered) colours prepared with water only, and the two sorts of plaster, the rendering and finishing coats on which the picture is to be painted, the painter's mind must be full of his subject; everything must be pre-determined on, as no alteration or amendment can take place: he must have a rapid and decisive execution, and be well acquainted with the qualities of his colours, as they dry lighter when laid on . . .. The colours must be dashed on at once, in a broad, bold and general manner, that with which an able artist must produce a grand style.[19]

In the end, Tenniel did complete a fresco sample, which he sent with his coloured sketch and a half-finished drawing for his cartoon, and an apologetic note to the committee secretary, the noted history painter Charles Eastlake. Despite his late entry and his half-finished cartoon, he still hoped to be considered for the premiums: "According to the requisition published by the Commissioners of the Fine Arts, I beg to send herewith a colour'd sketch of the Allegory of Justice together with a specimen in fresco – and a cartoon – which last I regret to say, owing to illness, is but a sketch."[20]

Tenniel's entry design was a clever synthesis of those High Art models he had long admired. His Spirit of Justice borrowed from Raphael's famous fresco stanzas in the Vatican, with classical draped figures skilfully posed in a formal architectural setting, as well as more familiar devices used by contemporary history painters. In fact his design echoed his rival Daniel Maclise's "Spirit of Justice" entry, although Maclise's figures were not as firmly classical, well-drawn and noble as Tenniel's. He chose a winged angel for Justice to dominate a rising staircase, mounted to the right by her good subjects, to the left by the evil.

Tenniel's award-winning design, "The Spirit of Justice" which was lithographed but never fresco painted

It was a bold, confident if derivative performance, especially by an unknown artist of twenty-five.

Much to Tenniel's delight, his design was chosen for one of the £200 premiums (the other two going to Edward Armitage and Joseph Noel Paton for designs depicting the Spirit of Religion). It was a short-lived triumph, however. As with most of the previous competitions, the results were riddled with controversy and ill-feeling. Nine of the unsuccessful competitors petitioned for a division of the proceeds earned by the entrance fees charged to the exhibition of their work – a familiar disagreement which helped to sour the art world against these and further competitions. More to the point, Tenniel's triumph was turned into farce when his abilities to paint in fresco in such an important building were called into question. Although he retained his prize money, he was tactfully requested to give way to the more accomplished Daniel Maclise, whose inferior Spirit of Justice fresco was eventually completed in 1849. Tenniel, on the other hand, was asked to provide designs for a new and smaller (8' x 5$\frac{1}{2}$') fresco to help fill the Upper Waiting Hall of the House of Lords. Again the subject was dictated – one of six on poetic themes – but unlike so many previous competition winners, Tenniel's designs were now actually carried out. He chose Dryden's muse of music, St Cecilia, borrowed from his "A Song for St Cecilia's Day", and attempted an oil sketch of his subject before work began on the fresco itself. To help placate any ill-feelings he might have, the committee awarded him £400 for his trouble.

The money and commission allowed Tenniel to visit the continent for the first time in his life. He set his sights on Germany, that home of monumental fresco designs, and planned a visit to Munich, where the supreme master Cornelius and his assistants had established a highly organized school of fresco painters under the keen tutorage of their patron King Ludwig. Tenniel was joined on the journey by such budding artists as the painter Edward Henry Corbould, soon to become Instructor of Historical Painting to the Royal Family, and several less successful colleagues. All were intent on learning first-hand this difficult new medium, for although fresco went back as far as ancient Greece, it had only recently been revived in Europe. Tenniel's German experience was to have unlimited influence over his future work. There he came into contact with work by the celebrated Nazarenes, who attempted to revive through religious themes the elemental yet romantic medievalism of the early Italian painters. There too he discovered Dürer's hard-edged mastery over woodcut line, those heavy yet intricate designs which his disciple Burgmeyer perfected in his "Triumph of Maximilian" series of equestrian woodcuts which Tenniel, in later years, would own and "discourse lovingly" over as the jewels in his collection of medieval art.

Tenniel returned to London fired with renewed determination to emulate his German mentors, not only in his fresco of St Cecilia, but the book illustrations which would occupy him over the next thirty years. Unlike his fellow fresco painters, he was meticulous and thorough, and had learned his technical lessons in Germany well. The quick-drying lime and plaster which he spread on the framework of laths to take his design did not suffer the fate of his less careful colleagues, whose work was destroyed by the ubiquitous English dampness which seeped into the lathwork. In fact Tenniel's St Cecilia survived valiantly; well into the twentieth century his design remained unfaded and undamaged by dampness in its niche in the Gallery of Poets, a faint yet reproving presence which would, he hoped, establish his artistic reputation.[21]

Not everyone accepted the value of German art, however. Some felt it undermined national virtues with a forced sense of piety; it was that "New German dandy-pietical school" according to Thackeray's acidic Mr Michelangelo Titmarsh. Richard Doyle also parodied the public's blind acceptance of the High Art ideals implicit in the Westminster fresco competition entries in his *Punch* cartoons and his book, *The Rejected Cartoons*, 1848. But with royal approval, the Teutonic invasion gained momentum and, as the Queen bought paintings by Dyce and Maclise and those disciples who borrowed from this new fashionable style, it found its way into books and prints, illustrated translations of medieval German tales, and wood-engraved drawings of fashionable German artists like Ludwig Richter, Otto Speckter or Alfred Menzel.

It was in this spirit that Tenniel's next book illustrations were created. His developing interest in all things medieval and German was to gain him Ruskin's double-edged compliment: "I said that had Tenniel been rightly trained, there might have been the making of a Holbein, or nearly a Holbein in him."[22] This first published experiment with Germanic themes appeared in a new translation of the favourite German folktale, Undine. The Queen loved the story and in fact had recently given her beloved Albert a birthday painting of Undine by Maclise. The version by Friedrich Baron de la Motte Fouque, the German romantic writer of medieval tales, had enjoyed great popularity in Germany, and later in England, where it first appeared illustrated with Dürer woodcuts. Tenniel was asked to illustrate a new edition which, from the design, format and binding, was clearly intended to appeal to the medievalist vogue of the time. His designs were surrounded by rusticated borders of dense, intertwined branches suggestive of those medieval manuscripts that he had studied at the British Museum. His wood-engraved frontispiece of courtiers in coloured tunics on horseback set against a dense foliage background was engraved in a style the Dalziel brothers called the Germanic "shaded outline school", and showed Tenniel's clear homage to Dürer and the German Old Masters. He provided eleven drawings for these engravers, mostly used as chapter headings. The figures remain poor, their poses wooden, while only their costumes are carefully rendered; but their horses – the most successful of his drawings – are bold and powerful. The story of the ill-fated marriage between the good knight Huldbrand von Ringstetten and Undine, the sylph daughter of the wicked water goblin Kühleborn, had all the gothic and supernatural elements which would in time appeal to Tenniel's inner nature. It combined his favourite strain of historic romanticism with his love of knights and chivalry. While his illustrated version of the story went into several printings during his lifetime, later critics dismissed his illustrations as insignificant hackwork. It was a mere period piece which had suffered too much from heavy-handed engraving and fashionable medievalism. It pointed Tenniel in the right direction though and gave him an encouraging outlet for his growing illustrator's skills; for this he was soon to be extremely grateful.

Tenniel's "Chivalry", an early parliamentary spoof, chalk drawing 6 x 9" (Christie's)

2   In Search of a Name
1846–1860

By the late 1840s Tenniel felt confident that his artistic career was well-established. Still intent upon a painter's life, he was practical enough to realize the financial benefits of the occasional illustration commission which would allow him time to paint. He had the advantage of a courteous, gentlemanly manner which impressed many prospective patrons – and their daughters. When Tenniel called on the prosperous print publisher Mr Lloyd of Lloyd Brothers, Ludgate Hill, he impressed this valuable acquaintance well enough to be invited home to meet his daughter and to discuss with him a possible print from one of Tenniel's paintings. Miss Lloyd was immediately taken by the handsome artist in his mid-twenties then in his "salad days", as she later recalled; she was obviously fascinated by such "a good-looking, dapper, bright, well-set-up young artist". [1] Indeed had he been more sociable, he would have been regarded as one of the more eligible bachelors of his generation. Instead, he generally remained distant and aloof from the world, devoted solely to his artistic and sporting interests.

A rare display of Tenniel's public spirit combined with a boyish love of adventure took the form of his application for a special constable post during the terrible Chartist riots in London in April 1848. Tenniel joined several of his friends to help the Duke of Wellington defend the city and was given a decidedly dangerous beat in Kennington, South London, where it was said a monstrous demonstration was to be held on 10 April, with the possible rioting of citizens set against the police. It was not something Tenniel relished, for afterwards, when fewer demonstrators turned up than were expected and the meeting ended quietly, he breathed a sigh of relief. He had only taken the position "hoping I shouldn't have to fight anybody"; and he would remain a life-long opponent of violence. He shared this view with the artist John Leech, who had also joined the forces and been given the ominous nocturnal patrol (10pm–1.00am). Afterwards he too decided "only loyalty and extreme love of peace and order made me do it". [2]

With the growth in the number of illustrated editions of poetry on publishers' lists and booksellers' shelves came a demand for competent draughtsmen illustrators who could turn their talents to a diversity of poetic subjects. Tenniel was soon regarded as just such an artist, and he agreed to contribute illustrations to five new volumes by 1848. These were experimental works, which allowed him to perfect his medievalism and the technical skills necessary to draw quickly and clearly on wood blocks, working under the pressure of deadlines.

The first volume was for a minor children's poetry anthology series *Poems and Pictures*, in which Tenniel's illustrations to "The Children in the Wood" appeared in 1846. It was followed by four more significant volumes in 1848. For an edition of Milton's *L'Allegro and Il Penseroso* he created a composition of knights bowing to their enthroned King. He set it within a curved arch which echoed his Spirit of Justice fresco design, to accompany lines in Milton's *L'Allegro*: "Towered cities please use us then, And the busy hum of men, where throngs of knights and barons bold, In deeds of peace, high triumph hold." It was engraved on wood by the Dalziel brothers, set alongside work by some of his most talented contemporaries, like Richard Doyle, J. Absolon, Frederick Goodall, E.H. Corbould and Kenny Meadows. It was published in a large folio edition by the Art Union of London, to help support their invaluable work commissioning new artists, selling their prints and holding the lotteries which often offered books as prizes. That same year Tenniel reused the equestrian knights theme in the three drawings for "The Death of King Henry III" and "The Price and the

Tenniel's design to Milton's "L'Allegro" for the Art Union of London, 1848

"The Dog Invited to Supper" from *Aesop's Fables*, 1848

Outlaw", which appeared in *The Juvenile Verse and Picture Book*. Here he experimented further with page design and planned the illustrations to run alongside and to separate the blocks of text.

This preoccupation with page design was perfected in a third book that year; one which marked a turning point in his illustration career. It was announced as "a new version" of Aesop's Fables, taken "chiefly from original sources" by the Reverend Thomas James, MA and published by John Murray. Tenniel's friend Leopold Martin had introduced him to Murray and eventually it was agreed he would provide a hundred and six drawings to the ninety-six page book. Most of these were based upon his early animal sketches done while visiting the London zoological gardens in Regent's Park and drawn (according to the author's preface) with "a kindly spirit . . . the happy results of his skill". They remain some of Tenniel's most accomplished early animal drawings, despite glaring anatomical errors like poorly proportioned arms and legs – a problem which would plague his entire career. The book sold well, and only when a new edition was compiled in 1851 did Tenniel agree to make necessary corrections to his animal drawings to harmonize with the twenty new cuts added by the accomplished bird and animal painter Joseph Wolf. The *Art Journal* called Tenniel's Aesop "Germanic" and pointed out how his figures as well as animals relied upon areas of deep shadow and sharp, clear sculpted outline. Especially good were the drawings of lions, foxes and goats, a splendid camel and a sinewy weasel, as well as a bravura single-page composition of flying beasts from hawks to bats that would catch the eye of Lewis Carroll and convince him of Tenniel's suitability for his Alice book.

The printers of the Aesop were Bradbury and Evans, who printed Tenniel's fourth and most prestigious book of drawings that year. For several years Charles Dickens had produced an annual Christmas story which he published with illustrations by his friends Daniel Maclise, Clarkson Stanfield, John Leech and Richard Doyle. 1848 was to be no exception, and Tenniel was asked to submit five drawings to his latest Christmas story, *The Haunted Man and the Ghost's Bargain,* to appear alongside drawings by Clarkson Stanfield, Frank Stone and John Leech. Tenniel's work unfortunately suffered from weakness and was overtly derivative. Moreover, he found his friend Dickens a hard taskmaster with artists and a serious judge of illustration as well as a man who demanded complete obedience to his dictates. Tenniel's frontispiece medallion of swirling gnomes encircling a seated man, overshadowed by a ghostly figure, was intended to set the tone of the story, but it lacked the invention and strength of more accomplished fairy illustrators like Doyle or Maclise. Indeed his witch drawings and curiously tortured gnomes echoed Doyle's drawings to Dickens's *The Chimes* three years earlier. Yet Tenniel's trailing chapter headings and swirling initial letters, in which he incorporated aspects of the story, are distinct hints as to where his illustrative talents lay. The book itself was, as always with a Dickens story, a popular success; it sold 18,000 copies on publication day (19 December 1848) alone. This was followed by a successful dramatization by Mark Lemon at the Adelphi Theatre and a joyful celebration "Christening" party for the book at Dickens's Devonshire Terrace home in early January, which Tenniel attended with his fellow illustrators.

Among the numerous recent illustrated comic papers which attracted the most devoted readers was the popular satiric weekly *Punch, or The London Charivari*. Founded in 1841 upon a Parisian model, *Punch* soon became the most successful and respected satiric paper, filled with witty observations on current events, numerous puns, fiery attacks on the church and government (which soon lost their strength), and a mixed assortment of wood-engraved illustrations, comic initials and full-page political cartoons. The *Punch* staff of journalists and illustrators occupied positions of considerable power in the eyes of their devoted middle-class readers. By the mid-1840s the political and social cartoons were provided by the talented and prolific John Leech, while the decorative initials and comic illustrations were drawn by that remarkable prodigy Richard "Dicky" Doyle, who astonishingly had joined the paper in 1843 at the age of nineteen and quickly gained a devoted public. His travel series, "Brown, Jones and Robinson", set a fashion for parodies upon the typical English tourist abroad; his gentle, respectful views and careful political portraits tempered the fiery tone of *Punch*'s more radical staff members.

In November 1850 Doyle shocked his fellow *Punch* staff members and his public by resigning from what had become one of the most prestigious posts in

Tenniel's early pen and ink design for *Punch* uses favourite animals (Victoria and Albert Museum)

illustrated journalism. He protested against the paper's recent scathing attacks on the Catholic Church, in particular the Pope's decision to re-instate an English cardinal. A member of a staunch Irish Catholic family, Doyle could not reconcile the paper's position with his family's devout religious stance. By remaining on the *Punch* staff, he compromised his religion, which he refused to do. Such were the strengths of his argument that he refused to reconsider his position, despite pleas from colleagues, Thackeray and *Punch*'s editor Mark Lemon. In fact his resignation left Lemon in considerable difficulties. Doyle had neglected to complete his annual almanack designs before he left, and the annual *Punch* almanack was eagerly awaited by its devoted readers. The editor was left in a desperate position, unable to find a replacement for Doyle at very short notice. The staff too had turned against "Dicky" Doyle and they continued to publish stinging attacks on the papacy and even attacked Doyle's resignation as "Very Ridiculous".[3]

During the frantic course of events that November, Mark Lemon was shown Tenniel's Aesop illustrations (probably by the fierce anti-papist Douglas Jerrold). At first glance it is difficult to imagine how these almost classic animal drawings should suggest to Lemon a suitable comic replacement for Doyle, but then Lemon was in a desperate position with a weekly paper of over thirty pages to fill as well as a growing circulation of readers devoted to Doyle's comic inventions. The almanack drawings were equally important since its annual publication alone accounted for considerable sales and once boosted *Punch*'s circulation figures from 6,000 to 90,000 in one week. Doyle and Leech had created a much awaited work in a finished style where Doyle's elaborate and intricate borders of fantasy or social themes competed with Leech's half-page social satires. So in some desperation, Lemon wrote to the Aesop publisher, John Murray: "Dear Murray – Who is this young man whom you have found to illustrate Aesop? He seems the sort of person we want: please send him to us."[4]

Meanwhile, Tenniel was unaware of the *Punch* crisis and considerably taken aback when Lemon's invitation arrived. It was a flattering offer to join *Punch*'s senior artists like Kenny Meadows, John Gilbert and Alfred Crowquill, whose work he had admired while collaborating on *The Book of British Ballads* commission. But joining *Punch* meant he would have to compromise his High Art ideals and painter's ambitions by taking up a full-time position as an illustrator. True, his painting had been pushed further into the background over the recent years and he now found little time to paint as he struggled to earn a living from illustration, and the Aesop illustrations were obviously much admired. In the end Tenniel accepted the *Punch* offer, reluctantly at first, as he suggested to a friend: "Do they suppose there is anything funny about *me*?" He doubted his abilities to create humorous sketches on demand, "mere foolings" as he called them, to satisfy the dictates of *Punch*. The paper's staff was eagerly awaiting his decision; and years later he recalled his surprise when "I went down to the Punch office forthwith, with a letter from John Murray introducing him to Lemon, and I was engaged there and then".[5] His first drawing in fact appeared on 30 November, three days after Doyle's resignation. It was a small but distinctive initial letter with a cavalier about to mount his horse – an appropriate subject for one about to launch a fifty-year long career of obedience to the powerful dictates of Mr Punch.

In some respects Tenniel was right to doubt his comic potential; his later *Punch* cartoons were often criticized for their stiff, austere classicism. Yet over the years he enjoyed a considerable reputation for his dry wit and benign presence on the paper. This convinced him he had a special type of humour to contribute: "Now I believe that I have a very keen sense of humour and that my drawings are sometimes really funny", he retorted to his critics in the 1880s.[6] It was not easy to take up where his inimitable predecessor had left off, however. Dicky Doyle's endearingly boyish view of the world in "Manners and Customs of Ye English", his clever storybook initials filled with dragons and knights, ladies in peril or suitors in pursuit, were favourites with *Punch* readers. At first Tenniel wisely chose merely to imitate Doyle's fantasy style, although he drew these on the wood block in a firmer, more evenly shaded line with occasional inventions from the medieval world gradually to suggest that a newcomer had supplanted Dicky Doyle. He even initiated his own travelogue variant of Doyle's popular Brown, Jones and Robinson, and invented the ineffectual yet intrepid foreign traveller Peter Piper, a bumbling sportsman who hunted buffalo across the American prairie and Bengal tigers atop an elephant in India – all with the inevitably disastrous results.

St. George and the Dragon, initial "S" for *Punch*, 1857

The break in Tenniel's reliance upon Doyle's formula came in the issue of 1 February, where Tenniel's first full-page political cartoon appeared. It was in fact a blatant attack on Doyle's religious stance and used Doyle's favourite Jack-the-Giant-Killer theme to depict Lord John Russell as Jack, and Doyle's friend Cardinal Wiseman (the new English cardinal) as the menacing giant. Later it was said that this was the only *Punch* cartoon with a scriptural basis, but Tenniel dismissed it as "awfully bad", obviously embarrassed by its crude conception. It is not known whether Tenniel was fully aware of his position with respect to Doyle's resignation, or indeed whether he had firm religious beliefs. One recalls his French Huguenot ancestry, and later his religious paintings of Christ and Adam and Eve in "The Expulsion". What is certain is that this first cartoon was an effective attempt to purge himself of the Doyle legacy and to declare his own hand as the new *Punch* illustrator. The work that followed – full and double-page political cartoons, half-page comic spoofs on current fashions, and even his own satiric article on the meeting of the Philoperisteron Society of pigeon breeders in London – firmly established Tenniel as a solid, reliable and conscientious worker on *Punch*. His success was measured by the fact that some of his earliest cartoons were republished that same year in the *Punch* tenth anniversary issue, as well as in the issue commemorating the Great Exhibition of 1851. His first almanack borders were by then composed of distinctive Tenniel subjects: medieval scenes from life around the countryside with knights and serfs in the fields enjoying seasonal country pleasures, celebrating harvest festival, and in the December segment the king and his loyal subjects ice-skate on the local pond. They were strong, confident linear designs, engraved on wood by *Punch*'s engraver Joseph Swain, who did much to clean and simplify Tenniel's early style. As for Tenniel, he later looked back upon his early *Punch* career with horror, telling an interviewer "in fact, all my work, at that particular time NOW seems to me about as bad as bad could be, and fills me with wonder and amazement".[7]

He also discovered his *Punch* work inspired new plans for paintings and exhibition work. In May 1851 he broke an eight year gap at the Royal Academy by exhibiting a topical design called "Sketch for a large Picture in Progress, Representing Allegorically the Great Industrial Meeting of All Nations in 1851". The *Art Journal* (now edited by his old patron S.C. Hall) enthusiastically praised such a worthy idea, with its "pyramidal composition, the apex of which is occupied by Britannia and Peace". It was in one sense a restatement of his early Westminster Hall fresco success. This perfectly suited the theme of the Great Exhibition, while "an examination of the figures shows great command of resource, and an inexhaustible fund of invention".[8]

By the end of 1851 Tenniel found himself more dependent upon *Punch* than he had at first anticipated. He was now well-paid (Doyle had received £200 a year, Tenniel's annual salary was £500 by 1861), and the large number of drawings required each week, while a strain, provided him with some financial security at last. He felt he could at least afford to leave home and he took rooms at 24 Newman Street, north of Oxford Street, within streets of the Clipstone Academy where he could conveniently continue to sketch from models.[9] The move was a considerable step upward for the thirty-one-year-old bachelor; it marked a further sign of his need for independence, especially from his past. On days when he was not occupied drawing for *Punch* he frequented the theatre and opera. With a small notebook on his knee, he made quick sketches from the productions which he hoped to incorporate into *Punch* cartoons. Throughout the 1840s and 1850s he fed this passion for the theatre by regularly attending performances. He heard and marvelled at the melodic brilliance of Jenny Lind, who had taken London by storm. He continued to befriend actors like Charles Kean and William Macready. He was also a keen opera fan and was especially delighted by the virtuosity of Giulia Grisi when she appeared in "Norma" in 1855; he also marvelled at the astonishing breath control of the Neapolitan bass Luigi Lablanche. The world of the theatre became his treasured means of escape and as it happened a rare source of occasional true happiness. Not until total blindness and old age prevented it did he abandon these visits to the theatre and the opera; even then he treasured the theatrical photographs he had carefully collected over the years and the memories of past performances they represented.

There is also evidence that despite Tenniel's reserve he could have become an impressive actor. When Charles Dickens invited him to play Hodge, servant to Sir Geoffrey Thornside, in a special amateur production of Bulwer Lytton's five-act costume drama, "Not So Bad as We Seem", Tenniel agreed and achieved critical acclaim for his performance. Although an amateur production the play was far from makeshift and even received a royal premiere. As with all of Dickens's theatricals, it was the result of long rehearsals and arduous planning by the author as well as his talented actor and artist friends. The performance was in aid of the Guild of Literature and Art , a charitable fund set up by Dickens to assist artists and writers in need. For three days a week Tenniel interrupted his *Punch* work and joined Dickens to rehearse his part on a converted stage in the library of Devonshire House, where it was to be staged. These were gruelling, prolonged sessions for both actors and their director. Dickens moaned

> My legs swell so, with standing on the stage for hours together, that my stockings won't come off. I get so covered with sawdust among the carpenters, that my infants don't know me. I am so astonishingly familiar with everybody else's part, that I forget my own. I roar to the troupe in general, to the extent that the excellent Duke (who is deaf) thinks in the remoteness of his own little library that the wind is blowing hard.[10]

Finally, after a dress rehearsal on 14 May, two days later the play was premiered before the Queen. A large audience paid five guineas each for their seats and as the overture, played by the Duke's private band, heralded a remarkable evening, the curtain rose. The scented footlights shone on sets designed by David Roberts

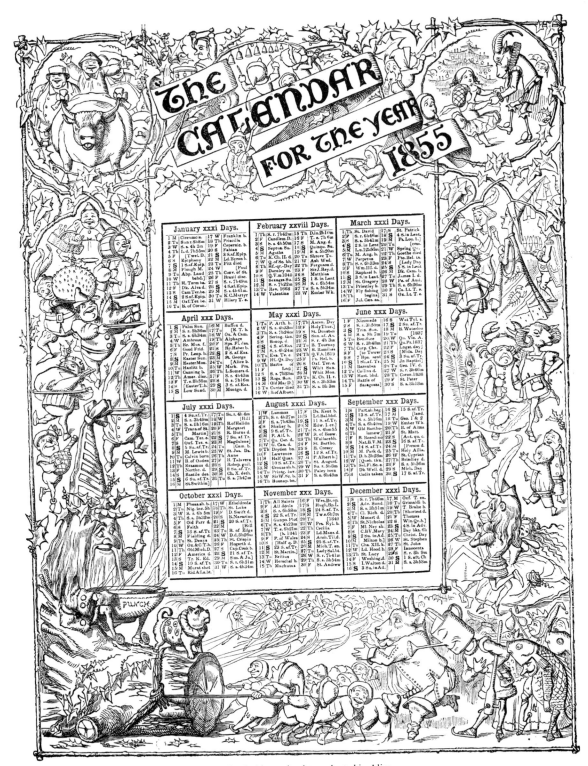

Tenniel's *Punch* almanack design for 1855 uses whimsical invention later adopted in Alice

and Clarkson Stanfield, and eighteenth-century period costumes designed by Augustus Egg. Dickens took the lead assisted by Tenniel, Topham and Wilkie Collins, and their performance ended in rapturous applause. Afterwards the Queen dined beneath a gothic archway decorated with roses, magnolias and jasmine and festooned in orchids, with opals scattered to simulate dew. It was one of the most inspired evenings of Tenniel's short acting career. Their patron, the Duke, was so pleased he insisted upon a second performance in his house on 21 May, which was followed by an even more sumptuous ball and supper; then the play moved to Hanover Square and opened to the general public until early August.

As the Christmas season approached Tenniel rushed through his *Punch* almanack designs in order to free himself for a return to his acting role when the play toured the provinces. He performed first in Bath, then Clifton in November 1851. Then followed sporadic performances throughout 1852 in Manchester and in Liverpool, which the company left "blinded by excitement, gas, and waving hats and handkerchiefs". In May they were in Shrewsbury and Birmingham before ending the tour in the Midlands and North, with a grand total of some £3,000 raised for the Guild. Dickens was thrilled by their success and delighted that his actors made such a good impression. "You have no idea how good Tenniel, Topham and Collins have been in what they have to do", he wrote to Forester from Sunderland. In Manchester Tenniel's performance alone was singled out for praise in the local press. On tour the thirty-plus company of actors, stage-hands and director took over the principal hotel in each city and after the performance those of Tenniel's *Punch* colleagues who followed the tour appeared backstage for hilarious dinners with local dignitaries and amused fans. These high-spirited evenings echoed their own *Punch* editorial dinners, the childish antics of their friends, the games of leap-frog around the supper table shocked yet delighted the guests, especially once when the devilish Mark Lemon made a "high back" to prevent anyone from clambering over his massive frame.[11]

Elements of romance appeared in Tenniel's work at this time, clear indications of a growing desire to express his inner feelings in his work. Although he had learned the value of suppression and restraint from an early age, and his classical style echoed that tendency, occasionally he lashed out and drew strong melodramatic poses – expressions of frustration, pain, or the grotesque suffering of the gothic aspects of life which surprisingly attracted him. Struggle seemed to highlight his own dilemma: he drew women struggling against evil, knights battling enemies, prisoners fighting to escape. Inevitably, the aftermath of battle, the peaceful end to suffering, and the lure of death were also favourite Tenniel themes. He chose one, based upon a significant religious story, for his next Royal Academy entry. This was accepted for hanging in 1853, and was called "The Expulsion from Eden", the theme undoubtedly borrowed from John Martin as much as his beloved Dürer's medievalism. Here Adam and Eve cower beneath the oppressive gaze of a large hovering angel, which was "a very grand realisation" according to the *Art Journal*. He chose Milton's verse to accompany the painting: "The world was all before them, where to choose their place of rest". It was a well-conceived entry, for critics that year noted how many of the Academy's entries had strong religious themes ("scriptural themes have this year met with new exponents"). Here too impassioned Pre-Raphaelite longings were represented by such works as Millais's "The Order of Release" and Holman Hunt's "Claudio and Isabella". Tenniel's entry again received considerable

"Figures in a Park", early watercolour, 8 x 10", on a romantic theme by Tenniel
(Huntington Art Gallery)

critical attention, the prestigious *Athenaeum* reviewer pointed out his Adam and Eve was "lofty in sentiment, skilful in composition, correct in drawing, and forcible in expression". But in an age of German artistic influence which made many suspicious, and with standards at the Academy having fallen dramatically over the past four years and High Art suffering from too many imitations, the *Athenaeum* stuffily concluded its review: "Mr. J. Tenniel, whose cartoon has shown what he can do in the higher regions of Art, justifies his pretentions. He has a fine conception of his subject, his figures are admirably drawn, and the colouring appropriate." Unfortunately the painting was hidden away in the North Gallery, alongside watercolours by Edward Lear and John Linnell, which the *Art Journal* critic thought very unfair: "The picture merits a better place." [12]

Romance played a vital role in those subjects Tenniel now chose to illustrate. The seventeen allegorical designs he provided for Martin Tupper's *Proverbial Philosophy*, 1854, were published alongside those by John Gilbert, Birket Foster and Thomas Dalziel (John Martin had promised to contribute but failed to deliver designs). Tenniel chose those subjects most representative of his own personal approach to the world. For the chapter "Of Thinking", he drew a dreamy, pensive bachelor in love, while above him flew the tempting spectre of lust, a bearded lecherous satyr clutching a terrified woman's breast as he floats through the air. The text preached discipline and restraint, hallmarks of Tenniel's view of the world and of the true gentleman in love:

> But liker to the passions of man, which rejoice and expand
> in exertion;
> Yet live not wholly on thine own ideas lest they lead thee astray.

Similarly, for the chapter "Of Joy", he drew a beautiful, dark, hauntingly

"Of Thinking" from Tupper's *Proverbial Philosophy*, 1854, on the theme of lust

seductive Italianate woman being lifted aloft by angels: "His love is pure and single, sincere, and knoweth not change." Here was his ideal woman, a foreshadowment of the woman who was soon to become his own beloved wife.

The Victorian vogue for chivalry, which raged throughout the 1840s, with full expression at the Eglinton Tournament – a fully staged medieval joust – represented to many those inspired "old world" virtues of courtesy and respect for tradition. It was a philosophy which also played an important role in Tenniel's art and life. He regarded himself as a supreme gentleman, not unlike those whom his father had trained. As a result, he kept himself aloof from those things (or people) that he did not find worthy of his attention. A struggling freelance, he also found the precarious financial worries especially trying. In 1854, for example, he had completed drawings for the publisher F.M. Evans and still remained unpaid. Finally in August the money arrived and his response was typical:

My Dear Evans, This is to thank you very much indeed for the cheques and to say that if my frequent applications have been in any way troublesome and annoying to you – how much I regret it – and to assure you that they have been no less so to myself. I quite agree with you that the present mode of settlement is more agreeable to me, decidedly so.

He was polite at all times, but cold and even harsh in his judgement of the unsympathetic changes in the world. He preferred the past, when knights worshipped fair damsels and virtuous ladies waited patiently for their return from battle. Such stereotype images inspired many of the period's most stirring works of art; reactions against the loss of virtue and romance in an era of social "progress": "The stage, the drawing academy, and the costume-book, have always intervened between him and the outer world", his fellow reactionary artist and medievalist, the painter H.S. Marks recalled of Tenniel. "His sympathies are less with the present than the past. Modern dress is awkward and uncouth to Tenniel's way of thinking." [13]

Part of Tenniel's retraction from the world was related to his own sense of alienation; that he was an outsider kept firmly from the pressures of the present by his belief in the past. He honoured social conventions and was devoted to his friends; yet he might shun them in favour of very private longings. When emotional upsets threatened he turned further inward, away from the world: so it was that he chose to marry a woman on the outside of conventional life. Her name was Julia Giani, an Italian-born spinster of twenty-nine, five years his junior, who suffered from poor health. She no doubt appealed to Tenniel's chivalrous instincts with her weak constitution and, by Victorian standards, ageing spinsterhood. When in 1854 he proposed marriage to her, he was clearly echoing the man in love from "Of Thinking" in *Proverbial Philosophy*. They married probably outside London (the marriage was not recorded in the city), and spent a short yet blissful two years together in a very private happiness. Tenniel chose a large house for them on the northern edges of London, at 3 Portsdown Road, Maida Hill (now Vale). This was of an impressive size, and over the years he filled it with his collection of armour and antiques, bronzes, casts of favourite equestrian statues and hung his workroom ("my den") with unsold paintings and drawings; he still had room for a studio adjoining the house. There, he and Julia spent what one source described as a "vividly happy married life". Curiously Tenniel kept his wife very much to himself, not even letting his most intimate friends know about his happy marriage and its mounting complications.

Indeed, by the end of their first year of married life Julia began to show alarming signs of weakness. Tenniel's illustrations perhaps hinted at his worry and frustration at this period. He was thrust into a seemingly defenceless position, trapped by his wife's ill health, yet unable to help her. He chose a passage from Byron's *Childe Harold* and drew a stern self-portrait in battle armour; a knight about to leave his frantic love for the dangers and uncertainty of battle. In *Punch* he selected a scene from Shakespeare's *Henry VIII* and drew the evil Henry in a carriage alongside a bound and trapped Anne Boleyn: "Sweetheart, I were unmannerly to take you out, and not to kiss you."

Then, as Julia endured bouts of coughing and the loss of weight which were symptoms of a most serious illness, Tenniel was forced to watch helplessly. The doctor had diagnosed phthisis – that all too familiar Victorian disease commonly known as tuberculosis which, according to law, had to be certified. For several

"Of Beauty" from Tupper's *Proverbial Philosophy*, 1854, recalls Tenniel's own contentment

months Tenniel nursed and watched over his beloved wife as she slipped further from him; a victim of a disease that claimed 13 per cent of London's population at the time and was especially prevalent in persons, like Julia, under forty-five. Then on 23 January 1856, Julia Tenniel died, aged just thirty-one. Her tragic death left Tenniel crushed; according to a close friend "he seemed never to forget his bereavement".[14] It marked a low point in his life and seriously undermined his career; he stopped work on *Punch* and went into mourning for several months. When he did reappear in *Punch* in early March, it was with a series of prophetic, doom-ridden images: for example, he chose a significant scene from Shakespeare's *Romeo and Juliet* to portray a grief-struck Romeo staring into a shop window selling poison so "that the life-weary taker may fall dead".

No new book illustrations appeared the year of Julia's death; the prolonged period of mourning Tenniel observed would only be interrupted by his weekly *Punch* duties. Fortunately, Julia's mother, Eve Giani, was a sympathetic soul concerned by her son-in-law's extreme grief, and she agreed to move into their Portsdown Road house to serve as his housekeeper and friend. She remained there for the next twenty-three years, as devoted to Tenniel as he was to her.

The offers of book illustrations which arrived over the next three years were in one sense a godsend, for they helped temporarily to take Tenniel's mind off his grief. Again the subjects he chose showed his preoccupation with the turbulent world of romance, the struggles to conquer heartbreak and evil. The element of gothic horror, of supernatural forces, ghosts and unexplained presences which lay under the surface of so many of Tenniel's drawings now resurfaced in a stronger light and provided the basis for some of his most powerful if exaggerated drawings. It is not, therefore, surprising that Tenniel struck up a friendship with Richard Doyle this year, for Doyle was not only his talented predecessor on *Punch* but an avid collector of supernatural tales and legends, which he turned into eerie fantasy watercolours much admired by Tenniel. His new friend visited Doyle's studio to exchange tales of the supernatural and over the years to see the remarkable fairy compositions Doyle created using luminous lighting effects; the glow of moonlight shining through white cloud which Tenniel – himself a keen student of atmospheric effect – found so appealing. He loved Doyle's more distant, ethereal effects: so much better, he decided, than the usual halo round the moon used by less talented artists.[15]

During the early months of 1857, the wood-engravers the Dalziel brothers tactlessly sent Tenniel a series of deeply painful romantic subjects to draw on wood blocks. He was still immersed in mourning his beloved Julia and, despite efforts to draw what was required – scenes of beautiful Italian women with their suitors on bended knees, proposing marriage – he objected that they were too reminiscent of his recent loss. Yet he did not entirely refuse the offers at first; he

Richard Doyle's "A Midsummer Knight's Dream", in a style admired by Tenniel

admired the Dalziels' work and wished, characteristically, to please them. In fact he completed three book commissions for them by the end of the year: *The Course of Time* by Robert Pollock, *Dramatic Scenes* by Barry Cornwall, and the anthology *The Poets of the Nineteenth Century*. This last book was a source of unexpected traumas, when the Dalziels wrote to ask for two new subjects to add to the six Italian and equestrian subjects he had already completed. One was to accompany the deeply suggestive poem "The Coronation of Inez de Castro" by Felicia Hemans, in which King Pedro mourns his lovely Inez's death, the dark-haired beauty so reminiscent of Tenniel's beloved Julia ("under the parted ebony hair. . ."). Pedro's despair took the form of a painfully suggestive eulogy:

> Death! Death! Death! Canst thou be lovely
> Unto the eye of life?

He passionately addresses his beloved Inez:

> Who call'd thee strong as death, O Love? Mightier thou wast and art.

It was this twelve-stanza poem which Tenniel refused to illustrate and returned to the Dalziels for, "although a good one" he found it "*very* painful. I should not like doing it on that account." The poem was subsequently illustrated by his

"And thou wilt then be mine?" from Barry Cornwall's *Dramatic Scenes*, 1857, 3½ x 3⅛"

colleague John Gilbert. Subjects of a similar mournful and poignant nature continued to arrive from the Dalziels until Tenniel grew so impatient with them he flatly refused to cooperate further: "I wish you would find me two subjects instead of those which I return herewith – something with more action or incident in them. I am quite tired of *love subjects*, they permit so little variety of treat-

Douglas Jerrold, the influential *Punch* journalist

Death scenes dominated Tenniel's career, here to "The Norse Princess" by Alex Smith, *Good Words*, March 1963, p. 201

ment."[16] Even the seemingly innocent anthology Barry Cornwall's *Dramatic Scenes* proved too suggestive, although Tenniel did agree to draw for the melodramatic "Ludovico Sforza", in which Frederico, the handsome Italian suitor, drops on his knees to beg the love of the beautiful Italian Giana (surely a name suggestive of Tenniel's beloved Julia Giani) and poignantly asks her: "And thou *wilt* be mine, my beautiful? How fondly will we love through life together; and wander heart-linked thro' the busy world, like birds in an eastern story."

This sense of loss plagued the year and was compounded by the news in June of the death of his first champion on *Punch*, the fiery-tongued journalist Douglas Jerrold. This effusive, controversial playwright, journalist and author had devoted the last sixteen years of his life to *Punch* where he achieved popularity and success for his celebrated "Mrs Caudle Lectures" series, and notoriety for upsetting Richard Doyle with his stinging attacks on the Catholic Church. Above all his death marked the passing of the radical element in *Punch*, which was soon replaced by the more gentle, respectful satires of Tenniel's generation. Tenniel therefore agreed to attend Jerrold's funeral with his colleagues, while Dickens, Thackeray and Mark Lemon were pallbearers. The ceremony and final resting place in Norwood Cemetery was "thronged with gentlemen celebrated in literature, the drama, and fine arts", according to one observer. It was yet another poignant reminder of the tragic side of life, when death and the supernatural could unexpectedly force its way into Tenniel's carefully ordered life.

It was not surprising that the following year Tenniel's work continued to be preoccupied with death. The dark mystery of unknown forces in nature would always fascinate him; if only to provide an excuse for his more accomplished experiments with atmosphere and lighting effects. Ghosts and spirits played a part in some recent work, like the full-page colour-plate "The Unexpected Guest" he produced for the *Illustrated London News* at the end of 1857. It was an effective experiment with spectral effects suggested by light – here the bright light of a guardsman's lamp shone on the heavily cloaked ghost of a returning soldier long assumed dead. Although as a colour-plate it was poorly wood-engraved and printed, it does show Tenniel was willing to put the lessons he learned from Doyle into practice at this time. His skills in manipulating effects of highlights and deep shadows to define moods were best confined to black and white, however.

Those book designs Tenniel produced in 1858 were ghoulish variations upon the same theme. He agreed to provide four illustrations to a new edition of Robert Blair's *The Grave*, which later critics praised for their clear, even outlines, drawn "in his best Alice manner". Atmospheric effects predominated the four brooding drawings to Edgar Allen Poe's *The Raven*, where he combined an intensity and mood of latent terror achieved through the exaggerated facial expressions of the tormented man. He was more confident, however, with medieval subjects; those groupings of knights in battle or the carnage of war which borrowed heavily from the Germans. These first appeared in the prestigious new vehicle for major illustrators, *Once a Week*, from 1859–1861. He chose Scandinavian legends, translations from Goethe, as well as poems inspired by medieval England: "The Song of Courtesy" by George Meredith inspired a sketch of Sir Gawain in the issue of 9 July 1859. They appeared alongside work by such noted masters of the rising generation of "Sixties School" illustrators as Millais and Phiz. The intention of *Once a Week* was to rival the success of Dickens's popular magazine *All the Year Round*. Tenniel's drawings were generally published as page fillers,

Tenniel mastered atmospheric terror in Poe's "The Raven": "And the silken sad uncertain rustling of each purple curtain/Thrilled me – filled me with fantastic terrors never felt before."

but they contained valuable and suggestive hints of his preoccupations at the time. Such was his classical tribute to the death of love, in which a chubby cupid lies dying, to accompany the poem "Lament for Eros ('Eros is Dead')". His drawing to the ghost story, "A Railway Journey", depicted a beautiful, dark-haired woman seated opposite an astonished man in a railway carriage. In this bizarre and ghoulish fantasy the woman is in fact the ghost of a bereaved widow who had died "almost paralyzed to idiocy" after witnessing her husband's death as he lay bleeding in her lap on just such a railway. Again melodrama gave him a chance for exaggeration and attracted Tenniel to the more bizarre contributions in the paper. Fairies and goblins were also a popular preoccupation at the time and Tenniel provided his version in "Eckhart the Trusty". As one recent critic remarked, "Tenniel of course is just one of a number of Victorian illustrators whose childhood fears and delusions seem to smoulder under the surface, only to burst out in zany worlds where children and hobgoblins have complete control."[17]

The horror-struck lover tormented by the loss of his love was now a recurrent theme in Tenniel's work. He drew it in several guises, but generally as variations upon the *pieta*, the dead or dying figure lying limp in the lap of the lover. The best

The supernatural dominated the bizarre "A Railway Journey", *Once a Week*, 8 October, 1859, p. 285.

example appeared in *Once a Week* on 18 January 1860, to accompany the gripping classical melodrama, "The Pythagorean". The tragic fate of Glaucus imprisoned with his beloved Virginia and her subsequent death in his lap was too poignant a reminder of Tenniel's own loss to go unnoticed. He provided several

The imprisoned Virginia and Glaucus in Tenniel's haunting melodrama "The Pythagorean", *Once a Week*, 28 January, 1860, p. 99

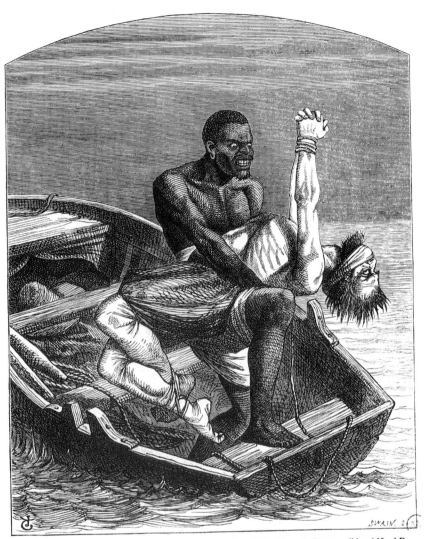

Bondage and terror become familiar Tenniel themes, here "The Negro's Revenge" by Alfred B. Richards, *Once a Week*, 7 July, 1860, p. 52.

strong, remarkably confident drawings of a despairing Glaucus bent over Virginia "in her sleep of death", and his descent into grief-filled madness: "I saw it coming now! A giddiness seized me – It went away – I saw it nearer. I stopped to kiss her lips. It was nearer still again". Then followed his final wishful prayer, "Virginia! I come – I come!" and his own death. In a similar melodramatic vein he drew a tormented Negro for "The Negro's Revenge" (7 July 1860), who had bound and gagged his captor and was in the gleeful act of throwing him to the sharks.

Tenniel rarely agreed to illustrate serials; those extended stories in numerous chapters which appeared in magazines to attract readership he found time-consuming and tedious. When he did, he displayed a strong, confident talent for following an author's story and enhanced the flow of the narrative with his drawings – marks of the true illustrator. The most successful is generally agreed to be his twenty-two illustrations to *The Gordian Knot* by Shirley Brooks, which

Preliminary drawing for Tenniel's etching "The Iron Pit", (6¹/₄ x 4¹/₄") published in *The Gordian Knot*, 1860 (Victoria and Albert Museum). He notes "bite it *tenderly*".

appeared in monthly instalments from 1858, published by Bentley, and in a book edition later in 1860. What is interesting about these designs, which were all etched upon steel rather than wood-engraved, is how clearly they show Tenniel's talent for the recently revived etching process as a reproductive technique for books. His etching technique suggests renewed experiments with atmosphere and outline; in some he relied too heavily upon outline, echoing his wood-engraving training. This left critics divided about which were his best plates in the serial. Forrest Reid was convinced "The Duke's Grandfather" was "like an early Charles Keene" and rich in domestic detail; while the final melodramatic struggle between a young woman in the clutches of the villain in "The Iron Pit" was "an extraordinarily powerful and even terrible design".[18] Yet he was hesitant to recommend Tenniel's achievements on the whole.

Tenniel's second serial commission, for Brooks's *The Silver Cord*, appeared in ninety-seven chapters in *Once a Week* from 1860–61. These were also etched and according to Reid

> interesting rather than attractive. What the subject of that romance in 97 chapters may be I have lacked the courage to discover, but Tenniel seems to have seized on all its more stormy moments for the purposes of illustration. There is hardly a picture that does not confront us with wrath, horror or despair. There is one, indeed, depicting a wasp-waisted, gaol-cropped Frenchman, who has been disarmed in a duel (apparently fought in a parlour), literally grinning with rage, and showing quite a dozen of his teeth as he glares at his opponent. Tenniel, who could put so much beauty into a horse's head, never found it easy to give beauty to his human figures. For female beauty especially, he relied entirely on regular features and unnaturally long eyelashes.[19]

By mid November 1860 Tenniel turned the exaggerated theatrical aspects of his recent work into more restrained drawings of considerable merit for a book which many of his admirers consider his best. This was a new illustrated edition of *Lalla Rookh*, with sixty-nine Tenniel illustrations to accompany Thomas Moore's popular series of five oriental verse tales. First published in 1817, the collection had become a favourite gift-book among enterprising publishers who issued their own lavish editions with Westall, Turner and Maclise steel engravings. More stylish variants included the lavish *Pearls of the East, or Beauties from Lalla Rookh*, 1837, with twelve colour lithograph "beauties" by Fanny Corbaux, "to embody the female characters of Lalla Rookh – to render those bright creations of the poet's fancy as familiar as they already are to the mind and heart".[20] More recently, Routledge had issued a highly-praised edition in 1857, compiled from work by some of the period's most prominent draughtsmen on wood, and it was this edition with which Tenniel's now had to compete.

Tenniel received a copy of Moore's text from John Murray, his Aesop publisher. There were blank spaces left where illustrations might fit and he quickly made sketches of the exotic backgrounds, the harem girls and grotesque creatures of Moore's stories and transferred them onto wood blocks before sending them on to the Dalziels for engraving.[21] His early years of costume study and detail for the Indian and Muslim architectural backgrounds helped him to speed through the work. Yet he was extremely careful with elements of details which he instructed the Dalziels to retain. He restrained himself from the usual melodramatic poses of his recent work and produced charming romantic pastiches, like the lovers in "The Veiled Prophet of Khorassan". He let his grotesque preoccupations loose on the evil Mokanna, whose glaring eyes and bare jutting skull threatened all who looked upon him. There were chances to explore more classical subjects like the angelic spirits in "Paradise and the Peri" – the peri being spirits of the air, agents of good and beauty. He drew a familiar battle scene for the Persian story "The Fire-Worshippers" and filled the pages of the delightful love story "The Light of the Harem" with atmospheric yet carefully delineated interiors, heavily decorated furniture and costumes. He used light in a clearer, more confident manner, no doubt learned from his recent etchings, although one critic blamed the Dalziels for spoiling the delicacy of Tenniel's original compositions. In the end Tenniel's *Lalla Rookh* was a striking production, a lavish yet not over-fussy pastiche of the exotic and the grotesque, which reached the bookshops early in November, in time for Christmas. That same year another illustrated edition also appeared, illustrated by the inferior G.H. Thomas, but it was Tenniel's which captured the most critical attention. In an age of grey, uninspired gift-books, elaborately bound but full of derivative drawings indifferently engraved, Tenniel's book stood well above the average. *The Times* critic went into rapturous praises and ended by calling it "the greatest illustrative achievement of any single hand". The *Art Journal*, still under his friend S.C. Hall's editorship, gave it a full notice and encouraging review. In the end the

Tenniel's "The Light of the Harem" for *Lalla Rookh*, 1861

The classical "Paradise and the Peri" sequence in *Lalla Rookh*, 1861

book marked a further step upward in Tenniel's illustration career.[22] He had survived the terrible period of mourning and produced a work of considerable strength to expiate his private loss and propel him further in the world of the illustrator. Under the dominance of Mr Punch, and with a steady flow of new commissions offered to him, he now reached a reassuring plateau in his career.

The familiar grief-struck lover used in "The Fire-worshippers" for *Lalla Rookh*, 1861

3 Mr Punch Commands 1861–1864

By the middle of 1861 Tenniel felt confident that his career as an illustrator was truly launched. His status can be measured by the substantial fees he asked for his drawings – at least £5 each. His bill for *The Silver Cord* alone was £215 or almost half his annual *Punch* salary, which the book's publisher grudgingly paid. In fact Tenniel had by this time contributed to over twenty books of varying quality.

He had worked on *Punch* now for over ten years, and during that time had attracted a considerable following for his comic cuts and occasional political cartoons. He watched with growing dismay as the career of his superior, John Leech, went rapidly downhill, and wondered at the outcome. Leech had grown dissatisfied with his *Punch* work and the gruelling weekly demands for political "Big Cuts" as well as numerous social cartoons which left him disillusioned and overworked. He began to spend time in pursuit of a more rewarding gallery career and turned his *Punch* cartoons into feeble paintings for public exhibition which generally failed to attract notice. His position on *Punch* suffered yet he seemed bent upon bouts of overwork to support his ambitions. Nervous strain and the stress of varied work eventually forced him into a tragic early death in 1864.

Even before Leech's death it became clear that a replacement political cartoonist was necessary. Mark Lemon inevitably turned to Tenniel and in 1861 offered him the new position at a salary of £500 a year (Leech received £1,000). Tenniel agreed reluctantly, and dropped his usual mixed assortment of comic fillers to work exclusively upon the weekly full-page cartoon. It was not surprising that his first efforts were greatly influenced by his predecessor. The Leech mastery of line, his unmistakable concern for detail, and most of all his skill at drawing to order, to a deadline, were admirable attributes of the once dedicated *Punch* artist. He had brought to *Punch* a solid, restrained approach to political issues which helped to temper the more fiery rebels and turned the paper into a good-humoured showplace for the middle-classes – their virtues and their foibles. John Ruskin shrewdly noted it was Leech, Tenniel and their disciples who contributed to what he called "the great softening of the English mind" by introducing some sense of decorum and restraint into the heated social and political issues of the day.

Moreover Leech shared Tenniel's belief in conservative values. The Leech signature on a *Punch* parody of sports, fashions or political follies of the day gave it his unconscious approval – at least to the eyes of his many fans. Having joined *Punch* in 1841, he had built up an unrivalled reputation for satiric cartoons and drawn over 3,000 subjects for the paper – an amount which in time would

John Leech by Millais, 1854
(National Portrait Gallery)

46

compare in number only with Tenniel. Indeed Tenniel learned much from his colleague and the two men respected each other's talents. Leech was strong on social detail and could turn a slight domestic scene between two parlour maids into a hilarious parody of class values. He was a quick worker: it was said he often sent three completed drawings on wood to the *Punch* engraver before dinner. He shared Tenniel's aversion to drawing from models and proudly claimed to have produced only a half dozen drawings from nature. They shared a preoccupation with detail: Leech took special care with his figures' feet; Tenniel's critics later attacked his feet drawings as too large. Praise from Leech was therefore very welcome. "Talk of drawing!" he once exclaimed to the artist William Powell Frith, "what is my drawing compared to Tenniel's? Look at the way that chap can draw a boot; why I couldn't do that to save my life!" Yet Leech disliked politics – a curious deficiency in a political cartoonist – and generally failed to understand the political issues he drew, while Tenniel kept well-versed on current events, especially the political personalities he was asked to draw, and whose portraits he took such pains to perfect. As one critic pointed out, Leech and Tenniel were "admirable foils to one another . . . Leech sketched and Tenniel drew; Leech gave us farce and drama, and Tenniel high comedy and tragedy; and the freedom of the one heightened the severer beauties of the other".[1] At a time when less accomplished comic papers existed for the literal joke without concern for the quality of their cartoons, the two artists brought a new degree of professionalism to elevate a mundane and ephemeral art into the realms of true artistic expression.

Indeed, in the past *Punch*'s illustrators were mere hacks, who financed their fine art ambitions by drawing quick, careless sketches for money. Even the more competent men like Kenny Meadows or the opinionated John Gilbert merely dashed off their weekly offerings. Gilbert was especially upset when threatened by more conscientious newcomers and once snapped angrily, "We don't want a Rubens on our staff!" The editor Mark Lemon was content to let the illustrations occupy a secondary position; since he was a literary man, he best understood writers, not artists. This was the key to Leech's and eventually Tenniel's success: theirs was essentially a literary talent. Their clever social and political cartoons told a story or supported a joke and could rarely stand on their own without a text. And yet Tenniel's approach was more sophisticated and artistic, for he took great pains with his drawings' style and finish. A Tenniel cartoon was well-conceived and expertly modelled in the best classical tradition. Lemon warmed to this approach, especially when Leech's work grew sloppy and uninspired. At first to help fill in gaps, he had asked Tenniel to do the occasional political cartoon, which was carefully drawn and well-composed. Then when Tenniel became chief cartoonist, Lemon relied more upon freelance contributors for the comic fillers Tenniel had once provided. Between 1841 and 1895, while just twenty artists had been on the *Punch* staff itself, over 170 freelances had their work published in *Punch*. Among them were Tenniel's friends Charles Martin, who had three drawings published in 1853, and Thomas Harrington Wilson, who not only appeared in *Punch* but drew for the famous *Punch Pocket Books* as well.

Tenniel's acceptance of the chief political cartoonist position was a major boost to his career, one which he greatly valued during the forty years he held the post. It was a measure of his reputation now, that he agreed to sit for one of the fashionable *carte-de-viste* photographs of famous artist personalities which were so avidly collected by fans of the art world, and he took special, if not obsessive care with his appearance on this occasion. The weekly cartoon he

Mark Lemon, Tenniel's friend and editor on *Punch*

The *Punch* table by Linley Sambourne. Left to right (standing) F. Burnand, F. Anstey, H. Lucy, E.T. Reed, Gilbert à Beckett, E.J. Milliken, Sir W. Agnew, W.H. Bradbury, G. Du Maurier, H. Furniss, R.C. Lehmann, Arthur à Beckett, L. Sambourne, J. Tenniel (with dog). The portraits and busts on the wall (left to right) are of Mark Lemon, Gilbert à Beckett; (below) Douglas Jerrold; (busts): Thackeray, R. Doyle, T. Hood, J. Leech, Shirley Brooks, Tom Taylor and (on easel) Charles Keene.

provided had by this time become a major factor in the paper's popularity and was held in such high regard that its subject was the sole basis for the notorious *Punch* editorial dinner. These famous Wednesday evening meetings are among the most documented and intriguing events in this period of illustrated journalism. They were attended by roughly two groups at the time: those older generation journalists like Shirley Brooks, Tom Taylor, Horace "Ponny" Mayhew, Percival Leigh ("The Professor"); and a second group of younger writers, like Francis Burnand, and artists like Charles Keene (from 1860), Tenniel, later George Du Maurier and Linley Sambourne, who brought a useful air of purposefulness to what had traditionally become hilarious smoke and drink-filled evenings. At the time that the nineteen-year-old Richard Doyle was admitted to the staff in 1843, his father had begged the editor to excuse his son from these exhausting (and no doubt corrupting) editorial evenings, for fear of upsetting his "delicate health".

One suspects Tenniel viewed the antics of his colleagues with a mixture of voyeuristic interest and silent disapproval. His brief stint as an actor had taught him about the less dignified behaviour of the theatrical world, and his bohemian days as an art student had subjected him to the more unseemly elements around Fitzroy Street. Whatever his feelings, in time he grew to relish these weekly dinners and he rarely missed one. They became the high-point in his carefully organized, rather dull weekly routine and even in old age he cherished the memories of such welcomed breaks in his isolated life. Here he met some of his closest friends and renewed his acquaintances with the occasional special dinner guests, like Dickens, Millais or on one occasion Gladstone. In a sense *Punch* was an exclusive gentlemen's club with a diverse and highly talented if eccentric membership. Impromptu comedy highlighted these evenings, during as well as after dinner. It was usually sparked off by those members Burnard called "the Boozers", whose tongues had been sufficiently loosened by drink to let flow a fund of ribald stories, shocking puns and amusing if occasionally scandalous anecdotes. "They were not drunkards: they were not Teetotallers: they were simply Boozers", he recalled.[2] The wittiest was undoubtedly Shirley Brooks, the talented author of those melodramatic domestic serials Tenniel had illustrated. A frustrated and unhappy gossip, he told the dirtiest jokes, displayed an unrivalled mastery of puns and epigrams, and loved scandal. His own notoriety included a painfully unhappy marriage which precipitated the string of young and beautiful, talented women admirers he collected around him, to whom he played "sugar-daddy". Another was Percival Leigh, the eccentric author of *Mr. Pips' Diary*, who was noted for his "dog-latin" verses, his dry sense of humour (he was an ex-academic), a passion for mysticism and a collection of prize-winning fungi. As a "Boozer" he once joined forces with Horace Mayhew in a drunken stupor which ended by them both falling downstairs on top of one another. Afterwards they solemnly picked each other up, smiled knowingly and shook hands.

Less obvious but still hilarious contributors to the evening were the dramatists Tom Taylor and the jovial, round-faced and rotund Mark Lemon. As editor he was an amiable father-figure to many aspiring contributors, while to his critics he suffered from an unfortunate manner. Some called him a "humbug", others a "sycophant", although he was well-meaning and willing to understand the trials of becoming established as a writer. As a member of Dickens's circle (he helped to dramatize the Christmas stories), a successful playwright and journalist as well as *Punch* editor, he commanded great respect in the literary world. With his younger artists, though, he was occasionally puzzled, uncertain of his position when asked to decide which drawings went into *Punch*. "Here I sit like a great ogre, eating up other peoples' little hopes", he once told a hopeful freelance, then pointed to his wastepaper basket full of rejected drawings. Yet from the start Tenniel found him an understanding and highly amusing editor. He likened him to Shakespeare's Falstaff, and once drew Lemon as that fat, witty old knight who loved jests and self-indulgent sprees, drawn waving a tankard of ale in the air and grinning.[3]

The *Punch* dinners began at 6.30 on Wednesday evenings at the paper's offices in Bouverie Street, near Fleet Street. There from 1867 a special banquet hall was constructed, the room dominated by a massive mahogany table (Thackeray called it the "Mahogany Tree") into which each staff member carved his initials when invited to join the paper. On the walls hung a series of special drawings including some of Tenniel's early almanack designs. The dinner was usually for the paper's staff only, although there were occasional guests from Mark Lemon's wide circle of friends. The dinner itself was a hearty affair, usually capped off with such delicacies as new strawberries, pineapples from Joseph Paxton's greenhouses, or oranges sent by doting admirers; followed by port and cigars, when Tenniel and Keene puffed away contentedly on their

Tenniel smoking his favourite
churchwarden pipe "when at the
Punch table", ink drawing by
Harry Furniss (National Portrait
Gallery)

famous long clay pipes. The evening's conversation was spiked with gossip, as
the *Punch* journalist Henry Silver duly recorded after each dinner he attended in
his invaluable diary (that still survives). Jokes generally centred around art world
gossip: the sexual eccentricities of Rossetti's circle, the more obscene dwelling
upon Ruskin's supposed impotence, Watts's ill-starred marriage to the young
actress Ellen Terry or Swinburne's relationship with Adah Isaacs Menken, the
American actress married four times and divorced three. Silver recalled the
schoolboy humour, the ridiculous jokes and insults which even the junior
members hurled at one another as the evening heated up: "When it was
announced Arthur Lewis had a daughter on the 6th – Du Maurier piped up, 'Born
with spectacles and grey hair like Tom Taylor's'" – a gentle but carefully aimed
insult at that staid member of *Punch*'s staff. Then the topics turned more personal:

> D.M[aurier] says boys have big bums – F.C.B[urnand] doubts – '*You* had at any
> rate' says Kiki [Du Maurier]. F.C.B. retorts something about Christopher Columbus
> – apropos de quoi? Shirley Brooks cuts in with 'Christopher could look a long way
> round this table before he discovered the Continent!' Good![4]

In time reports of these jolly evenings became exaggerated and *Punch* fans eagerly waited at the door to see their favourite writers and artists and catch a
snippet of comic brilliance as they passed. Sometimes, especially in summer, the
dinners were held in Greenwich, or at The Mitre, Hampton Court, or the Star and
Garter along the Thames at Richmond. By the time George Du Maurier attended
his first dinner in 1864, they had become notorious, as he informed a friend
afterwards:

> The Wednesday dinners are a great institution & very jolly. Old Mark [Lemon] I
> like immensely, the most genial old fellow that ever lived; Shirley Brooks is a
> deuced amusing fellow, but rather snarling & sarcastic; Sir Tom de Taylor, very
> jolly too, but so beastly well informed that he rather embeasts one at times; The
> nicest of all is Percival Leigh I think, and old [Frederick] Evans whom we call
> Pater, next to whom I sit. The dinner gets uncommonly jolly towards cigar time;
> the other day we all stood up on our chairs to drink success to the Almanack with
> 3 times 3 . . . .[5]

As an effective antidote to hilarity and noise, a small group of more dignified
individuals puffed away quietly on their cigars and pipes with rarely a word.
These unnerving members were much watched and respected, especially on
those rare occasions when they offered a comment. The group was comprised of
Leech and Tenniel, and those like-minded individuals who became Tenniel's
close friends – Henry Silver, Charles Keene and Francis Burnand. As Du
Maurier recalled from the start, there was much more behind their silence:

> Tenniel is a delightful fellow though very quiet – Burnand very amusing, Horace
> Mayhew often very drunk; *bon enfant mais bête* [Henry] Silver rarely opens his
> lips, at which I wonder for he's got lots to say for himself. Our dear old stiff-necked
> Keene doesn't get quite in tune with the others, and I think these dinners haven't
> as much charm for him as for this child.

After Leech's death Tenniel became the acknowledged leader of the silent group:
they sat around the table listening and nodding but rarely rose to offer an opinion.
Tenniel was given several apt nicknames as the result of his influence; a favourite

one was "Jackides" suggested by the inventive Shirley Brooks, after Mark Lemon's quip about Lord John Russell – "No longer Jack, hereforth Jackides call". Another was "Colonel Newcome", an apt expression for the dignified presence Tenniel brought to the *Punch* table, which was modelled after Thackeray's supreme gentleman character in *The Newcomes*. Such was Tenniel's position among his colleagues that they soon adopted his habit of clay pipe smoking as well. Earlier Charles Keene had taught him the delights of puffing on a churchwarden, and had given Tenniel one from his large collection formed by fishing old Charles II pipes out of the Thames mud. Tenniel proudly scratched his initials into his new pipe and took it down from the mantelpiece each Wednesday evening after dinner.

The jovial antics and good-humoured insults came to an abrupt halt when the editorial meeting began, and the weekly political cartoon, or "Big Cut", was discussed. During these occasions Leech had learned to keep silent while long and infuriating arguments ensued over the exact details of his drawing. It was significant that for all his seven hundred plus political cartoons he had suggested just eleven, between 1845–47. Tenniel learned to do the same: he kept relatively quiet while subjects were suggested, each one discussed then rejected until only the few remaining were fully and formally debated. The entire proceedings took as much as two hours and even when the subject was selected, the details of the drawing – the exact number of figures, the setting, style of costumes, and characters – had to be agreed. During Leech's term he became famous for cartoons with as few figures as possible during the hunting season; he made it clear that more than two figures seriously hampered his weekend hunting plans. Then the cartoon title or legend ("Cackle" as the staff called it) was argued and finally written down, placed in a sealed envelope and given to Tenniel to take home to his studio.

This selection process, with its heated arguments and prolonged indecision, was alien to Tenniel's fair-minded, carefully considered approach to work. "I don't remember that he ever suggested a subject himself for the cartoon", one member recalled, then added,

sometimes he would object with a kind of humorous petulance 'Now you're refining! You'd got quite a good cut, and you want to spoil it!' He occasionally objected strongly and was never asked to draw those he objected totally to. He was not fond of what he called 'perfunctory' cuts, especially those in which royalty figured, and these were certainly the least satisfactory of his drawings, but I am sure he enjoyed representing the British Lion or the Russian Bear, or for that matter any animal, in a cartoon, and I think he had a fondness too for any subject connected with Shakespeare's plays.[6]

In later years his even temper and sound judgement proved invaluable to the new generation of less experienced staff. The sporting writer R.C. Lehmann, who joined the staff in 1890, recalled

more than a few occasions when he broke in upon our deadlock with a new and happy suggestion of his own which was eventually adopted *nem. con.* Very often, too, when we thought we had reached the term of our labours and referred the suggested picture to him, he crushed it with the one word 'impossible', very scornfully delivered. From this judgement there was rarely an appeal.

Throughout his career as political cartoonist he relied successfully upon silence and tactful reserve, as Lehmann remembered:

My memory of him during these cartoon discussions presents him to me as the embodiment of an almost deferential courtesy, about which there was something rather formidable, as though it sometimes cost him an effort to restrain himself from breaking his churchwarden over the head of someone who was pushing a futile suggestion beyond reasonable limits. The churchwarden never *was* broken, but it continued to inspire respect.[7]

Tenniel cultivated the impression of a courteous, reserved yet confident stranger with a remarkable talent in the presence of his colleagues. "Few men have been so reserved", Henry Silver recalled. "Even his most intimate friends knew nothing of him in the intimate sense."[8] It was a strange yet significant remark from one whom Tenniel regarded as one of his most respected friends; one who could remember the exact conversations of *Punch* dinners long after they had broken up. One cannot help wondering at such resolve to remain aloof, at the obsessive privacy and self-control which Tenniel maintained all his life, despite the unseemly temptations of what some called "the age of publicity". "In him, the disparity (if disparity there were) seems emotional; one is led to suspect that Tenniel, behind the ordered surface, hid a considerable nervous intensity of feeling," his first biographer suggested.

> This degree of reserve, maintained even with close friends, might characterize a man who felt that, expressing his feelings, he would find himself uncomprehended and perhaps questioned in alien terms. But a compromise could be made. Reserve, courtesy, dignity could be employed to protect intimacy from the encroachments of friendship; and so it seems Tenniel used them. [9]

Another theory for his reserve centred round Tenniel's French ancestry, which emotionally may have isolated him from his more prejudiced colleagues. It was (and still is) after all, a familiar social bias, as his friend and colleague the French-born Du Maurier was to discover when he struggled to set up in London.

Consequently Tenniel had the reputation for being the supreme English gentleman, whose exemplary courtesy and self-effacing manner fascinated his long-standing colleagues as well as brief acquaintances. His life-long "Healthy

OUR FRIEND TOM NODDY HAS A DAY WITH THE BROOKSIDE HARRIERS.—WITH HIS USUAL PRUDENCE HE GETS A HORSE ACCUSTOMED TO THE HILLS!

A typical Leech equestrian social satire, from *Punch's Almanack, 1857* horror of interviews" made his eventual fame difficult to accept, but he successfully managed to preserve his privacy to the end. To the young *Punch* journalist and future friend, Fred Anstey Guthrie, Tenniel represented

> the best type of cavalry colonel. He was tall, slim and upright, clean-shaven except for long drooping moustaches, quietly courteous and dignified, with a peculiar distinguished voice. Bernard Partridge always said, and I fully agree, that no-one speaks more perfect English than Tenniel. One had only to look at him to recognise that any pettiness or meanness, even in thought, was absolutely impossible to him; he was as much loved as he was honoured by all who knew him, and to the end of his days he was extraordinarily modest as to his powers as a draughtsman and illustrator.[10]

OVER!

Tenniel used his riding for cartoons, here depicting Gladstone's majority horse scaling the locked gate marked "obstruction" (*Punch*, 18 November, 1882)

The role (or charade) of the supreme English gentleman meant certain social expectations had to be fulfilled: Tenniel was, after all, an acknowledged actor. The thoroughly appropriate masculine world of sport, especially horseback riding, played a vital role in Tenniel's life. Like Leech, he relied upon it to escape his gruelling *Punch* routine and provide social pleasures. As Lehmann recalled, "All things that were manly, upright and honourable had an irresistible attraction to him".[11] He loved to join John Leech for weekly rides in Hyde Park and was amused at how avidly Leech pursued his own quest for the gentlemanly role. Although a passionate horse rider and huntsman, Leech was less accomplished than Tenniel, and yet he embraced the sports of the country gentleman with a single-mindedness which he hoped would help to alleviate the prejudices surrounding one whose socially inferior position was that of a mere comic illustrator. He joined the more elevated hunting circles and was a keen member of the Puckeridge Hunt, adopting the experiences of racing through the Hertfordshire countryside in his *Punch* drawings. And yet Leech brought to the sport an endearing exuberance which Tenniel admired, and his many fans followed through his drawings of the hunt disasters of the bumbling horseman Mr Briggs. In fact the two men brought greater respectability to the sports of riding and the hunt through their *Punch* drawings. Together Tenniel and Leech pursued their riding with singular dedication; their motto was "art and the open air". Sometimes they joined forces with the artist Millais and the novelist Trollope and rode down Rotten Row, or into the nearby countryside to exercise their horses. Tenniel loved the endearing mock-rivalry Leech seemed to show with him, especially since the latter was never a match for Tenniel's superior horsemanship. The headstrong Leech would challenge his friend or make wild declarations about those less competent than himself. He poked fun at Millais, whose bowlegged stance after riding provoked the promise that he would draw a new series of "triangular landscapes" – views seen between the curves of his friend's legs. On the other hand, Leech could joke about his own obvious weaknesses. Once he delighted Tenniel with a plan to buy a broken-winded horse, because he was sure then it would not carry him too far if it bolted. He called his favourite horse "Red Mullet" and rode confidently if unevenly alongside Tenniel, whose own favourite was "Miss Brown", a carefully tended obedient animal. When the mare died Tenniel sent her body to the zoo for lion meat - "as some return to his 'models'" he noted, referring to the lion drawing he perfected in *Punch*.

On other occasions Tenniel bore the irrational brunt of Leech's temper. He was told that he took his jumps recklessly and without careful thought for the horse's welfare, a remark which Tenniel still remembered years later, obviously crushed by the attack on his superior horsemanship. On the other hand, Tenniel felt unease in Trollope's company, for he was flagrantly reckless. He would ride his horse at a five-barred gate and while it was being opened for a spectator, he would take the obstacle to the astonished anger of his friends. Such episodes filled Tenniel's routine life with momentary excitement, and in later years were among his favourite memories. He loved to recall the favourite horses he owned, like the one he carefully kept stabled and rode weekly for sixteen years. There was also the obstinate mare whose mouth had been "spoilt by a stupid and cruel groom" so that she nearly threw him in the Regent's Park Canal when she bolted. "And after that she always bolted and I had to get rid of her", he recalled with dismay. Such incidents also helped to inspire his *Punch* drawings, especially those cartoons in which politicians took to the hunting fields in expert parodies of his favourite sport.

*   *   *   *   *

Tenniel had worked as *Punch*'s chief cartoonist for nearly twenty years when the news of Leech's sudden death reached him on 29 October 1864. His friend and mentor had succumbed to nervous exhaustion and died aged just forty-seven. According to Shirley Brooks, Tenniel "was stunned by the news, totally unexpected by him".[12] The loss brought sadness and mourning to the entire *Punch* staff, as well as to Leech's numerous fans. The funeral was a scene of "overwhelming grief" according to the *Morning Star*, with Tenniel joining Mark Lemon, Shirley Brooks, Tom Taylor, Henry Silver and Millais as pallbearers. Millais, who had shared many hours riding with Leech and Tenniel, was openly crushed by the loss of so dear a friend and tears streamed down his face. In fact, the service was temporarily halted "by convulsions of grief" from his many friends and admirers. Afterwards another observer noted how London was

> perhaps more shocked at the sudden and unexpected death of John Leech than even when Thackeray was smitten [the previous year, when Tenniel also attended his funeral]. The shock radiated all over the country; for there was not a household in the land in which his name was not familiar as a household word.[13]

It was then discovered that Leech had left his wife and children without provision, so Tenniel, Millais, Richard Doyle and other mutual friends campaigned hard among their politician friends and prominent art world figures until a pension was granted to the artist's dependants.

Tenniel was overcome with grief for his friend. In fact it was in this period that he broke down and failed to deliver the promised Alice drawings to Lewis Carroll, as we shall see. Fortunately he received some comfort from Henry Silver: their friendship had grown steadily since Silver's entry on the staff in 1857 (following Douglas Jerrold's death). Silver was a sympathetic soul who, although eight years Tenniel's junior, understood the loss which Leech's death brought to his older friend. Moreover, he shared Tenniel's interests in rowing and in the theatre – he acted as *Punch*'s drama correspondent – and he wrote the satiric "History of Costume" series (which Tenniel illustrated) as well as originating the "Essence of Parliament" series. But it was his rowing, or "oarsmanship" as they called it, which helped to bind their friendship, especially on those delightful early summer escapes from London, rowing up the Thames together.

Henry Silver, the *Punch* diarist

Tenniel especially loved these excursions, like the time in June 1865 when he rowed twenty-nine miles to Streatley for supper with Dickens's son. The day had begun slowly, but the pace quickened around Abingdon, Nuneham and Clifton so they were in time for a lunchtime swim and picnic under the lee of a haystack to get out of the wind. On another occasion they rowed to Henley by seven, having stopped for the ritual bathe in the river and lunch; on the following day rain threatened the route to Cookham and lunch had to be eaten in Lord Boston's boathouse, well out of the wet. There they battled a colony of moths disturbed by their intrusion and had to light their pipes to keep warm. Then Tenniel and Silver insisted on racing further; "through steaming showers by misty wooded banks", according to Silver's diary. They finally reached Maidenhead for a chicken and champagne celebration by a warm fireside before catching the 8.45 train back to London for the following day's *Punch* dinner. These were relaxed, congenial occasions when Tenniel forgot the pressures of deadlines and enjoyed the high spirits and ribald jokes of his companions.[14] They were a carefully selected group, usually from among the *Punch* staff or their immediate friends. Once Fred Evans, son of the *Punch* proprietor, joined them, together with Dickens, Tenniel, and his early patron's son Louis, of Lloyd's the printseller. George Du Maurier considered it an honour to be asked to join the group and recalled with relish his unforgettable rowing weekend:

George Du Maurier, Tenniel's friend and rival

> On Friday last I went down to Oxford, to meet Tenniel, young Charles Dickens and 3 others to row back to Windsor; one of the most splendid holidays I ever recollect, and I wish I could do it a little oftener – you will soon see I hope some burlesque account of it in *Punch* like the hunting. The weather for the first two days was lovely; on the third day it poured, but we caught no harm rowing – 70 miles – *ce n'est pas mal.*[15]

The gap which Leech left as a social satirist was soon filled by Tenniel's old friend Charles Keene – at the instigation of Tenniel and Silver. Keene, or "Carlo" to his friends, had earlier tried to help Silver adapt his crude drawings onto wood blocks, and had been invited over the years to contribute to *Punch* himself. As Leech's successor he was asked to provide weekly observations on the fashionable, the comic and the most outrageous of society's whims which he did with exemplary if individual skill. His total *Punch* output amounted to 5–6,000 drawings, for which he insisted on payment per drawing. He remained freelance until his death in 1891; his frugal habits left an estate of £30,000 from his *Punch* work alone.

Another new staff member proposed at the death of Leech was the eager and ambitious George Du Maurier. Again Tenniel, Silver and Keene proposed his membership of the staff, knowing he "was anxious to join us", and he was taken on as a social cartoonist under Keene. Mark Lemon told him his cartoons must not be too funny and more graceful; he must become "the romantic tenor in Mr. Punch's opera bouffe company" in which Keene was "the basso singing the real comic songs". Since he had struggled long and hard to reach a staff position by first contributing occasional sketches to the paper, Du Maurier accepted this secondary role; but not for long. He was ambitious enough to aim for the top positions – if he worked hard enough, he reasoned, he might take over from Tenniel himself.

Not surprisingly Tenniel's relationship with this new, ambitious artist was cautious from the start. Du Maurier, or "Kiki" as his friends called him, was fourteen years his junior, had been born and well-trained in France (under Gleyre in Paris) and set up in London as a black and white illustrator in the early 1860s. He began drawing for *Punch* in May 1861, when he explained to his mother how his early *Punch* initials were carefully conceived to compete with such admired senior rivals as Leech, Tenniel and Keene. They were intended to be "something so much better than what is ever done there in that line (now that Tenniel has left off) that I hope to keep on and get enough for an existence. They are very little paid (15/- each) but do not take me more than a couple of hours." His work was encouraged by Mark Lemon, who promised to take larger drawings "when they were very much better than theirs [Leech, Tenniel, Keene]".[16] So as early as 1 June 1861 he admitted his sights were firmly set upon a staff position: "I am trying to make a dead set at that paper, so as to be one of the regular staff someday."[17]

When the offer came, Du Maurier got off to a decidedly bad start with Tenniel and his fellow staff members. At his first *Punch* dinner he was apparently nervous and over-excited, and managed to upset and offend both Tenniel and his· colleagues without knowing it. He rose to give his inaugural speech and to receive the toast and good wishes of his new colleagues and took the occasion to make his own handicapped position clear from the beginning. He explained how he was blind in his left eye and "begged them to pardon him if he failed at any time to 'see' a subject that might be suggested for his pencil". By referring to his disability he unknowingly cast doubts about Tenniel's performance on the paper, and embarrassed his senior colleague, who had managed to draw so well over fourteen years, also with the use of just one eye. Shirley Brooks finally rose to break the embarrassed silence, and noted how

> Tenniel has only one eye left, and it really *is* the left, for he lost his right while fencing, whilst you have your right eye left. So you see you two fellows have two good eyes between you, and a pair of good eyes are better than a score of bad ones. In the country of the blind, you know the one-eyed man is king, and here we're blind as bats – to one another's failings. So I drink to your good health, you two one-eyed royal Majesties.[18]

On the other hand Tenniel found Du Maurier's enthusiasm wearing, and he remained aloof during their early days together on *Punch*. Perhaps he sensed competition in the air, for Du Maurier had written to his mother within months of his new appointment, "Shouldn't I like to do political cuts for Punch some day, *ca viendre j' espere* without any damage to that jolly fellow Tenniel". But he soon gave up the idea and had no real interest in politics; his outspoken opinions were dubbed mere "dilettante radicalism" by his friends.[19] He was well-trained to draw with an academic sureness of line which attracted Tenniel. Moreover, he created gothic fantasies and grotesque, nightmarish creatures of the type which appealed to the latter's darker nature, and these alone inspired some of the more powerful grotesques in Tenniel's weekly political cartoons – like the ghostly figure of Napoleon standing in the path of the infatuated German emperor which was entirely Du Maurier's idea.[20] In time the two men warmed to each other, united no doubt by a common love of France. Once Du Maurier attempted a parody of his friend's stern, aloof manner by drawing Tenniel's face with a bulbous tinted nose, obviously in a state of intoxication as he puffed away silently on his long churchwarden.[21] He even tried to invite Tenniel to Paris with him, but failed to persuade the elder artist enough to abandon his carefully maintained London routine, even for a few days.

Another of Tenniel's young protégés during the 1860s was the inventive gunsmith turned artist, Robert Taylor Pritchett. He was eight years Tenniel's junior and a keen sportsman with a considerable reputation as an inventor – he helped to perfect the Enfield rifle and invented the "Pritchett bullet" for which the government awarded him £1,000. This windfall helped convince him to throw up his guns for the drawing board and Tenniel agreed to help launch him on an illustrator's career. They first met at one of Arthur Lewis's notorious bachelor evenings at Moray Lodge, Campden Hill, and soon Pritchett was invited to visit Tenniel's studio – itself a rare privilege. There he received his first lesson in drawing upon wood: "He had been watching the Master drawing his cartoon, and was busy sketching the top of his amiable head, when its owner told him he would be much better occupied in drawing on the wood, and threw him over a piece." He completed this and Tenniel was pleased enough to take it to Swain, the *Punch* engraver, who cut it well enough for it to appear in the magazine. Thus began Pritchett's career as an illustrator, which in time included drawings for other prestigious magazines like *Once a Week* and *Good Words*. Eventually he illustrated his own travel books and drew for the Queen, who awarded him a Jubilee medal.[22]

R.T. Pritchett was taught drawing by Tenniel

Tenniel entered his forties a tall, lean, clean-shaven figure with a striking military bearing. He had borrowed from Leech the thick set of sideboard whiskers of which his friend was inordinately proud, but generally preferred an immaculate appearance suggestive of a stern military training. He was to a great degree vain about his appearance and took great pains to dress and appear in public in the most dignified way possible. In response to the numerous flattering requests for his portrait photograph, he eventually agreed to sit for the firm of Messrs J. & C. Watkins, London, and had several poses taken for *carte-de-viste*. These were prominently displayed in the photographer's window, and an angry Tenniel passed one day, upset by what he saw:

> I saw one of my portraits in a window yesterday & confess to have felt decidedly the reverse of gratified at finding that it was the one I *especially dislike*. The one sitting, with the chin on the hand and the head turned round. The position is constrained and affected, and as all my friends agree – not a bit characteristic of the "party".

He urged the photographer to stop printing from this negative, "or better still, cancel the image altogether, the pose is so evidently got up that it annoys me whenever I see it". He preferred the far more dignified standing pose, with only his hat and riding whip as props.[23]

As a result changes in his appearance were made only after great consideration. The long, drooping moustaches, for example, which remained his most characteristic feature in middle age, were the result of a rebellious act of defiance, instigated by his friend Prichett. Tenniel and Leech had often sworn to remain clean-shaven and not be taken in by "the great beard movement" which dominated society following the Crimean War. Beards and moustaches were reserved for the military, they believed, despite the recent outcrop of hair in even the most polite social circles – expressions it was said of solidarity with the army. Leech strongly objected that moustaches should be reserved only for members of "the crack cavalry regiments", and he continued to shave his face around his bushy mutton-chop whiskers, and Tenniel did the same. *Punch* savaged the great beard movement and Charles Keene used it to draw a little girl's appeal to her father for their guests' long drooping moustaches, to use "for a tail for her horse". In such an atmosphere Tenniel joined with Leech and Prichett and made a solemn pact while riding (which they swore on their riding crops) never to wear "hair on the lip or chin". They remained true to their promise until a year after Leech's death, when Prichett returned from a painting holiday on Skye with full moustaches. He knocked at Tenniel's door to get his reaction, and when Tenniel opened the door he could only stutter, "You scoundrel", then added, "then *I must!*" From 1865 onward Tenniel began to grow and carefully groom those now familiar long bushy moustaches which grew silvery and grey with age.[24]

Although never socially gregarious, Tenniel especially enjoyed the company of his fellow artists. He joined the Arts Club in Hanover Square, founded by younger artists like Du Maurier to provide a social atmosphere and exhibition space for talented members, who over the years included Randolph Caldecott, Charles Keene and Frederick Walker as well as the painters Frederic Leighton and William Frank Calderon, the talented animal painter. Members paid a substantial ten guinea annual subscription and met over dinner or, like Tenniel, on Saturday evenings after his *Punch* drawing was sent off to the engraver, to share in the gossip and exchange views about politics or fine art. On the whole, though, Tenniel remained most loyal to that more exclusive club, *Punch,* and felt no need to join the more prestigious gentlemen's clubs in Pall Mall. He was, however, a guest at Moray Lodge, the bachelor home of the art patron and wealthy silk-mercer Arthur Lewis on Campden Hill. Here Lewis gathered together an astonishing variety of characters during these notorious monthly evenings, when the famous and infamous met under his roof. Tenniel met old colleagues and made brief acquaintances here: the guests included, over the years, Dickens, Thackeray, Richard Doyle, Landseer, Frith, Millais, Leighton and Keene, as well as royalty and sportsmen. George Du Maurier joined the group by the early 1860s and wrote in 1863, after a particularly sumptuous evening, how things "are getting more and more gorgeous; half the peerage will be there tonight, and very likely the Prince of Wales".[25] In addition the Moray Minstrels performed ("Music at 8.30 Oysters at 11"), who were a select group of Lewis's friends famed for their voices. Even the more reserved, like Tenniel and his colleague Frederic Leighton, eventually lost their restraint in such an atmosphere; Leighton inspired the remark: "we used to say at Moray Lodge his appearances were like those of a beautiful meteor – in flashes, as it were."[26]

There were still chances to escape to the theatre as well, for Tenniel's *Punch* colleagues were also among the more popular dramatists working in London. He felt obliged to attend their productions and there he dreamt of reviving his own acting ambitions. He was in fact given a second chance to perform in 1867, for the *Punch* benefit in aid of the artist Charles Bennett. Although Bennett had contributed to *Punch* for just two years, his endearing manner and talent as a draughtsman – Tenniel probably borrowed from his work – made his premature death a tragic blow to the staff. Moreover, he had died young, aged just forty-two, leaving a wife and eight children without provision. The *Punch* staff rallied round and organized an impressive theatrical benefit and collected together some of the most talented young musicians and actors within its acquaintance. Tenniel agreed to play opposite Du Maurier, with the Terry sisters Ellen and Kate, Mark Lemon and Francis Burnand in attendance, in a performance of Tom Taylor's one-act melodrama "A Sheep in Wolf's Clothing". For his performance Tenniel donned a cavalier's costume of the type he loved to wear: its wide brimmed plumed hat, slashed doublet and tight knee breeches with bright buckled shoes, those of the dashing Colonel Lord Churchill of the Life Guards. The cast

Cast of Charles Bennett's benefit performance, with Tenniel (standing third from right) dressed as Colonel Lord Churchill. Others are (standing left to right): R.T. Pritchett, Shirley Brooks, Arthur Lewis, Mark Lemon (in hat), Mr. Twiss, Tenniel, Arthur Cecil, Henry Silver. Seated left to right: Sir Arthur Sullivan, Ellen Terry, George Du Maurier, Kate Terry and Tom Taylor.

assembled for a portrait photograph which showed Tenniel as the tall, elegantly dressed and most handsome figure in the group. The entire performance was a tremendous theatrical and financial success. The music was composed and conducted by Arthur Sullivan, who also wrote the comic operetta "Cox and Box" which followed, with Du Maurier in a debut singing lead. The first performance was held in the afternoon of 11 May 1867, at the Adelphi Theatre. In the audience was the recent author of *Alice in Wonderland*, Charles Lutwidge Dodgson, who watched over Tenniel's performance with the same sharp critical eye he had earlier focused upon Tenniel's Alice drawings. In the interval Dodgson joined his friends, the Terry sisters, in their box and afterwards confided in his diary how much he enjoyed the performances: "Tom Taylor was good but a little tame, Mark Lemon was first rate. Tenniel seemed nervous and was hardly audible, Miss Terry was, in parts, very pathetic . . . "[27]

A second performance was staged in July in Manchester's Theatre Royal. For this Tenniel joined the cast on the five-hour rail journey they turned into a song-fest, singing all the way: "Of the row made . . . no idea can be given", Shirley Brooks recalled with glee.[28] This time Tenniel was more confident on stage and after his performance the audience "warmly cheered", although one observer cryptically added "probably those stalwarts of liberalism were also applauding the work of the cartoonist". At any rate the two performances raised £1,000 for the widowed Bennett family which the *Punch* staff proudly claimed was a record.[29]

*   *   *   *   *

Some of Tenniel's best magazine illustrations were done during the 1860s, despite the fact that they were completed alongside his *Punch* cartoons and the growing number of requests from admirers for sketches and autographs. Although these requests were often delayed he usually complied, as in the case of the small yet meticulous pencil sketch of a knight in armour, a plumed hat and a tankard of ale in his hands, which he sent to a fan with apologies for the delay: "At last I have managed to make you a little sketch", he confessed, "and now that it *is* made I feel positively ashamed to send it. I very much wish that I could have done something better worth your acceptance – as it is, I can only hope you will kindly take the will for the deed."[30]

Sporadic drawings were engraved in *Good Words* between 1862 and 1864,

"Bacchus and the Water-Thieves" by W.T. from *Once a Week*, 4 June, 1864, p. 658

supplanted by designs for poetry and serials in *Once a Week* and eventually the Alice book which would occupy all his spare moments. Yet in 1867 he made a curious reappearance in *Once a Week* with an elaborate border design to "Lord Aythan", in which the pleasures of summer idleness – playing croquet, attending flower shows, picnicking – serve as the frontispiece to launch the magazine's new volume, the entire plate printed in garish green ink. And yet Tenniel discovered that such work offered more creative outlets than *Punch*, when he could find the time. In other instances he offered to use his valuable publishing connections to help newcomers and less fortunate aspiring artists and writers to break into the more prestigious papers. When one young woman writer appealed to him for help he wrote to his old employer, the editor of *Once a Week*: "A young lady – Miss Selina Gaye – is very anxious to contribute to 'Once a Week' with a view to profitable employment. I am told she has considerable talent . . .. You will confer a favour on me, in that I shall have fulfilled my charge in triumphant manner", he concluded, after asking him to consider Miss Gaye's work.[31]

Tenniel's book illustrations during this period confirm how meticulous was the care he took with the drawing, engraving and the printing when unhurried by the seemingly ceaseless deadlines of weekly *Punch* work. His drawings are clearer, the atmospheric effects more carefully rendered, more thoughtful effects of light and shade, with perhaps a subtle character line upon a face, or a wholly successful pose. In Bryant's *Poems*, or the later *Lays of the Holy Land* drawings, he concentrated upon the nocturnal effects of bodies on a battlefield, lit only by the diffused glow of the moon – that familiar Doyle device – which he nursed through the engraving and printing stages. In later *Ingoldsby Legends* and *Legends and Lyrics* drawings he used single torches and candles to concentrate the light and exaggerate facial expressions. This was achieved with care; the resulting proofs which his engravers returned to him for checking were heavily marked with notes in the margins for even slight corrections or modulations in tone. "I'm not a first rate artist, I know; but I'm not half as bad as those fellows the woodcutters, make me", he once snapped.

Over the years Tenniel established an invaluable relationship with two groups of wood-engravers, the Swains and the Dalziel brothers, upon whom he could depend for sympathetic interpretations of his designs. His *Punch* engraver Joseph Swain and his son, were responsible for introducing the clear outline style which his public came to expect from a Tenniel cartoon. Swain was treated with complete respect, as in fact Tenniel treated most of his printers and engravers; he clearly knew the value of tact and could appreciate the technical difficulties of the engraver's art. Some of his proof comments to Swain or the Dalziels are characteristic of that approach: "In most respects capital", "Very good indeed"; or even when improvements were needed they were suggested not told: "There is something to worry about the knee. It had better be lost in the gloom." Once he asked Swain to be especially careful with a block, but tempered his remark by praising the engraver's abilities, with whom "he *knew* he could place his complete trust".[32]

Similarly the Dalziel brothers admired Tenniel's talent and understood his brief comments to improve their engravings. They had engraved some of his earliest anthology drawings as well as the justly famous Alice series. During that period they had come to appreciate his meticulous approach to the wood block, later noting how he "was never very effusive in his observations, though his remarks were invariably complimentary".[33] From a selection of his proof com-

The frizzy-haired Pre-Raphaelite "Dividend" from *Puck on Pegasus*, 1861

ments it is clear he was most concerned with sharp definition and occasionally took them to task for heavy-handedness. For example, his frizzy-haired Pre-Raphaelite allegorical figure Dividend for *Puck on Pegasus* was too crudely cut in its proof form: "The figure should be lighter throughout – softer more radiant. Split all the dark lines and lighten shadows". This alone involved a tedious, time-consuming process whereby each raised wooden line on the block had to be incised carefully to make two lines from one – a considerable feat.

Ironically this pursuit of clarity and atmosphere was most successful on the etched plate, not on the wood block at all. One of his most effective etchings was the smoke-filled tavern scene, "Modern Druids" from *The Gordian Knot*. Tenniel wished the surly down-at-heal drinkers to emerge from their own tobacco smoke and he noted this on the first etched proof: "This upper part to be kept quite light. It is meant to represent tobacco smoke. I shall scratch it all even with *dry point*. Please don't make it *too* dark." Also, in the melodramatic struggle between villain and heroin called "Iron Pit", he noted:

> N.B. This subject should be grey and dark in tone throughout but please bite it *tenderly* as the work is very close and I don't want the lines to go all together in the darker parts. The *pit* is the darkest part of the picture. [34]

The first of the strong, clear commissions was in fact for *Puck and Pegasus* in 1861. Tenniel's round-faced characters and comic burlesque to "Lord Jolly Green's Courtship" were admirable foils to the sketchier styles of fellow contributors like Leech and Phiz and Cruikshank's comic frontispiece. This anthology of comic verses was itself a popular book which had gone to several editions, although critics dismissed the verses as dismal attempts to rival Tom Hood. Tenniel began work on his contributions in 1861 and produced a mixture of *Punch*-inspired comedy and restrained domestic vignettes, some of which echoed the more melodramatic poses of favourite romantic stage productions, with feuding lovers and love-torn suitors on bended knees. The drawings were quickly engraved by the Dalziels, who returned them to Tenniel for comments; they lay in his studio for days before the publishers prodded him and he acted

Preliminary pencil design and completed etching for "Modern Druids" in *The Gordian Knot*, 1860, 6¼ x 4¼" (Victoria and Albert Museum)

upon them. "I am really quite ashamed of myself", he wrote back apologetically, his letter marked "Haste!" "Dalziel sent the proofs the other day – I think he has engraved the drawings very nicely." He thought for the sake of lost time that two drawings might be condensed onto one page: "Lord Jollygreen's agony at the window would tell better in every way – as a tailpiece".[35] It was his rather feeble attempt to merge text with drawings. The book appeared by the summer, and Tenniel curiously received just seven guineas for the drawings – well below his usual £5 per drawing standard. The reviews were mixed: The *Art Journal* dismissed the verses and even neglected to mention the illustrations specifically, saying only that on the whole they were worthy of *Punch*, "which is the highest compliment we can pay them". The more cautious *Athenaeum* noted dryly, "the humour of the writing falls below the illustrations". In fact the *Athenaeum* found the whole venture a mixture of the ridiculous and the sumptuous:

> The author of *Puck on Pegasus*, although heralded as funny, is only foolish.... This volume has fared sumptuously at the publisher's hands; inside a creamy luxury; outside a glory of magenta and gold! .... The humour of the writing falls far below that of the illustrations.[36]

The religious strain in Tenniel's paintings re-surfaced in several relatively minor book commissions. He provided slight drawings to Mrs Gatty's *Parables from Nature*, a popular anthology which went into several editions and placed Tenniel's work alongside such prestigious and successful artists as Millais and Holman Hunt. His first steel-engraved plates appeared as frontispieces in the moralistic collection of stories in the "Standard Library" series for Hurst and Blackett; first for Frederic W. Robinson's *No Church,* 1862, then *Grandmother's Money* the same year, followed by Dinah Mullock's *A Noble Life* in 1869. Although most were mere domestic scenes of no real merit, Tenniel's frontispiece to *Grandmother's Money*, with its old woman and guests leaving a house as "Grandmother Treasdaile's Coup d'etat", was copied by the famous steel-engraver John Saddler, who exhibited his plate after Tenniel's design at the Royal Academy in 1863. The *Athenaeum* critic pronounced that particular book "a good novel" and praised it for "throughout a healthy tone of morality". Later critics dismissed Tenniel's designs: Gleeson White concluded, "The steel en-

"Penance" from *Ingoldsby Legends*, 1864, was typical of Tenniel's use of bizarre lighting

graving bestowed upon most of these obliterated all character from the designs, and superseded the artist's touch by hard unsympathetic details; but all the same, the compositions by men of such eminence deserve mention".[37] He included Tenniel and other artists such as Millais, Holman Hunt and Frederick Sandys in that group. Finally Tenniel agreed to illustrate for the Religious Tract Society and had his work published in their *English Sacred Poetry of the Olden Time*, 1864, alongside that of such noted Sixties School men as J.W. North, Frederick Walker, J.D. Watson and Du Maurier.

The commission which provided the greatest challenge, considering Tenniel's preoccupation with medievalism, was Richard Harris Barham's *Ingoldsby Legends*. These hilarious parodies on familiar medieval legends by the one-time Canon of St Paul's had captivated audiences since their publication, despite critics who attacked them for their irreverence. Leech's friend Richard Bentley had originally published them as a serial in *Bentley's Miscellany* in 1837, then had issued them in three illustrated volumes in 1840. Some twenty-four years later it was thought a single, more manageable volume was needed, and Tenniel was asked to supply drawings to accompany the original ones by Leech and Cruikshank. Of the sixty drawings in total, he could find time to do only seventeen. Work began after he sent a list of those tales he wished to illustrate

"The Sleeping Genie and the Lady" from Dalziel's *Arabian Nights*, 1865

to George Bentley on 1 May 1862, noting they were those "I am prepared to carry out without delay". The Dalziels again engraved his drawings and Tenniel, as always, went over their proofs carefully. Some he dismissed and sent back as "very hurried and loose"; in others he worried about an eye or the dark leg of a horse which should have been lighter when the animal's breath enveloped it.[38] The Dalziels patiently complied with his wishes, later calling these "exceptionally clever drawings" which were among the many they had "the good fortune to engrave". The book went into several editions and survived well into the 1880s as a mark of Tenniel's success. His Sir Rupert, the moustachioed hero he admired and later painted with such skill; the grotesque exaggerated chase scenes and the carnage after battle all helped him to perfect subjects and compositions similar to those he had done earlier.

The Dalziels were also anxious to secure Tenniel's illustrations for their own ambitious publishing ventures. As engravers they occasionally initiated projects, commissioned the artists, then sold the finished work to publishers for distribution. Such was the case with their *Arabian Nights' Entertainments*, an elaborate and grandiose scheme to be issued in 104 weekly parts with two wood-engraved plates and eight pages per part, which was eventually compiled into a two volume edition in October 1864. This book remains one of the true classics of the Sixties

School of illustration and helped to make the reputation of its primary contributor, Arthur Boyd Houghton. Other artists included Millais, Pinwell, Watson, the Dalziels themselves and Tenniel, with eight drawings.[39] These they considered "an act of kindness to ourselves", despite the fact that they were greatly delayed and did not appear until the later weekly numbers. They remain some of Tenniel's most intriguing, inventive and densely conceived fantasies. The *Athenaeum* decided the venture

> marks an era of importance in the history of its class . . . is what is required to bring English book-illustration to the level of the practise of our German and French neighbours. Several of the designs of Mr. Tenniel are admirable in conception and execution.[40]

Critics later pointed out the merits of "The Sleeping Genie and the Lady" on page five, a bizarre yet powerful composition that would have made the reputation of a lesser man.[41]

Each of these book commissions was shared with the strain and pressure of *Punch* deadlines. Throughout the 1860s and for most of his professional life Tenniel struggled to keep several projects going at once; his letters to friends as well as business associates are almost always headed "In Haste" or "Haste". While most of these books were competently conceived and admirable examples of Sixties School illustration, the true test of his abilities lay with a fastidious, infuriatingly tiresome Oxford don and his inimitable childish fantasies. They would try Tenniel's abilities to the limit over the years until he would emerge broken and disillusioned with book illustration. The results of this struggle – the Alice illustrations – remain, for many, Tenniel's masterpiece.

4   Alice 1864–1872

Enchanting Alice! Black-and-white
Has made your charm perennial;
And nought save "Chaos and old Night"
Can part you now from Tenniel.

                        Austin Dobson

Tenniel's enchanting Alice

At the end of 1863, an Oxford mathematics don wrote from Christ Church College to the *Punch* journalist Tom Taylor, asking for advice on a very special matter:

> Do you know Mr. Tenniel well enough to say whether he could undertake such a thing as drawing a dozen wood-cuts to illustrate a child's book, and if so, could you put me into communication with him? The reasons for which I ask (which however can be of little interest if your answer be in the negative) are that I have written such a tale for a young friend, and illustrated it in pen and ink. It has been read and liked by so many children, and I have been so often asked to publish it, that I have decided on doing so. I have tried my hand at drawing on the wood, and come to the conclusion that it would take much more time than I can afford, and that the result would not be satisfactory after all. I want some figure-pictures done in pure outline, or nearly so, and of all artists on wood, I should prefer Mr. Tenniel. If he should be willing to undertake them, I would send him the book to look over, not that he should at all follow my pictures, but simply to give him an idea of the sort of thing I want. I should be much obliged if you would find out for me what he thinks about it and remain, Very truly yours, C.L. Dodgson.[1]

Lewis Carroll in middle age

The book was, of course, what Dodgson called *Alice's Adventures Underground*, and later became *Alice's Adventures in Wonderland*. Its author is better known as Lewis Carroll. Dodgson had spent much of that year writing up his imaginary fantasy which he hoped to fill with ink drawings in a presentation copy for his beloved child friend, Alice Liddell, who had inspired the story. The tale of Alice in Wonderland is now so familiar as to remain a classic amongst adults as well as children around the world. Its genesis is well-documented from Dodgson's side of the story, but has been much overlooked from his artist–illustrator's point of view. Tenniel's role in creating what many still regard as his greatest illustrations was a tortured, difficult and at times almost impossible one. It needs to be explained in the light of his troubled life, if only to put his achievements firmly into perspective.

    The idyllic summer day Dodgson spent on the river rowing to Godstowe with the Liddell sisters in July 1862, when Alice and her sisters asked for a story and Dodgson began the Alice adventures, remained freshly implanted in Dodgson's

Carroll's photograph of Alice
Liddell as a street urchin

Carroll's ink sketches of birds, 7¹/₄ x 4¹/₄" (Christ Church College Library, Oxford)

mind. A quarter of a century later he still recalled their genesis:

> I can call it up as clearly as if it were yesterday – the cloudless blue above, the watery mirror below, the boat drifting idly on its way, the tinkle of the drops that fell from the oars, as they waved so sleepily to and from, and (the one bright gleam of life in all the slumbrous scene) the three eager faces, Hungry for news of Fairyland, and who would not be said 'nay' to: from those lips 'tell us a story, please' had the stern immutability of Fate! [2]

The following day he organized his tale and wrote up chapter headings, and on further outings he continued to spin out what he now called the "interminable fairy-tale". He even hoped to have it entirely written up and illustrated to present to Alice in time for Christmas. He worked earnestly upon this labour of love throughout November 1862, but unfortunately failed to complete the project in time. Nevertheless he refused to give up and finished the text by 10 February of the following year, although even then he still struggled over his thirty-seven crude ink illustrations. Dodgson was not without some artistic talent although it was of a decidedly amateurish nature. He had illustrated all his schoolboy inventions with sinewy exaggerated comic drawings and clearly enjoyed the challenge. He found the numerous animals in the Alice story a particular problem and had to borrow a natural history book from his colleague at the deanery to help to get their details right. He especially struggled over the White Rabbit which he redrew several times (his pencil sketches are now at Christ Church Library) with long floppy ears and a mouse-like face. His style, if there was one, was more inspired by the spontaneous inventions of Edward Lear rather than by more sophisticated artist contemporaries, although he admired and attempted to emulate his Pre-Raphaelite friends' work as well. Like a true amateur he laboured over intricate detail at the expense of overall composition; he concentrated upon Alice's frizzy Pre-Raphaelite tresses, wide eyes and childish features rather than upon her correct proportions and convincing backgrounds. In the end, she emerged as different characters from his consecutive drawings. Fortunately Dodgson was self-critical enough to recognize his failings. On the other hand, he sent his completed text to his friend George Macdonald to read to his young family to see whether the story itself was successful. They pronounced it delightful and urged publication which, by mid-July 1863, Dodgson decided to do, at his own expense.

He knew that his drawings, however feeble, would have to be transferred onto wood blocks for wood-engraving, and he began this laborious process after receiving a sample title-page from his printer, Thomas Combe, of the Oxford Clarendon Press. He visited Combe to show his drawings and received stern yet well-meaning advice from Combe's visitor, the Pre-Raphaelite sculptor Thomas Woolner, who was then sculpting the printer's portrait. He was urged to draw only from life – echoing the cardinal Pre-Raphaelite tenet of "Truth to Nature". Earlier the supreme champion of the Pre-Raphaelites John Ruskin had attempted to teach Dodgson a similar lesson, but could only conclude he "had not enough talent to make it worth his while to devote much time to sketching". It was frustrating for Dodgson's sharp, critical eye, his love of printing and illustration, and his fastidious nature. It proved a severe handicap to his ambitions, and in the end he was a better critic than an artist. Yet he persisted with the wood block Alice drawings, and within three weeks he was far enough advanced to take his first block to London for engraving by the Camden Town wood-engraver Orlando Jewitt. He had engraved some mathematical diagrams for Dodgson in 1859 and

Carroll's "Alice and the White Rabbit" from his original Alice manuscript

built up a solid reputation for meticulous, intricate architectural and scientific wood-engravings. Dodgson greatly respected Jewitt's expertise and had bought a collection of wood blocks and pencils from him, knowing they would be the most suitable for his work. It was probably Jewitt who finally convinced him if he intended to publish his illustrated story, he should consider the services of a professional draughtsman. Dodgson thought about the suggestion and, after meeting with his publisher, Macmillan, he wrote his appeal for Tenniel's services, which he sent to Tom Taylor.

Dodgson's choice of Tenniel for his Alice illustrator is an interesting one. Most sources point to Tenniel's strong talent for drawing animals; Dodgson probably admired Tenniel's Aesop with its profusion of creatures which have undoubted parallels to his thwarted animal scenes in Alice. He also admired what he called Tenniel's "grotesqueness"; those dark atmospheric compositions of exaggerated fantasy creatures carefully drawn in outline which would culminate in Tenniel's famous Jabberwock drawing in Alice. Indeed Dodgson would test all his potential illustrators by their ability to combine what he called "the pretty" with the grotesque. Writing years later to Henry Holiday, illustrator of *The Hunting of the Snark*, he lamented, "If *only* he can draw grotesques, it would be all I should desire – the grace and beauty of the pictures would quite rival Tenniel, I think."[3] Moreover, Dodgson was an avid reader of *Punch* and had once hoped to have one of his poems published there (an example survives of a trial poem scribbled on the back of a *Punch* cartoon). It is tempting to search for sources in *Punch* for his early Alice inventions as well as for those he and Tenniel created together. Parallels appear in such forms as Tenniel's *Punch* drawing (21 December 1861) of the frog smoking two enormous pipes which prefigures the caterpillar on the mushroom in Alice; or his frequent use of gaping-mouthed fish dressed as people, or the round-faced wide-eyed clown figures which he drew in almanack borders – both echoes of the fish-messenger and Tweedledee in Alice. Similarly there is a jolly pole-balancer with a long nose in Tenniel's *Punch* which reappears as a snake rising above Father William's nose in Alice. Tenniel's almanack borders, especially those of the early 1850s, however unknowingly, remain a rich source of Carrollean fantasy, drawn and engraved in the "pure outline" Dodgson so much admired. Such inventions made Tenniel the ideal candidate for Alice.

The whimsical Tenniel in *Punch* page fillers which attracted Carroll

From the start Dodgson's relations with Tenniel were courteous and business-like. He had waited over a month before he actually contacted the artist, using the letter of introduction Tom Taylor had obtained for him. Then, on 25 January 1864, he went to London to call on Tenniel in person at his studio. He found him "receptive" to the Alice illustrations, although typically cautious until he had seen the manuscript. Despite his reserve Dodgson was clearly optimistic; his diary entry records how Tenniel "was very friendly and seemed to think favourably of undertaking the pictures". Yet he allowed a further two months to pass before pressing Tenniel for his final decision, hoping it would be an agreement to take on the project. This he finally received on 5 April.[4] However, from Tenniel's point of view, the new offer came at a very bad time. At that moment he was rushed to complete his neglected *Ingoldsby Legends* drawings, which he supervised in between his equally trying weekly *Punch* duties. Here too his cartoons demanded greater detail of the "grotesque" nature Dodgson admired. They were filled with dark, shaded backgrounds, grotesque spectres of evil and heavy, brooding atmosphere. Some were sharp comments on the

Tenniel worked on *The Ingoldsby Legends*, 1864, as well as Alice. Here "The Nurse's Story", p. 80, was typical of the emotive terror themes he used at the time.

American Civil War which raged on to the disgust and horror of the British nation, and which Tenniel drew as the prophetic "American Juggernaut", the pathetic allegory "Ave Caesar" and "Britannia's Sympathy with Columbia". He created some of his strongest, most powerful evocations of the senseless horror of war; works which were deeply upsetting to the American people as the conflict dragged on. Moreover, just as Tenniel completed the *Ingoldsby Legends* drawings, the Dalziels pressed him for his promised *Arabian Nights* illustrations, "which were wanted immediately", Tenniel sighed, in a troubled letter to Pritchett.[5] It seemed he could just not get ahead. His commitments outnumbered the small amount of time left to him after Mr Punch demanded his share. Yet it was not until the end of 1864 – the year of Alice – that he realized how much more demanding and traumatic the year would be – one of the most difficult, in fact, of his entire career.

The problems began when Dodgson received Tenniel's agreement to undertake the Alice drawings. This gave him the ambitious idea that, since he now had a professional to interpolate his story, whom he would pay well, his original manuscript might be lengthened from 18,000 to 35,000 words – almost twice its length. His delight at having Tenniel's professional expertise can be measured by his own frank criticism of his original efforts to draw Alice: "I printed in manuscript and illustrated with my own crude designs – designs that rebelled against every law of Anatomy and Art (for I never had a lesson in drawing)." Of the expansion he added "in writing it out, I added many fresh ideas, which seemed to grow of themselves upon the original stock; and many more added themselves when, years afterwards (sic), I wrote it all again for publication."[6] The first chapter was largely unaltered, however, and he delivered it for printing on 6 May, four days after sending the first galley proofs (from the beginning of Chapter III) to Tenniel for the first illustrations. Meanwhile Dodgson worked upon his presentation copy for Alice Liddell and, reaching the end, he drew her on the final page, then had second thoughts and pasted her photograph over the drawing.[7] He wished to reserve the title "Alice's Adventures Underground" for this presentation copy alone, and toyed with alternative titles for the published version and considered such stilted ideas as "Alice's Hour in Elfland" before finally settling on the famous "Alice's Adventures in Wonderland". This published edition he still hoped to have completed in time for Christmas, despite the worrying silence of nearly two months from Tenniel's studio. Eventually he called upon his illustrator to see for himself just how much work had been done on Alice. He was severely disappointed, for Tenniel had not even begun work on the book. Although obviously upset, Dodgson found some comfort in the fact that the book's format could still be changed and Macmillan, his publisher, persuaded him to adopt the small size used by the successful second edition of Charles Kingsley's *The Water Babies*. It seemed a good idea, the book now smaller, more suitable for children, and after consultation with Tenniel, he also agreed. The pressure momentarily seemed to subside.

The reasons for Tenniel's neglect of Alice were various and disturbing. During the late summer Tenniel's thoughts were far from work of any kind as private sorrows and bitter morbid memories haunted his days. Most worrying of all was the recent news of his mother's serious illness. It brought back those painful memories of nursing his dying wife, and now at an especially poignant time since this year would have been their tenth wedding anniversary, had she lived. In fact Tenniel still mourned his beloved Julia. He continued to use black-

Carroll's sketches for fantasy characters and Alice(?), 4¼ x 7¼" (Christ Church College Library, Oxford)

Carroll's original title-page design for Alice (Christ Church College Library, Oxford)

Prophetic preoccupations with death in Tenniel's "The Way in the Wood" by Isa Green, *Good Words*, July 1864, p. 552

edged mourning stationery and refused to mention her to his friends. Now his beloved mother threatened to follow the path of his deceased dear wife, to leave him with only memories and renewed bouts of morbid depression. His drawing at this painful period echoed this new preoccupation with death. He chose a prophetic, distraught maiden wandering in a dark wood, overcome by the death of her lover, to accompany Isa Craig's mournful verse, "The Way in the Wood" in *Good Words*, which ended:

> Yellow, yellow leaves,
> Falling, falling, falling!
> Death is best, when hope
> There is no recalling,
> Yet, O yellow leaves,
> How the parting grieves!

Dodgson tried to keep in close contact with his artist during this difficult period, but Tenniel was far from forthcoming. His frustrations could also be seen in the dark brooding grotesques he produced for *Punch*, especially the macabre "American Juggernaut" cartoon (3 September 1864) with its wheels of death and the spectre of destruction as it rolled further into the smoke and carnage of battle. Six months had passed since he had agreed to draw for Alice but produced nothing. Then in mid-October Tenniel reached breaking point. He yearned for some relief from the personal worry as well as the guilt at not fulfilling his promise to Dodgson – all overshadowed by the ceaseless weekly demands of *Punch*. Of the Alice drawings he half-heartedly started, he chose the prophetic "pool of tears" scene in which Alice, deserted by the White Rabbit, sits by a pool of her own tears. Dodgson tried to understand the delay and recalled after another disappointing visit to Tenniel's studio: "Thence I went to Tenniel's, who showed me one drawing on wood, the only thing he had, of Alice sitting by the pool of tears, and rabbit hurrying away. We discussed the book and agreed on about thirty-four pictures."[8] It was also at this point, while Tenniel worried and nursed his dying mother, that news of his dear friend John Leech's tragic death left him deeply shocked and grief-stricken. Significantly, for the first time since he had taken Leech's place on *Punch*, he now faltered and failed to provide his usual weekly cartoon – such was the magnitude of his grief for his friend.

Then, within days of Leech's funeral, Mrs Tenniel died. Her son had been devoted to his loyal mother who had supported him and her large family for over forty years, and her death, although expected, left Tenniel deeply crushed. He wrote to Dodgson "in great distress" and although unable to explain fully his reasons, it was now clear that a Christmas Alice was impossible. And so Dodgson sent his sympathetic good wishes and begged Tenniel to put aside work on their book; "a magnanimous gesture for the Liddells were growing up so fast that he was anxious to press on with publication", according to his recent biographer.[9] Next Dodgson wrote to Macmillan explaining the delay:

> I fear my little book Alice's Adventures in Wonderland cannot appear this year. Mr. Tenniel writes that he is hopeless of completing the pictures by Christmas. The cause I do not know, but he writes in great trouble, having just lost his mother, and I have begged him to put the thing aside for the present.[10]

Instead Dodgson pressed on at least to finish his manuscript illustrations for Alice Liddell; these he completed on 26 November, in time for Christmas. It was some small consolation; and by finishing his own drawings for her gift he was able to synthesize his original ideas and prepare for the time, some time soon he hoped, when Tenniel would again be free to fulfil his Alice obligations.

Eventually Tenniel rallied round and completed all forty-two Alice drawings in about six months, submitting the last one on 18 June 1865. It had been a protracted yet revealing collaboration which in time taught him much about Dodgson, who had retained the upper hand throughout. It was clear that Tenniel was merely the hired workman, who might be asked for ideas or sketches or to supervise the engraving and printing; but in the end he remained in Dodgson's employ. Alice was, after all, published at the author's expense. Tenniel accepted his position gracefully and adopted his familiar gentlemanly air of good mannered courtesy. But in time he showed signs of strain, his intransigence and slow methods of work upset the equally stubborn and fastidious Dodgson. The two men, though, shared similar personalities, marked to the greatest extent by their insular lives; Dodgson rarely left Oxford during term time, and then he spent his summers usually at Eastbourne; Tenniel went abroad only three times in his life and proudly remained in London. "London's good enough for me!" he once snapped when a *Punch* colleague asked about his holidays. Dodgson was twelve years Tenniel's junior, but there was much of the stubborn old man in him despite his middle-age at this time. His staunch conservatism, myopia and his obsessive concern for detail were characteristics which Tenniel also shared and could at least appreciate, if not agree with.

In the end it was this mutual obsession with detail which helped to smoothe occasional bouts of pique and anger during their long collaboration. Tenniel approached his task with characteristic thoroughness and first studied the text carefully to provide the correct detail mentioned as well as those imaginative fantasies which Dodgson left up to his reader's imagination. Indeed Dodgson was never strong on description in either Alice book; he preferred dialogue and what he hoped would be strong, clear illustrations to make his points. He sent Tenniel his own rough sketches and occasional photographs for models, but these were generally ignored since Tenniel, as always, declined models of any kind. When the drawings were finished Dodgson surprised his artist by his ability to criticize and suggest alterations and expensive changes further to marry illustrations to his text. Dodgson was, after all, an avid collector of illustrations: his Oxford library contained a number of valuable aids, from works by Gillray, Seymour and Cruikshank of the older generation artists, to his much admired collection of Noel Paton's classical Shakespeare illustrations, a copy of Richard Doyle's *King of the Golden River* and work by later toybook artists like Randolph Caldecott and Kate Greenaway's imitator T. Pym. His preoccupation with accurate detail was inspired by his Pre-Raphaelite friends: he owned *The Germ*, had photographed Rossetti and later Burne-Jones drawings, and owned paintings by Rossetti and Arthur Hughes. They, like Tenniel (who also had Pre-Raphaelites as acquaintances), spurred him on to demand more meticulous and carefully considered drawings for his Alice.[11]

While Dodgson was undoubtedly the greatest single influence upon Tenniel's Alice drawings, much has been made of their similarity to the anthropomorphic inventions of the French master caricaturist Jean-Ignace Isidore Gerard Grandville. It is possible that Tenniel knew Grandville's work (and for that matter Dodgson as well), since the French artist once worked for the Parisian *Le Charivari* (upon which *Punch* was based) and his books of satiric fantasies, *Metamorphoses du Jour*, *Scènes de la vie privée et publique des animaux* and *Un Autre Monde* were published and well-known in Britain throughout the 1840s and 1850s. A recent

Grandville's anthropomorphic illustrations to his *Scènes de la vie privée*, 1842, have been compared with Tenniel's

"The Animal Caucus" from Alice in Grandville's style

critic has explored the visual similarities at length between Grandville and Tenniel's Alice drawings. But, unlike the clear evidence that exists that artists like Richard Doyle borrowed from Grandville, there is no such evidence for Tenniel, and the critic could only offer intriguing conjectures:

> Standing between the two in the realm of art as he did in time, he brought Carroll and Grandville together . . .. The white rabbit is of the prolific family of Grandville's coated, waistcoated and hatted rabbits; in the title vignettes of the Caucus-Race the animals are disposed exactly as they are in many a ring in "La vie privee et publique des animaux" or "Un Autre Monde"; The Dodo proffers his "elegant thimble" to Alice with the very gesture of the Reverend Father Cormorant that officiates at Grandville's bird wedding; the big hand reaching out of an unseen window for the white rabbit has nothing in common with Carroll's sketch of Alice's arm but much with the hand that in Grandville's cartoon [for *Le Charivari*] drops from the sky a Louis-Phillippe 'pear' to clamours of the frog kingdom; these in turn are first cousins of the frog footman and one wears the very hat and coat of the fish footman in Pig and Pepper; the pig-body carried by Alice is a near relative of Grandville's baby-pig in arms of an animal-nurse. Carroll's mock turtle had something of a seal's face but Tenniel's is like the calf in 'Un Autre Monde' . . . Humpty Dumpty belongs to the family of merry egg-shaped money-boxes in 'Un Autre Monde'.[12]

The greatest source of argument between Tenniel and Dodgson was over use of models; "Mr. Tenniel is the only artist who has drawn for me, who has resolutely refused to use a model, and declared he no more needed one than I should need a multiplication table to work a mathematical problem!" Dodgson told his protégée Gertrude Thomson years later. "I venture to think that he was mistaken and that for want of a model, he drew several pictures of 'Alice' entirely out of proportion – head decidedly too large and feet decidedly too small." Despite continual objections from Dodgson, Tenniel refused to comply.[13] His firm stand on questions of technique helped him retain some small but important hold over his employer. During the months Tenniel realized he had been hired not as an imaginative illustrator but as a drawing machine; someone to polish and perfect Dodgson's own ideas and prepare them for the engraver. His proprietorial air took the form of an irritating fastidiousness which grated upon Tenniel's independent nature. Dodgson even sent Tenniel a detailed list of all drawings required for Alice, with their exact dimensions and placement upon the page, carefully written in a mathematical code.[14] In fact he managed to get Tenniel to agree to use the majority of his original manuscript drawing ideas. A comparison between the shorter manuscript Alice (published in facsimile in 1886) and the final Tenniel Alice is very revealing. Although Dodgson's original drawings are crude, the compositions are often exactly as Tenniel's final versions, or at best only with slight variations. It was clearly Dodgson's book, and he rarely gave in to Tenniel's more imaginative expertise. Years later this same intransigence irritated Harry Furniss, the illustrator of Dodgson's *Sylvie and Bruno*. Tenniel had warned his friend against working for Dodgson, and Furniss soon discovered why. He protested to Dodgson that he and Tenniel had their own individual styles and approaches which must not be ignored; but Dodgson refused to listen or give in to such flights of artistic temperament.[15]

Moreover, Tenniel's task was even more difficult in those passages where the text gave no description of the characters or fantastic creatures required. The Alice text is filled with passages which leave most descriptions to the imagination, for Dodgson refused to pamper or talk down to his readers, however young. "If you don't know what a Gryphon is, look at the picture", was a characteristic aside

Tenniel's "Expanded Alice" compared with Carroll's claustrophobic composition, which indicates the differences between the true illustrator and the amateur.

addressed to readers in Dodgson's typical schoolmasterly tone, which he adopted in the Mock Turtle and March Hare episodes as well. Fortunately both artist and author agreed upon the importance of characters over backgrounds; that the figures should dominate their settings. Tenniel would never be a strong landscape artist; he preferred to leave his backgrounds to the discretion of his engravers. Similarly Dodgson allowed Tenniel to use his firm outline style for the rather wooden figures he placed, like actors on a stage, into their settings. These were enhanced by the Dalziels, the Alice engravers, who were by now familiar with Tenniel's obsession with engraved outline or tonal clarity. And yet critics attacked the drawings for their lack of spatial depth, that his figures were more cut-outs than carefully shaded solids.

Part of the reason for this was that Tenniel chose to imitate his *Punch* drawing techniques with Alice. He drew brief preliminary pencil sketches to perfect a composition or pose, later returning to these preliminary drawings with ink and Chinese white to simulate the engraver's line. Once satisfied, he used tracing paper to transfer the bare pencil outline of his composition onto the wood block, then finish the shading on the block, using his own specially made 6H pencils, which gave a silvery sheen to the surface, despite a preliminary whitening of the block's face for necessary contrast. These blocks were a genuine challenge to the Dalziels who peered through the sheen to cut around each densely drawn pencil line. Moreover, they endured the numerous expensive changes ordered by Dodgson, as well as Tenniel's short proof notes and corrections in pencil or red with Chinese white to point out special areas for improvement. His proof comments reveal how meticulous he and Dodgson could be. His changes are often so minute – the curl of a mouth, turn of an eyelash, twist of Alice's hair – that only the most accomplished illustrator would have detected the weaknesses, and only after years of working with their engravers. In time Dodgson too learned to recognize these subtle improvements and, much to Tenniel's dismay, he began to order more and more changes. This encroached upon Tenniel's technical expertise, and left him irritated, as his curt comments to the Dalziels in the margins of some proofs suggest.

It is significant that in later years, long after Alice was published, Tenniel returned to his original pencil sketches to re-finish and work them into his own versions of familiar plates to give friends and collectors. Was he then reasserting his authority over ground which Dodgson took away from him? Perhaps he hoped to make his original intentions known even at this late stage. Certainly the frustrations increased with the number of corrections Dodgson ordered. Moreover, it has been recently suggested that Tenniel (in pique?) supplied the Dalziels with a mere traced outline on the wood blocks using the type of artist's shorthand familiar to them and from which they were expected to work out a fully shaded and detailed finished engraving, much like his *Punch* engravings were done with the Swains. If this is true, Tenniel did reassert his authority over Dodgson with the book's printers, for only he could assess properly whether the blocks had been adequately inked and run through the presses. From the start too he had his doubts about the abilities of Dodgson's chosen printer; the Oxford University Press was an academic press capable of producing scientific and mathematical diagrams, but not the subtleties of printing children and animal illustrations.[16] But this was a small concession to such a long and difficult period working under Dodgson's complete control.

The Illustrations: Alice

Tenniel's Alice begins with a delightful and skilfully composed frontispiece. This courtroom scene, dominated by the stern gazes of the Queen of Hearts and her jittery King, is a formal composition of the type where Tenniel loved to contrast a classical sense of decorum with exaggerated comedy. His bird barristers sit obediently, their hands folded before the evidence, a large tray of tarts; the frog juror waits patiently, pen poised to record the facts. It is a very regal setting, one which a recent critic has suggested Tenniel borrowed from his talented illustrator colleague Charles Henry Bennett – then about to join the *Punch* staff. (There is a remarkable similarity with Bennett's courtroom frontispiece for *The Fables of Aesop and other Tales Translated into Human Nature*, 1857, and Tenniel's Alice frontispiece.) It would be nice to believe he used Bennett's invention, in light of the tribute he paid to the artist when he acted for his widowed family's benefit three years later.[17]

On the whole, sources for most of Tenniel's Alice illustrations came from Dodgson himself from either his original sketches or suggestions sent to the artist. Many believe that the model for Alice herself was a photograph Dodgson sent to Tenniel of the canon's blonde daughter Mary Hilton Badcock – although typically Tenniel does not seem to have copied it. Another theory is that Dodgson at least modelled his Alice upon Edith Liddell, the seven-and-a-half-year-old sister of Alice Liddell, who was herself too old for the part at the time. Tenniel, however, chose a distinctly adult-looking Alice, whom some believed to be his niece, but even this seems unlikely in view of his aversion to models of any kind. Indeed, children were not his favourite subjects, and his *Punch* work throughout 1864 suggests that he worked hard to bring his juveniles up to scratch. A childless widower for the remainder of his life, he rarely had the opportunity to study children first-hand, although he loved the visits of his young nieces and nephews. He never actually chose to illustrate children's books, apart from the Alice volumes, although he made a curious attempt to design a set of playing cards for children, which he called "Happy Families" – each card a stark cut-out face presumably to imitate medieval models.[18] In the end his Alice is far from Dodgson's original Pre-Raphaelite girl with the long, frizzy tresses and haunting eyes. Tenniel's Alice echoed the china-doll features of those flawless classical

Tenniel's touched-up proof with note instructing his engraver: "One touch right corner of mouth *above*. One touch under right lower eyelash." (Victoria and Albert Museum)

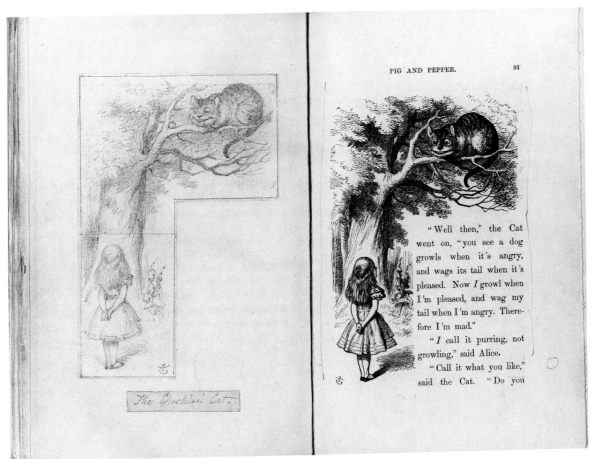

Original preliminary pencil drawing mounted beside published engraving of "The Cheshire Cat" (Private Collection)

Within the image, the published engraving reads:

PIG AND PEPPER.   91

"Well then," the Cat went on, "you see a dog growls when it's angry, and wags its tail when it's pleased. Now *I* growl when I'm pleased, and wag my tail when I'm angry. Therefore I'm mad."

"*I* call it purring, not growling," said Alice.

"Call it what you like," said the Cat. "Do you

The pencil caption reads: *The Cheshire Cat*

beauties he so successfully portrayed in *Lalla Rookh*; she was an enigmatic child–adult well suited to her fits of very adult petulance and outraged anger as well as the expressions of childish innocence which dominate the story.

Tenniel achieved greater success with the White Rabbit, one of the first subjects he drew. This endearing, bug-eyed, fancy waist-coated dandy with his pocket watch, umbrella and fan (a nosegay in Dodgson's original version) was well suited to Tenniel's anthropomorphic skills; a figure freely adopted from the full-faced inventions of his early *Punch* initials and almanack borders. Compared with Dodgson's original weak rabbit sketch in long trousers, even longer ears and mousey face, Tenniel's animal combined accuracy with the comic invention which would elevate this and subsequent drawings into the realms of the very special and make the White Rabbit one of the most popular characters in the book. Dodgson too was fond of this symbolic character, years later asking his inquisitive readers:

And what of the White Rabbit, what of him? Was *he* framed on the 'Alice' lines, or meant as a contrast? As a contrast, distinctly. For *her* "youth", "audacity", "vigour" and "swift directness of purpose", read "elderly", "timid", "feeble" and you will get *something* of what I meant him to be. I *think* the White Rabbit should wear spectacles [Tenniel omitted these]. I am sure his voice would quaver, and his knees quiver, and his whole air suggest a total inability to say 'Bo' to a goose![19]

George Edwards' copper engraved dodo, 1803 (Author's Collection)

Tenniel's pencil sketch possibly taken from Edwards' model

Final Alice-Dodo plate

In other instances Tenniel merely refined Dodgson's original idea – as was his role – particularly if the scene involved animals. Tenniel's "Animal Caucus" emerged a refined version of his *Punch* style and relied upon a vignette and cross-hatched background, familiar to *Punch* cartoons, to contrast with the carefully engraved feathered birds, furry mouse and shiny crab. In fact Dodgson added a number of new animal scenes when he revised his text, no doubt to make full use of Tenniel's zoological skills. Tenniel had the ability to convince yet add the subtle details which turned the scientific into the imaginative – like the stiff collar, human hands and foppish cane of the perfectly presentable Dodo. Dodgson wisely dropped some subsequent animal scenes, like the flight of birds which abandoned Alice on her water-washed island; Tenniel rarely drew birds in motion. Similarly he scrapped the delightful brandy to the lizard scene, which offered more opportunity for comedy; one can't help but think that this was a mistake.

Alice's erratic size presented Dodgson, at least, with serious problems. He was never skilled enough as a draughtsman to understand correct proportions, and here he relied instead upon altering details, like the voluminous drapery of Alice's dress; or the swirls of her hair which filled out his drawing in the original version and give the effect that Alice was too large for her surroundings. Tenniel, on the other hand, understood the tricks of scale drawing – no doubt learned from his nights at the theatre studying stage settings. In fact, he borrowed a favourite device used by Rossetti to suggest claustrophobia, by placing his Alice in a dark, doll-house-like interior with only a tiny leaded window opened to suggest escape. For added measure he propped Alice on her elbow to give a strong diagonal which helped, with stronger receding perspective lines, to send the eye inward toward the spaces into which Alice cowers. He also used the fairy-painter's trick of altering the scale of familiar objects, like the subsequent drawing of Alice chased under a perfectly drawn thistle by a well-proportioned life-sized puppy, while she is no taller than a blade of grass. The thistle was a rare instance of Tenniel's botanical studies and and it still survives in a double-page pencil sketch from one of his numerous pocket sketchbooks.[20]

Dodgson's love of the grotesque surfaced in his version of Alice expanding her body far above a forest, her twisted columnar neck like a stretched toffee on which pigeons could perch. Tenniel offered a more restrained version in which the rubbery neck sequence was dropped entirely and he concentrated instead upon Alice herself as she stands in amazement, her head seeming to pull her body upward "opening out like the largest telescope that ever was!" There were more appropriate opportunities for grotesques as well, like the cartilaginous face of a fish messenger or the bulging eyes of a frog footman which he made even more grotesque by dressing him in a meticulously realistic footman's uniform. The triumph of the bizarre was undoubtedly his Ugly Duchess, who was originally not in Dodgson's Alice; she was added later by Tenniel. Experts now agree in this instance he did use a model: the famous painting "A Grotesque Old Woman" by the fifteenth-century Flemish painter Quinten Massys. The painter himself sits comfortably within Tenniel's view of the world, for his paintings were inspired by such favourite masters as Leonardo and the early Italians. This particular portrait was reputed to be that of Margaretha Maultasch, Duchess of Carinthia and Tyrol, who was said to be the ugliest woman in history. Tenniel borrowed her rubbery frown – itself a suitable touch, for "Maultasch" translates as "pocket-mouth" – and her elaborate medieval head-dress, but replaced her withered

Alice and the dog, with preliminary pencil sketch of the thistle, indicate the care Tenniel took over sections of the Alice illustrations. (Huntington Art Gallery)

breasts and the symbolic rose bud in the original painting with a strategically placed screaming baby.[21]

Flowers and gardens played a considerable role in Tenniel's Alice illustrations, although, on the whole he rarely drew botanical subjects, apart from obligatory backgrounds. Even here he wisely concentrated upon detail, like the brilliant twist of Dodgson's original caterpillar on a mushroom into a subtle exercise in mystery, with Alice peering over the edge of the fungus and the caterpillar's legs forming a perfect profile face. Dodgson was clearly pleased with the care his illustrator took to get the flowers and plants to look right. Later, when he reissued Tenniel's drawings in his *Nursery Alice*, he pointed out Tenniel's careful drawing of a clump of foxgloves set behind Alice and the pig-baby. It was in fact a well-chosen fairyland flower: "Foxes do not wear gloves. The right word is 'Folk's Gloves'. Did you ever hear that Fairies used to be called 'the good Folk'?"

The Mad Hatter, March Hare and Dormouse chapter did not appear in Dodgson's original manuscript but was added later when he expanded the book. The source of the Mad Hatter has been the subject of considerable speculation. He may have been inspired by Dodgson's *Punch* reading; "Mad as a Hatter" (4 January 1862) ended suitably: "We think we can venture to observe that the madness of a hatter must be, from the nature of his calling, peculiarly one of those things that are said to be more easily *felt* than described". Other theories put forward are that he was a burlesque of Gladstone, the Prime Minister (although it has been overlooked that Gladstone did not become Prime Minister until 1868); or that, according to clerical circles, he was inspired by the Reverend Edward Bradley. Most convincing of all was that he was inspired by the local Oxford furniture dealer and eccentric inventor Theophilus Carter, known to his Oxford neighbours as the "Mad Hatter" because he always wore a top hat. Carter in fact invented such marvellous contraptions as an alarm clock bed (that woke a sleeper by throwing him out of bed) which was shown at the Great Exhibition in 1851. There Tenniel may have seen it or even Carter himself while he toured the halls, preparing drawings for his *Punch* Great Exhibition Number.

In contrast, Dodgson's original sketch for the Queen of Hearts resembled one eventually drawn by Tenniel. "I pictured to myself the Queen of Hearts as a sort of embodiment of ungovernable passion – a blind and aimless Fury", he once said.[22] His original drawing makes her look like a large-jawed nun in a flat, angular dress, presumably to imitate her playing card origins. This Tenniel softened, gave her a rounded profile, furled nostrils, gaping mouth and stern beady eyes; all suitable touches to this most terrifying woman. He called upon anthropomorphic skills learned while drawing his *Punch* political portraits (he refused to call them caricatures), to combine and exaggerate the distinctive elements of animals or humans. Examples survive in Alice – the gryphon and mock turtle. The fearsome gryphon was a legendary amalgamation of half eagle, half lion which he gave the sharp claws, scaly skin, sharp pointed ears and razor-like beak, a combination of two of Tenniel's favourite creatures. Dodgson was apparently pleased with the result, as he confidently told his readers, "If you don't know what a gryphon is, look at the picture". The mock turtle too was ripe for parody, and Tenniel used the familiar veal-based mock turtle soup to inspire his version of the creature, with the head, hooves and tail of a calf, the body of a turtle. It was a far more successful invention than Dodgson's original armour-plated, seal-faced turtle.

Tenniel took the greatest care over what was perhaps his most successful drawing in the book. This was Alice's trial by the animal jury which she accidentally overturns in their box, the twenty types of animal Tenniel drew toppling out onto the floor. Some were familiar creatures well-drawn, like the frog, dormouse, rat, ferret, duck and squirrel, while others left even Dodgson puzzled until Tenniel explained them: "Mr. Tenniel says the screaming bird is a storkling (of course you know what *that* is?) and the little white head is a Mousling. Isn' it a little darling?" he explained in the *Nursery Alice*. Tenniel's original pencil sketch for this illustration still survives. It was carefully shaded in ink and Chinese white, but eventually had to be completely re-drawn and condensed (Alice eventually loses her foot) before he transferred it onto the wood block. Even then he finished the original drawing, obviously pleased with the animals: it still exists in the clear firm pencil line on stiff board (now in the Harvard Library). It was a rare instance of Tenniel's use of suspended action in an otherwise rather static group of illustrations, a device which culminated in the final frenzied attack of playing cards sprayed over Alice and her animal jurors.

*   *   *   *   *

With the last illustration completed and Dodgson's approval of a specimen printed page and dummy volume bound in bright red cloth to appeal to his child readers, *Alice in Wonderland* was ready for final publication. By the end of June 1865 the Clarendon Press had printed 2,000 copies. Dodgson had the first one bound in white vellum which he presented to Alice Liddell at the deanery to mark the third anniversary of their famous river journey together. By some quirk of fate, Tenniel too had only recently toured the river banks where the Alice book had been born; his annual river row this year included a stop at Nuneham and those nearby areas familiar to Dodgson and his original Alice. It was as if he too paid an unconscious homage to Alice, to the two full years of prolonged struggle over her book. It was more likely he wished to extricate that far from happy experience from his memory. Meanwhile Dodgson had been to the publisher and, apparently satisfied with the copies he saw there, he inscribed about twenty for presentation to his closest friends.

Dodgson's satisfaction with the original printing was shattered by a letter he received from Tenniel in mid-July, after he had received his first copy. It was written in an alarmed tone, in which Tenniel explained he was "entirely dissatisfied with the printing of the pictures". Dodgson was understandably upset, not only for having overlooked the problem – if there was one – but at the embarrassing threat of a possible reprint, and the loss of a great deal of his own money. In fact, he had spent a total of £497 on Alice – almost Tenniel's annual *Punch* salary – of which the artist received £138, the Dalziels £142 for their engravings, the printers £137, and the binders and advertisers £80. For many years it has been assumed that the rejection of the first Alice edition was entirely due to Dodgson's fastidiousness. Critics pointed out his infuriating habits and perfectionist tendencies with his publishers; that Dodgson once wrote of publishers:

> The day they undertake a book for me is a *dies nefastus* for them. From that day till the book is out – an interval of some two or three years on an average – there is no pause in "the pelting of the pitiless storm" of directions and questions on every conceivable detail.[23]

With the Alice book he had plagued Macmillans about binding colours ("bright red will be best – not the best, perhaps, artistically, but the most attractive to childish eyes. Can this colour be managed with the same smooth, bright cloth you have in green?").[24] He suggested the book "would look better with the edges merely cut smooth, and no gilding".[25] He even insisted upon receiving fifty copies immediately after printing – proof of his acceptance of their quality – because, as he termed it, "his young friends . . . are all grown out of childhood so alarmingly fast".[26] But we know it was Tenniel's damning letter which rejected the first Alice, and left Dodgson despondent, confused and uncertain of his next move.

Dodgson's diary entry during this traumatic period is revealing. Despite the expense, he was obviously willing to bow to Tenniel's judgement, and sought only moral support from his publisher: "Called on Macmillan, and showed him Tenniel's letter about the fairy-tail – he is entirely dissatisfied with the printing of the pictures, and I suppose we shall have to do it all again." [27] Tenniel's objections have been analysed by bibliographers who compared the offending first edition with the subsequent printing. The result was that just nine of Tenniel's illustrations appear to be printed lighter and nine heavier, while the far more substantial group of twenty-four engravings were identical in both editions. [28] Surely eighteen misprints were slim grounds for losing so much money and time. Indeed speculation continues as to why Tenniel now decided to become so critical over the printing. He rarely gave his *Punch* engravings a second glance, never proofed them, and even accepted the poorly printed overall greyness of his early anthology drawings as part of commercial publishing. Could he have decided at the final hour to reassert himself over Dodgson after submitting to the author's demands for so long? Certainly Dodgson had the unfortunate talent of bringing out the worst in Tenniel, who suffered bouts of repressed anger. On the other hand, perhaps Tenniel did not truly believe Dodgson would accept his criticism, just as he often failed to do over the drawings themselves. By rejecting the edition he attempted to maintain his professional standards and if, as he maintained, the Alice printing was damaging to his career as an illustrator, this could damage Dodgson's reputation also. Months after Alice finally appeared Tenniel suggested as much to the Dalziels, who it seems were kept in the dark as to the fate of their Alice engravings. His letter to them merely hinted at his stand but it was enough: "Mr. Dodgson's book came out months ago; but I protested so strongly against the disgraceful printing that he *cancelled the edition*". [29]

Over the years, the Dalziel brothers shared in the traumas of getting Alice right for its author. They were instrumental in the final appearance of Tenniel's drawings which they transferred onto box-wood blocks (Tenniel transferred his own drawings onto blocks later on for *Through the Looking Glass*). When Tenniel's designs needed tightening up to fit the page spaces, the Dalziels condensed them (see "Alice's evidence" from *Alice*, which is known to have been drawn and engraved in two versions). Tenniel worked closely with them upon each block. Their engraved proofs (now in the Victoria and Albert Museum) indicate the care he took over the smallest line, the curve of Alice's face, or the change of a shadow. He even drew a fully finished ink version on the back of a text wood block which the Dalziels had sent him (this block is now in the Newberry Collection, Chicago). Years later Dodgson too recalled the Dalziels' role in his book and asked his publisher,

> By the way, who has the wood blocks? I can hardly doubt that they are being carefully kept, but, considering the sum I had to pay for them, I shall be glad to be certain that they are safe from all possibility of damage.

Tenniel's delicate pencil drawings were lost on the block, cut away by the Dalziels' engraving burins (tools). But the blocks have survived to this day, since only wax moulds were originally taken from them, and these were eventually turned into electrotypes for printing. [30]

Whatever the reason for Tenniel's objections the two men agreed to give their public the best Alice they could produce, regardless of the time or money spent. Several weeks passed until (on 2 August) it was decided to withdraw the first edition and reprint. It was a particularly painful decision for Dodgson: he had to write to those friends he had already sent copies to ask for their return, "as the pictures are so badly done". The new edition appeared by November 1865, still in time for Christmas and safely dated 1866. Dodgson received his first copy on 9 November, but Tenniel kept him waiting almost a month before writing on 28 November to approve the printing. Delighted by the news Dodgson was free at last to praise his new book, which he triumphantly declared "very *far* superior to the old, and in fact a perfect piece of artistic printing". Tenniel was less forthcoming, and he continued to watch over subsequent printed editions of his Alice to ensure an even standard from his original blocks, and the eventual electrotyped editions.[31] The question of disposing of the inferior first printing still plagued Dodgson, however. He had the idea he could sell them as waste paper and recoup some of his losses. Tenniel suggested selling them to America and eventually the first edition appeared in the autumn, issued by Appleton of New York, ironically even before the first English edition. Dodgson was further delighted by his printer, who magnanimously wrote off the outstanding £200 of the first inferior printing, so that by as early as 1866 Dodgson had recouped all of his losses and Alice began to earn him substantial sums of money.

The reviews of Alice stretched over a three-year period and at first were somewhat disappointing. The first appeared in *The Reader* (18 November 1865), followed by a more prestigious notice in the conservative literary paper the *Athenaeum* (where Tenniel's paintings had earlier been praised for their attempts at High Art). The reviewer compared Alice with the recent dearth of more suitable moral children's tales and dismissed Dodgson's fantasy as misguided. He had

> laboured hard to heap together strange adventures, and heterogeneous combina-
> tions; and we acknowledge the hard labour. Mr Tenniel, again, is square and grim,
> and uncouth in his illustrations, howbeit clever, even sometimes to the verge of
> grandeur, as is the artist's habit. We fancy that any real child might be more puzzled
> than enchanted by this stiff, over-wrought story.[32]

On the other hand, Tenniel's champion from *Lalla Rookh* days, *The Times*, gave a favourable account again to help promote his career. Barely mentioning the book's author, the *Times* critic announced:

> Mr Tenniel, who has illustrated a little work – *Alice's Adventures in Wonderland*,
> with extraordinary grace. Look at the first chapter of this volume, and note the
> rabbit at the head of it. His umbrella is tucked under his arm and he is taking the
> watch out of his pocket to see what o'clock it is. The neatness of touch may be seen
> in a dozen vignettes throughout the volume, the letterpress of which is by Mr Lewis
> Carroll, and may best be described as excellent nonsense.

Similarly the prestigious *Pall Mall Gazette* pronounced the entire venture "a children's feast and triumph of nonsense".[33]

Such enthusiastic reviews soon set the pace for the reading public's response. In fact new editions of Alice appeared annually from 1866–68, Dodgson receiving a handsome profit of £250 after just two years. From 1869–89 a series of twenty-six reprinted editions were issued, each one carefully supervised by Dodgson and, where the illustrations were concerned, by Tenniel (see Appendix). Such success centred on Dodgson's simple, entertaining story. Launched in an era of stern, worthy religious tracts and improving parables for children, it sought only to delight. Tenniel's clear animal creatures and exaggerated characters were a refreshing change in this all too earnest market; Dodgson's challenging text filled with puns, literary jokes and reworkings of familiar poets from

Southey to Wordsworth, tempted the most earnest adult as well as intriguing the innocent child. When the poet Christina Rossetti received her copy she characteristically pronounced it "a funny pretty book", and such responses echoed popular feeling. More exalted admirers included, according to legend, Queen Victoria herself. Since Alice had appeared while the Queen mourned the death of her beloved Albert, it seems Tenniel's drawings may have helped her briefly to forget her crushing sadness. One day a small three-and-a-half-year-old girl sat at the Queen's feet and turned over the pages of Alice, stopping over Tenniel's pool of tears drawing.

> Noticing this rapt doubled-up little creature in the fire-light so intent over her book, the Queen asked her what it was. She rose and carried it over, and standing at the royal knee opened it at the page where the diminutive Alice is swimming in the flood of her own tears . . .. This little girl, pointing out the picture, looked up into the Queen's face and said, "Do you think, please, *you* could cry as much as that?"

Although the Queen's exact response was not remembered, the incident proved a poignant reminder of her own sorrow. She expressed great enthusiasm for Carroll, and afterward sent a locket to this little girl who charmed her unknowingly to forget her grief.[34]

*   *   *   *   *

For the next two years, between 1866–68, Tenniel devoted most of his time to his *Punch* cartoons, with only occasional breaks for minor book illustrations. These again were largely for anthologies or religious works, the most notable being for Adelaide Anne Proctor's *Legends and Lyrics*, 1866. Tenniel consented to one drawing here, illustrating "A Legend of Bregenz", one of Miss Procter's collected poems (which were now in their tenth edition). She was the talented daughter of the noted literary lion Barry Cornwall and had achieved a considerable reputation writing on both literary and social issues. Charles Dickens agreed to introduce the new edition of her poems, while Tenniel's design, in his heavy gothic *Once a Week* style, depicted a woman appealing to a group of men in the torchlight. It again relied upon atmosphere, but unfortunately without the Dalziels to engrave it, the less accomplished Horace Harral turned his drawing in a rather heavy-handed, dull version of Tenniel's early more successful style.

His first full book commission after Alice involved twenty-nine full and half-page illustrations to W.H. Miller's *The Mirage of Life*, 1867, a religious tale published by the Religious Tract Society. Again he relied upon atmosphere and heavy background shading to suggest the mirage in the title, and had special difficulties with the book's eighteenth-century setting – a period generally overlooked by Tenniel. His figures dressed in powdered wigs and silk waistcoats, again suffered from inferior engraving, this time by the jobbing engravers Butterworth and Heath.

More literary themes, especially found in volumes of poetry, appealed to him because they offered greater scope for imaginative interpretations. Publishers realized this, but instead of commissioning new drawings, they re-issued his more successful earlier work in new guises: his three *Dramatic Scenes* illustrations reappeared now in a new edition of Longfellow's *Tales of the Wayside Inn*, 1867; his *Juvenile Verse* drawings reappeared in *Gems of National Poetry*, 1868; and even his early Dickens drawings were republished in a *Christmas Books* compilation in 1869. It remained clear that Tenniel was essentially a literary personality and illustrator. Those journalists, novelists and playwrights he befriended shared his affections and were second only to the artists he valued among his best friends. He most admired Dickens, who by now had become an impressive lecturer and American traveller as well as a prolific if indefatigable author. When Dickens proposed a second tour of America, Tenniel joined with his friends and organized a send-off banquet in his honour at the Freemason's Hall in November 1867. He was among the four hundred assembled actors, writers and artists; a hundred ladies were allowed to occupy the gallery after the dessert to listen to the speeches presided over by Lord Lytton, with Tennyson and Trollope as stewards. It was an overwhelming tribute which deeply touched Dickens, who rose to acknowledge their good wishes. Although Dickens was usually eloquent, on this occasion he found great difficulty speaking when faced by what he called "a living wall of friends".[35]

Tenniel's *Punch* work during the period was considerably eased by the support and advice he received from his good friend Charles Keene. Keene had infused *Punch* with a series of witty social satires for several years; now in 1866 he tried his hand at political cartoons and three Keene cartoons were published in place of Tenniel's. Gradually he helped to ease the weekly burden Tenniel felt; this left time for more ambitious schemes. These included a long, arched watercolour portrait of Leonardo da Vinci for a mosaic scheme at the South Kensington Museum (now the Victoria and Albert Museum). His single figure was dressed in a heavy brown fur-trimmed robe and held a palette, an elderly paragon of the Renaissance set against a shimmering gold mosaic background. The design remains as fresh, the colours minutely stippled and overlaid, as when it was painted a hundred and twenty-four years ago.[36]

"Leonardo da Vinci", Tenniel's watercolour for a mosaic, 1866, $36^1/_2$ x $26^1/_4$" (Victoria and Albert Museum)

*   *   *   *   *

The success and popularity of Tenniel's Alice quickly followed him to the *Punch* offices, where his colleagues convinced him to parody his familiar characters for political cartoons. He eventually agreed to a version of Alice, the gryphon and mock turtle published in the 1 February 1868 issue; and the Alice-inspired "Before the Tournament" in November that same year. During this time Dodgson had kept an occasional eye out for Tenniel's activities; like the time he attended the Charles Bennett benefit and criticized Tenniel's performance. Moreover, he was heartened by the popularity of their Alice collaboration, despite its problems. Within months of its publication he had written to Macmillan, "I have a floating idea of writing some sort of sequel". He completed several pages of what he soon called "the second volume of Alice" that same year, 1866, and approached Tenniel for help with the drawings to what would eventually become *Through the Looking-Glass*. Barely a year had passed since Tenniel breathed a sigh of relief after completing the first Alice drawings, and it was not surprising that he flatly refused Dodgson's new offer, politely but firmly pleading the pressures of overwork. He suggested his *Punch* predecessor Richard Doyle might agree; he recalled how Doyle now struggled to launch a gallery career with time-consuming watercolours of fairy landscapes, and that he

ALICE IN BLUNDERLAND.

(With Mr. Punch's *profoundest Apologies to "Alice in Wonderland.")*

Tenniel re-used Alice themes in *Punch* (30 October 1880)

needed the work. It was an inspired suggestion for, in fact, Dodgson had earlier approached Doyle over the first Alice illustrations, but was put off by Doyle's own claims of overwork. Dodgson clearly admired Doyle's fanciful style, and on 22 January 1867, he wrote to suggest the new project. Encouraged by the response he soon called upon Doyle at his London studio to examine his recently painted garish landscapes of swirling fairy figures, especially noting the re-worked pencil sketches of Doyle's childhood fantasies. Some of these were probably preparations for Doyle's masterpiece *In Fairyland,* 1870, but Dodgson was far from impressed, and he soon gave up the idea of using him.[37] He turned instead to another favourite artist – the master of clean classical outline, Joseph Noel Paton. Although a religious and historical painter, Paton was best known for his *Water Babies* illustrations and those large fairy-filled canvases which had earned him the recent accolade "Her Majesty's Limner for Scotland" and a knighthood. Dodgson had asked his Oxford colleague George Macdonald for an introduction to the artist, but when he approached Paton the painter refused his offer as well, pleading ill health: he added prophetically, "Tenniel's the man".

Despite these upsets Dodgson continued to work on the story he now called his "Looking-Glass House". As work progressed, it became clear that Tenniel was indeed "the man" to do this story justice. Determined to persuade Tenniel a second time, on 8 April 1868 he called upon him at his studio to press his case further. This time Tenniel was forced to confront Dodgson face to face, with the result that he was less doctrinaire, more unsure of his objections. Although he again refused the offer, he added a hopeful proviso: Dodgson later recalled how there was "no chance of his being able to do pictures for me till the year after next, if then". Dodgson outlined the apparent *impasse* in a letter to Mrs Macdonald, asking for advice and support from the woman who had urged him originally to publish the first Alice story:

> I shall try my luck again with Mr Tenniel, and if he fails me, I really don't know what to do. Doyle isn't good enough (look at any of his later pictures) and Arthur Hughes has not, so far as I know, any turn for the grotesque. However I haven't *quite* given up hope in Tenniel yet.[38]

He wrote next to Macmillan, outlining his dilemma and even asked about the decidedly minor talent of W.S. Gilbert ("Bab") as a suitable alternative to Tenniel. But it was clear that Tenniel was obviously the best choice, and Dodgson was so certain of this that he even offered to pay for five months of the artist's *Punch* time (a substantial £200) if he would agree.

It was probably Dodgson's characteristic persistence, now so familiar to Tenniel, which tipped the scales in his favour, and eventually the artist relented. He agreed to provide the new illustrations, but only in his own time. On this point he stood firm. His *Punch* responsibilities came first, despite the fact that he had again missed out a second political cartoon this year. Dodgson was elated, but not wishing to appear too enthusiastic and rather more businesslike, he agreed to think over Tenniel's offer. Only on 18 June 1868, a year and a half after first proposing the project to Tenniel, did he record in his diary: "I wrote to Tenniel accepting his kind offer to do the pictures (at such spare times as he can find) for the second volume of *Alice*. He thinks that it is possible (but not likely) that we might get it out by Christmas 1869."[39] In the end Tenniel's apprehensions were well-founded: it would take the next three years for the new Alice to appear. Perhaps he had a premonition about the difficulties of this new project; he certainly shared Doyle's belief in such things. Yet once he had given his word, he knew, like the true gentleman he was, he could never go back on his promise. His fate was sealed.

Again the long process of collaboration began. Tenniel believed for once he had the upper hand and sought to take full advantage of the fact. Dodgson, on the other hand, was clearly flattered by Tenniel's submission and anxious as always to proceed as quickly as possible. As late as 1 November 1868 he was still congratulating himself on his luck with Tenniel – a full four months after his agreement to collaborate – when he wrote in his diary: "The second volume of *Alice* will after all be illustrated by Tenniel, who has reluctantly consented, as his hands are full." It was as if he tried to convince himself of his good fortune.

Similarly a month later, on 11 December he wrote to Agnes Argles in a tone of thwarted pride, with his too familiar impatience evident: "Well, as to the new volume of *Alice*, I am just going to begin printing it – and I *hope* Mr Tenniel will manage to get the pictures done by Christmas next year – that's a long time to wait . . . " He had obviously been put off yet again by Tenniel, and his hope for a Christmas 1868 publication was now a faded dream.[40]

While waiting, Dodgson threw all his efforts into completing the manuscript of what he now called "Beyond the Looking-Glass", and eventually sent the first chapter to Macmillan in January 1869. There were encouraging signs that the sequel might share some of the popularity and financial success of the first volume, which continued to sell well and appeared in French and German editions this year. Dodgson's enthusiasm was dashed, however, when he visited Tenniel in March – almost a year after his promise to draw for him – and discovered that nothing had been done on the book. Moreover, Tenniel seemed far more intransigent, less willing to perform even after Dodgson's familiar goading remarks and insistent letters. Almost nine months further passed until Tenniel showed some small signs of progress. It seems strange that Tenniel, usually so thorough, should wait a full year before even consulting the Dalziels to ask whether they could engrave the new Alice commission; but such was the case. This occurred only after Dodgson's recent visit, when he thankfully found some rough sketches for about ten illustrations, and asked about engravers. Tenniel then felt it prudent to write to the Dalziels in a polite yet obviously harassed tone on 11 January 1870:

> Dear Dalziel,
>
> Are you disposed to undertake the engraving of another little book for Mr Dodgson — It is a continuation of "Alice's Adventures" and I am going to work upon it at once. Send line please to say *'Yes'* — and I'll let you know the size of blocks &c.
>
> > In much haste
> > Yours very truly
> >
> > J. Tenniel
>
> All good wishes for the New year!!![41]

Fortunately the Dalziels agreed. Two months later Dodgson returned more confident from a visit to Tenniel's studio. During such periods, Dodgson's characteristic impatience took various forms. It included a promise to the influential children's writer and editor of *Aunt Judy's Magazine* Margaret Gatty on 20 February: "I hope to be able to send you a copy of the English edition early in November, if not before the end of October. Mr Tenniel has gone to work at the pictures 'with a will', and is getting on capitally."[42] He and Tenniel had arranged for about thirty drawings and Tenniel sent off the first three to the Dalziels for engraving. Initially Dodgson had planned a total of forty-two pictures to fill eleven chapters; but again like the first Alice he enthusiastically expanded this to fifty illustrations over twelve chapters (eight more than the original Alice). Tenniel could not have been pleased with the extra work and his progress was painfully slow. Meanwhile, Dodgson turned his frustration on his publisher and with familiar fastidiousness plagued Macmillan with corrections to a title-page which he thought had misplaced letters, the wrong spaced lines and a comma and a full-stop set too high for his taste.[43]

Then, late in May Tenniel's steady progress was interrupted by the tragic death of his *Punch* editor and old friend Mark Lemon. It was in fact an emotionally trying period for the entire *Punch* staff, as the loss of such a long-suffering editor – and for Tenniel his first real employer with faith in his abilities – was difficult to accept. Yet Tenniel forced himself to return to his new Alice drawings throughout this sad period, no doubt aware of Dodgson's impatience.

Relations between the author and illustrator of *Through the Looking-Glass* have been compared to a chessgame: it is an apt metaphor for the book which opens with a chessboard, and the game dominates the story and Tenniel's drawings. Each man observed the familiar rules of courtesy and restraint towards one another; yet all the while one tried to gain the upper hand over the other – to play for time (in Tenniel's case) or to win a completed book (in Dodgson's). Again Dodgson irritated Tenniel with time-consuming demands to change small areas in his drawings or later sections of the engraved blocks. These were trying corrections: like the twist of a leg, the curl of an eyelash or the strengthening of an ear. He disliked Tenniel's choice of heavy crinoline for Alice's coronation dress and snapped "Don't give Alice so much crinoline", at such a late stage it meant expensive and costly re-drawing and re-engraving to satisfy the fastidious author. Tenniel in fact had to replace the tubular balloon-like rings previously used on the chess pieces drawings – which were cleverly used to indicate that Alice had joined the chessgame – with a more fashionable period dress of

Carroll objected to the balloon-crinoline Tenniel gave to Alice. Preliminary pencil sketch and final engraving for "Queen Alice" (Private Collection)

The Mad Hatter in prison was altered several times despite its engraving by the Dalziels. Engraved proof (Victoria and Albert Museum)

swagged and ruffled fabric (cut to the knee to suggest her youth). The change in this drawing alone involved five new blocks: the original engraved block was scraped of unwanted detail, a new piece of wood ("plug") inserted and re-engraved from Tenniel's newly transferred pencil drawing. In another instance, Tenniel's Mad Hatter in prison, drawn seated in profile as a forlorn character staring up at his hat, failed to satisfy. Dodgson asked for an entirely new pose, a more compact frontal view in which the Hatter's contorted face, twisted legs and dark shaded background could suggest obvious discomfort. This too had to be re-drawn, approved and re-engraved.

By 1 June Tenniel had reached the third chapter, "Looking-Glass Insects", which sparked off further difficulties with Dodgson. He had written the chapter so that Alice finds herself seated in a railway carriage with a goat, an old man and an elderly white-haired lady, with a ticket-collector staring in at them through binoculars. When the train lurched forward Alice was to grab hold of the old lady's hair – a most impolite and ungracious gesture according to Tenniel, who wrote to object. This time he succeeded in getting his way and the old lady was removed from the story. Similarly, the chapter continued with what is now called the "Wasp in the Wig" passage. Only recently has it been discovered exactly why Tenniel objected to it; in his opinion "a *wasp* in a *wig* is altogether beyond the appliances of art". He sent Dodgson the following letter and as a result the wasp chapter was duly removed from the text:

> My Dear Dodgson:
>
> I think that when the jump occurs in the railway scene you might very well make Alice lay hold of the goat's *beard* as being the object nearest to her hand – instead of the old lady's hair. The jerk would actually throw them together. Don't think me brutal, but I am bound to say that the "wasp" chapter does not interest me in the least, and I can't see my way to picture. If you want to shorten the book, I cant help thinking – with all submission – that *this* is your opportunity.
>
> In agony of haste,
>
> > Yours sincerely,
> > J. Tenniel[44]

Dodgson had the first seven completed illustrations in his possession by the end of June. This gave Tenniel a slight breathing space and he turned instead to troubles at *Punch*. The staff had begun work under their new editor, Shirley Brooks, but his disorganized, boisterous approach left much to be desired. Brooks was far from practical and his four year stint as editor helped to precipitate the steady downhill course *Punch* would take from now onwards. Tenniel's undying loyalty to the paper was to be tested during this period, and he understandably devoted most of his efforts toward maintaining good relations with his new editor. Moreover, it was a particularly trying time politically, with the rise of the Franco–Prussian war and reports of suffering across the Channel which stirred Tenniel's Francophile instincts. He eventually created some of his most stirring cartoons of war, filled with classical allegories, inspired patriotic virtues and humane sympathy which touched the hearts of his British and French readers. His position as chief cartoonist was duly recognized this year as well, when the *Punch* publishers re-issued a second volume of his most popular cartoons.

When he did return to Alice, he encountered fresh obstacles like Dodgson's

Tenniel's stirring *Punch* tribute to France during the Franco-Prussian War

instructions to have the chessboard landscape in chapter two re-drawn and re-engraved. Tenniel's original had Alice in the foreground surveying the patch-work fields, seated beneath the gnarled tree; but Dodgson now wanted a simple uncluttered landscape, free from figures. It was yet another instance of his infuriating whims and perfectionism; as always, Tenniel was placed firmly in the middle, between fastidious author and puzzled, over-worked engravers. He had to instruct the Dalziels' over each change and now wrote to them: "Please send me another proof of it. He [Dodgson] has the other, and don't send the block to Messrs. Macmillan till you have heard from me." All these negotiations, done by post, took time, and tried his patience. In another instance his famous garden fantasy for the Jabberwocky verse had the hairy badger-like corkscrew-nosed toves grazing with equally puzzling pig-like mome raths in a grassy patch of the wabe. Dodgson saw the engraved proof and was upset by the confused details, which he instructed Tenniel to alter, then re-engrave. Tenniel wrote in some exasperation to the Dalziels':

> Will you please clear away the ear of the centre animal [a tove] according to the enclosed proof. Mr Dodgson sees a second face, the ears forming the snout. Be so good as to send a rubbing of the head when you send the other proofs.[45]

This was just one of several misgivings Dodgson had over Tenniel's Jabberwocky drawings. Having finished his manuscript copy in 1871, he received printers' slips for all but the verses and sent these immediately on to Tenniel by 14 January. He still hoped to get the book out in time for Easter (9 April that year) but everything now clearly depended upon Tenniel. Total agreement on the remaining drawings was too much to hope for, as Dodgson should have known, and things did not go smoothly. He was understandably startled when Tenniel showed him his drawings of the ferocious monster Jabberwock, a half-dragon, half predatory bird which, though a true grotesque of the type Dodgson once admired in Tenniel's work, now seemed too fearsome for the book's frontis-piece. He feared for his child readers; that it would "alarm nervous and imaginative children". Tactfully he appealed to about thirty mothers to whom he sent a printed circular to survey their reactions, and he gave them three choices: to keep the drawing for the frontispiece, to put it in the book but find a new frontispiece or omit the work altogether (to which he noted this would be "a great sacrifice of the time and trouble which the picture has cost"). In the end he chose to use the drawing, but not as the frontispiece. Tenniel's Jabberwock nevertheless remains one of the most chilling inventions in children's literature.[46]

The planned April publication deadline came and passed with just twenty-seven of the fifty illustrations completed. Dodgson now set his sights upon a Christmas book; it was probably just as well for it would then capture the holiday market. He temporarily forgot Alice and tended to his own domestic worries. Now as the head of his large family (he had recently been elevated there on the death of his father in 1868), he assumed his duties with characteristic fervour and thoroughness, and even managed a holiday to visit relatives in Scotland. There he called on his favourite artist, now Sir Joseph Noel Paton, on the Isle of Arran and was given authority to look over the artist's studio whenever he wished. Dodgson relished this opportunity, no doubt to compare his impressions of Tenniel's skills with those of this equally talented illustrator. He recalled the thrill of his discoveries, "such a treat as I do not remember *ever* having had in any one day. The drawings are perfectly exquisite, and almost come up to *my* highest ideals of beauty".[47]

The ill-fated Jabberwocky illustration was moved from frontispiece position

The Illustrations: *Through the Looking-Glass*

Through the Looking-Glass and What Alice Found There was an ingenious tale filled with paradoxical allusions to what Dodgson called a "contrariwise" view of the world. Tenniel's illustrations echoed that preoccupation: with front to back reversals, duplicated images, expertly copied twins and imaginative reworkings of familiar objects – all attempts to twist reality into fantasy. When Alice peers through the looking-glass, perched on the mantelpiece, Tenniel turns the mirror into a stage onto which familiar domestic ornaments take new life: the dome-covered clock and flower vase smile knowingly, the arched fireplace ornament sports a grotesque gargoyle with his tongue stuck out. Tenniel reversed the setting perfectly, even remembering to transpose his signature from one side to the other (although the Dalziels failed to note this important touch; their name is still legible rather than reversed). The duplication device continues in Tenniel's numerous illustrations: like the pairs of chess pieces marching side by side, to which Tenniel added his own ecclesiastical bishops in voluminous robes,

A triumph of the "contrariwise" – Alice goes through the looking-glass

although they were not mentioned in Dodgson's text. The supreme example was his famous twins Tweedledum and Tweedledee, given mirror-like identical poses.

Again an ability to record accurate detail was Tenniel's greatest asset. His landscapes and especially the vital flower drawings are true to life, the tiger lily and roses looking like flowers despite their human faces and abilities to speak. One theory about their genesis was that the lilies and roses were borrowed by Dodgson from Tennyson's *Maud* with the botanical garden background borrowed from Oxford's domed conservatory.[48] The animals too have that element of accuracy for which Tenniel was now famous. Even his Jabberwocky creatures seem real rather than imaginary. This was partly due to the care he still took over the engravings. A proof of the final kitten drawing in which Alice watched the chess figures transformed into kittens elicited his careful comment to the Dalziels: "Kittens more *fluffy*. Less like *China*." Again the noses, eyelashes and Alice's eyes received his greatest attention at proof stage. In that same block he insisted a plug should be inserted to re-engrave and shorten Alice's eyelashes.

Tenniel possibly studied garden flowers to make such botanically accurate drawings for *Alice*

Tweedledum and Tweedledee as
enantiomorphs

Such were the perfectionist instincts in Tenniel, especially when goaded on by Dodgson.[49]

Tenniel again relied heavily upon formal compositions, carefully balancing each drawing for a restraining effect, which perfectly suited Dodgson's contrariwise world. The famous railway carriage scene, for example, has Alice and her purse carefully placed opposite two figures, the goat and man in white. But they are carefully shaded, subdued in the shadows to balance, yet return the emphasis to Alice, the sharpest, most detailed element in the drawing. Figures received familiar profiles, which in the case of the man in white resembled Tenniel's *Punch* drawings of Disraeli, his goat companion re-emphasizing the statesman's unmistakable profile. A recent critic has pointed out that Tenniel might have borrowed this composition from his friend Millais' popular painting "My First Sermon", in which a little girl sits piously in a pew, a Bible replacing Alice's purse, but otherwise remarkably similar in pose.[50] Formalism dominated Tenniel's version of the twins Tweedledum and Tweedledee, every detail of the enantiomorphs (mirror images of each other) carefully conceived. Tenniel's inscribed proof (now in the New York Public Library) suggests the extreme care taken over these two characters. Here the slightest tonal change or slip of the graver might damage his inventions, and he urged the Dalziels to highlight and emphasize "Mouth, Elbow, point of umbrella, Light touch between feet". When Alice dresses them both for battle, Tenniel managed to reverse the positions of each figure with expert clarity.

Dodgson occasionally gave Tenniel the upper hand to choose the subjects he might draw. The famous Walrus and Carpenter passage, for example, was the cause of Tenniel's objections to the original pairing. Dodgson had given him a choice of subjects – a carpenter, butterfly, or a baronet – each would fit his rhyme

Alice in the railway carriage was possibly based upon Millais's painting

and three syllable rhythm scheme and the nonsensical story. Yet Tenniel "remonstrated against the walrus and the carpenter as a hopeless combination and begged to have the carpenter abolished". He lost this battle and drew a curious carpenter with folded newspaper hat reminiscent of those worn by printers, his bag of tools carefully slung over his shoulder. Only the carpenter's poorly drawn legs, which needed strengthening to support such a sturdy body, kept him from being one of Tenniel's most convincing characters. Tenniel also tried to interject an element of propriety to Dodgson's verses, by objecting to "The Walrus and the Carpenter were walking hand-in-hand" which was changed to "were walking close at hand".

Tenniel hoped to abolish the Carpenter and, with the Walrus, pronounced them both "a hopeless combination"

Despite his objections to models, Tenniel probably used some for the sake of accuracy. It has been suggested, for example, that he used the small Oxford toy and sweet shop at 83 St Aldgate's Street, opposite Dodgson's Christ Church college. Indeed, Tenniel's drawing for the "Wool and Water" chapter with its bow-fronted window full of toys and sweets, in which he so carefully reversed even the "Tea 2 shillings" sign, seems to be a clear model for that Oxford shop, which still exists today. Humpty Dumpty was originally Dodgson's invention, born from a pen sketch (now at Harvard) in which the egg-headed creature gapes on his stool while a gaunt footman whispers to him. Tenniel's version used the egghead idea, but gave him more distinct, aged features which seem clearly modelled upon the round-faced Mark Lemon – if so a curious tribute to his recently deceased friend. Other critics have pointed to more obscure models. The Lion and the Unicorn battle scene, for example, suggests the figures in a famous Anglo-Saxon Caedmon Manuscript of the Junian codex in the Bodleian Library, which Dodgson and Tenniel may have known, but this is perhaps reading too much into that one drawing.[51] More convincing was the popular belief at the time that Tenniel's Lion and Unicorn were versions of Gladstone and Disraeli, those two sparring partners in real life, whom Dodgson's text and Tenniel's pictures so obviously seemed to suggest.

The most intriguing case of a model was that for the White Knight, who replaced the ill-fated Jabberwock drawing as the book's frontispiece. Tenniel's bumbling elderly knight was born out of his medieval preoccupations, especially those equestrian subjects by Dürer. His battle scene between the White and Red Knights was a skilful equestrian composition which suggested how closely Tenniel had read and followed Dodgson's text: both knights are drawn holding their clubs in the traditional Punch and Judy manner, under shoulder and forearm. It was the source of Tenniel's White Knight frontispiece which brought the greatest speculation: many believed the wispy-haired old gentleman of eccentric habits was Tenniel's parody of Dodgson, himself a finicky old man before his time, who functioned best in a convoluted world of his own invention. Dodgson once insisted Tenniel should cut off the White Knight's wispy hair; it offended his meticulous nature. Perhaps he noticed the similarity in character and wished to hide the slightest hint that he was in fact the White Knight. Others have pointed out a far more plausible theory, that Tenniel was in fact the model for the Knight. If one compares the long-moustached angular features of the artist with his elderly White Knight there is indeed a striking resemblance – although Tenniel was only fifty at the time. His *Punch* colleagues were quick to point out similarities to their beloved Horace "Ponny" Mayhew, the prematurely balding yet still handsome womanizer whom they knew as "the wicked old marquis". Tenniel flatly denied this; any similarity between his Knight and Mayhew was

Tenniel with drooping moustaches
of the White Knight

Another model for the White
Knight was Horace Mayhew

Alice's "White Knight" was possibly based upon Tenniel himself

"purely accidental, a mere unintentional caricature". It would have been a
prophetic tribute to his colleague, however, for Mayhew died in May 1872,
shortly after the book was published.[52]

*   *   *   *   *

Finally, on 1 November 1871, Tenniel completed all his proof corrections and
Through the Looking-Glass was printed. With less than two months before
Christmas, this still left a slim margin of time for errors but Tenniel was relieved
to be rid of the book at last. Not only did it leave him free again to concentrate

full-time on his *Punch* work, but more seriously it left him disillusioned by all future book illustration. The months he spent manoeuvring a pencil on hard wood blocks, only to see Dodgson change his design at the last expensive moment had weighed heavily upon his spirits, and he was completely worn out. He had spent nearly three of the last years on one small book. So when he received a flattering request for similar drawings on wood for *Once a Week* within days of delivering his last Alice proof, he wrote a frank and weary refusal to the paper's publisher, George Bentley:

> My dear sir:
>
> I am completely weary of drawing on wood; perfectly sick of wood engraving, and I have already more work on hand than I know what to do with. I am building a new roof to my studio, and I am "going in" for the real enjoyment of *painting*. Under all these circumstances I am forced to decline with much thanks – your kind and very flattering proposal.[53]

Fortunately the tedious delays and collaboration with Dodgson again paid off. By the end of November Macmillan proudly claimed pre-publication orders for *Through the Looking-Glass* accounted for 7,500 copies of the initial 9,000 print run, and a further 6,000 were ordered to meet projected demand. By January 1872 this ran to a total of 15,000 copies sold and orders for 500 more. Dodgson received his first copy on 8 December 1871, and was obviously pleased with the results; two days later he sent close friends (including Tennyson) one of three morocco leather-bound copies. Eventually he sent out a hundred cloth-bound copies to friends in a single day. Tenniel, it seems, did not object to the printing this time, although he did strongly criticize the poor appearance of a further 3,000 copies which Dodgson agreed were lamentably produced, probably the result of pressing the printed sheets between blank leaves to speed up their drying time. In fact then it was Dodgson who wrote in disgust to Macmillan, echoing his own and Tenniel's concern. Too much was sacrificed to meet rushed deadlines and fill larger orders "as fast as possible": "I have made up my mind that whatever be the *commercial* consequences, we must have no more artistic 'fiascos' – ", he told Macmillan.

> You will think me a lunatic for thus wishing to send away money from the doors; and will tell me perhaps that I shall thus lose thousands of would-be purchasers, who will not wait so long, but will go and buy other Christmas books. I wish I could put into words how entirely such arguments go for nothing with me. As to how many copies we sell I care absolutely nothing: the one thing I do care for is that all copies that *are* sold shall be artistically first-rate.[54]

In this respect he echoed Tenniel's perfectionist views. While many critics believe the Alice books were the finest work of Tenniel's career, he never forgot the strain these two small books of less than a total of a hundred drawings caused him. In consequence he refused to work on such a demanding project ever again. "It is a curious fact that with *Through the Looking-Glass* the faculty of making drawings for book illustrations parted from me, and notwithstanding all sorts of tempting inducements, I have done nothing in that direction since", he proudly admitted years later.[55] There was a hint of relief in this remark, for at last he had freed himself from the rigours of what would become a dying art – the drawing on wood blocks for wood-engravers.

Moreover he had freed himself from the debilitating demands of Dodgson, and he refused to work with him ever again. When his *Punch* colleague Harry Furniss

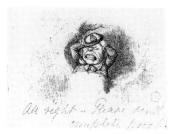

Tenniel was meticulous with proof engravings. He required details before the complete page was proofed. The text reads: "All right – Please send complete proof." (Victoria and Albert Museum)

explained in 1885 that he had been asked to collaborate with Dodgson on *Sylvie and Bruno*, Tenniel recoiled at the prospect: "I'll give you a week, old chap; you will never put up with that fellow a day longer." Furniss replied, innocently, "You will see. If I like the work I shall manage the author". But Tenniel shook his head and smiled knowingly: "Not a bit of it. Lewis Carroll is impossible. You will see that my prophecy will come true." Which, in the end, it did; for Furniss spent seven years under Dodgson's firm control, his drawings measured up against the standards set, in Dodgson's opinion, by the inimitable Tenniel. Dodgson went so far as to measure each new Furniss drawing and even counted the number of lines per inch to compare them with Tenniel's to make sure he received value for money. When Furniss grew enraged by such arrogant insensitivity, and told Dodgson, "John Tenniel, George Du Maurier, or Harry Furniss, must be accepted as they are – as the public are willing to accept them; you cannot alter them", Dodgson merely retorted that his beloved Tenniel was "an instance of the direct *contrary*! By the most curious coincidence, the very thing, which has upset all your plans, happened in *his* case!" For years Dodgson searched in vain for a new Tenniel, from among such varied talents as Luke Fildes, A.B. Frost and even Walter Crane. He was plagued by what he called "the apparent hopelessness of finding an artist worthy to succeed Mr. Tenniel, whose help he no longer had".[56]

On the other hand, Tenniel was clearly proud of his new Alice work once it appeared. Again his *Punch* colleagues convinced him to adapt his most recent inventions to fit political themes: a gryphon and Jabberwock appeared within months of *Through the Looking-Glass* in the *Punch* cartoon "The Monster Slain" (16 March 1872). These continued for years afterward, like the punning "Alice in Blunderland" (30 October 1880), or "Alice in Bumbleland" (8 March 1899). Tenniel also thought enough of his original Alice sketches to re-work them into finished drawings for friends and admirers; once he even re-drew Alice and the Ugly Duchess on the fly-leaf of a presentation copy to give authenticity to the gift – a rare instance of Tenniel accepting his Alice fame.[57]

Reviews of the new Alice book proved that the prolonged struggle and differences of opinion had again been worth the effort. Most surprising was the *Athenaeum* verdict, whose critic swallowed his pride after the attack on the first Alice, to pronounce its sequel "no mere book . . . but the potential of happiness for countless children of all ages". Generous reviews followed even more generous sales and future editions, which all helped to spread the Carroll–Tenniel formula of children's literature as pure, yet intriguingly childish entertainment. An Alice boom was born, with Tenniel's designs stolen for ephemera, pirated editions, and even Alice-inspired fine art prints, like the etching "Alice in Wonderland" after Albert Henry Payne which appeared at the Royal Academy the year after the second volume appeared. Nine of Tenniel's now familiar drawings were borrowed for the cover of "The Looking-Glass Quadrille", and parodies like *The Westminster Alice*, 1902, helped to keep Alice and indeed Tenniel's drawings perennially popular.

Dodgson was later to declare that of Tenniel's ninety-two drawings, he liked only one – Humpty Dumpty. It was a particularly back-handed compliment, since he had given Tenniel the idea for the eggheaded character himself. It was typical of Dodgson's quirky personality: Tenniel had found it almost impossible to keep up with his whims and infuriating criticisms. As a result, according to the artist's first biographer, his Alice character remained aloof and almost wooden; she lacked Dodgson's sympathetic invention and "is the least realised character in Wonderland . . .. His Alice is not creative but interpretative: the decisive mental impulse is that of Lewis Carroll." In this way Tenniel triumphed in the subsidiary role marked out for him by Dodgson from the start; he was the supreme Alice illustrator, the true interpreter of Dodgson's Wonderland. [58]

Carroll's favourite Humpty Dumpty

5 *Punch's* Don Quixote 1873–1893

When Tenniel reached his fifties, his *Punch* colleagues thought "Don Quixote" an appropriate nickname. Their senior staff member was still devoted to his duties and would bring an unfashionable sense of well-being, of solid virtues and reliable if at times eccentric viewpoints to the paper for the next twenty-eight years. When his older colleagues died or deserted *Punch* for more prestigious careers in art or journalism, to be replaced by high-spirited "New Generation" talent, he alone remained true to Mr Punch: a much respected "grand old man" who freely gave guidance to those less experienced and more ambitious than himself.

At the famous editorial dinners he sat in enigmatic silence, a benign presence recognized for his sound judgements of considerable power, whenever he broke silence. As chief political cartoonist he was much respected, for he alone was the source of those weekly satiric jabs at politicians which had been pioneered by *Punch* from those early days when the word "cartoon" was unknown and the less emotive terms "pencillings" or "sketches" were used to help excuse their decidedly slight, amateurish qualities. In fact the term "cartoon" for these weekly comic drawings was only coined from the 1840s, inspired by the misguided Westminster Hall fresco competitions of well-meaning national-styled "cartoons" which *Punch* thought a joke – and had the courage to say so. Gradually full and double-page satiric drawings by minor figures like A.S. Henning, W. Newman, Kenny Meadows, and Alfred Crowquill were published and set the stage for the more accomplished talents of Leech, Doyle, Tenniel, and their disciples Charles Keene and Linley Sambourne. It was Tenniel alone who surpassed even his most energetic disciples. The sheer number of political cartoons he produced over a forty-year period was inspiring: 1,860 full-page cartoons between 1851–1901, compared with Leech's 720 and Doyle's 70. Prolific and dedicated, he had over the years developed his own highly individual style and technique, which went virtually unaltered until his retirement. Rarely was he bothered by his editor while he worked just as Mark Lemon had seen the benefit of "inactivity and non-interference" with Leech in his later years. Tenniel was left on Thursday of each week to produce his own individual contribution to the paper.[1]

Although it was unusual for Tenniel to speak about his routine, he clearly preferred solitude and the reassuring distance of his Maida Vale studio rather than to work among his boisterous colleagues at the *Punch* offices. He gave a rare interview in 1889, in which he tried to explain how he went about this work. While he only briefly touched on matters of style, it remains the best account we have of his *Punch* methods:

A fine example of Tenniel's ability to finish a drawing was "Nuts to Crack", *Punch*, 11 February 1882. This was probably done after publication as a fold-out plate, since his weekly schedule didn't allow such work. It relates to parliamentarians considering the proposed changes in the governing of the City of London. (Chris Beetles)

I carry out my work thus: I never use models or Nature for the figure, drapery or anything else. But I have a wonderful memory of observations – not for dates, but anything I see I remember. Well, I get my subject on Wednesday night; I think it out carefully on Thursday, and make my rough sketch; on Friday morning I begin, and stick to it all day, with my nose well down on the block. By means of tracing-paper – on which I make all the alterations of composition and action I may consider necessary – I transfer my design to the wood, and draw on that. The first sketch I may, and often do, complete later on as a commission . . .. Well, the block being finished, it is handed over to Swain's boy at about 6.30 to 7 o'clock, who has been waiting for it for an hour or so, and at 7.30 it is put in hand for engraving. That is completed on the following night, and on Monday night I receive by post the copy of next Wednesday's paper. Although case-hardened in a sense, I have never the courage to open the packet. I always leave it to my sister, who opens it and hands it across to me, when I just take a glance at it, and receive my weekly pang.[2]

His greatest regret was not being allowed enough time to proof his work: a luxury he had insisted upon when drawing for books and magazines. Instead he was forced to work to a strict deadline which obviously grated against his perfectionist principles. During his later years on *Punch*, this resulted in some rather sketchy, if uninspired drawing, which saddened and even angered him. Writing in the heat of one rushed deadline he sent his *Punch* colleague "1000 thanks for taking so much trouble. D[a]resay it'll come out all right – but how the D.V.L. I'm to get the darn'd thing down by tomorrow afternoon – blest if I know! A hidgeous grind!!!"[3] The younger generation artists, hired now to fill in gaps and exert their considerable energies, were more willing to accept these restrictions. Linley Sambourne received his subjects by telegram at the very last minute, and he succeeded well enough to rival Tenniel's later cartoons and eventually take over from him. Much depended upon editorial requirements: under Francis Burnand, editor from 1880–1906, he was given special treatment when cartoons involved a more than average amount of work. Burnand recalled later:

> As time went on, for the satisfactory execution of double-cartoons, that in earlier days he would have thought out, designed, and produced within forty-eight hours, he became gradually convinced that an extension of twenty-four hours had become essential. In such cases, by pre-arrangement, the usual Wednesday's council would be transferred to the Tuesday in that week. Whenever some details at the time of discussion had escaped the attention of the deliberating assembly, Tenniel used to rely upon my coming round to him on Thursday morning, when, at an early hour, he would have already sketched out his tracing of the cartoon and then together, he and I would thoroughly rediscuss the subject, carefully considering every point. As a rule I would find him in his study, as he rarely availed himself of his studio, with drawing board before him, and on it the tracing of the cartoon well-nigh completed. The chief difficulties of the composition had been almost invariably surmounted, and then for half-an-hour or so we would discuss matters generally, the situation particularly.[4]

By this time Tenniel had accepted his influential role as a professional draughts-man on wood. Ironically by the 1870s and 1880s this profession was threatened. The number of artists and engravers on wood dropped dramatically with the advent of photo-engraving, or "process" as it was called, which eliminated the need for drawing onto wood by photographically transferring a drawing from stiff paper onto the engraved surface. Tenniel refused to adapt to this new technique, and continued to provide Swain with his usual silvery grey faint pencil covered blocks. Only by the early 1890s did he relent and draw in the pen and ink he always found difficult, for some of the first process plates in *Punch*, the earliest appearing in his *Pocketbook* and *Almanack* designs. He preferred the tactile sense of direct contact of pencil on the wood, and it was his engraver's continual problem to find enough wood blocks smooth enough to provide Tenniel's needs. No doubt Tenniel's greatest reason for shunning the process technique for so long was the necessity of providing highly finished, carefully shaded drawings which demanded much more time to complete, compared with his usual often rough outline sketch on the block which the Swains worked up into a finished engraving. The Swains, father and son, were indeed skilful craftsmen–engravers and printers, and for nineteen years they endured the precarious weekly ritual of cutting drawings as single block illustrations, until it was devised to split up each block into sections, engrave them individually and reassemble them for printing. Moreover, Swain managed to meet his weekly deadline for fifty years with little difficulty, despite the threat of a single damaged block which could spell disaster, for *Punch* was printed, unusually, directly from the blocks themselves and not electrotypes. If a last-minute gap occurred, he was a skilful enough draughtsman to work up and insert a drawing from a stock the *Punch* editor had given him for such emergencies. Often he was asked to train budding young freelances to draw on wood, like the nineteen-year-old Richard Doyle, who was terrified of his doctrinaire manner.

Although Tenniel had been trained to draw on wood before he joined *Punch*, he learned to adapt his preliminary sketches to the spare outline style and even lines of Swain's graver. The highly finished blocks he sent to Swain clearly could not be engraved in facsimile; there just wasn't enough time. Tenniel, in the end, provided short-hand drawings which, according to a series now in the Victoria and Albert Museum, suggest how little he needed to send to Swain to be sure of

More rapid preliminary cartoon sketch which Tenniel presented to his engraver to embellish. Published as "Battle of Frogs and Mice", 6¼ x 8⅛", *Punch*, 28 November, 1885, p. 259 (Victoria and Albert Museum)

clear interpretations of his original idea. In one his composition races across the page in spontaneous pencil line while the caption below was either illegible or ran off or up the side of the page.[5]

The Cartoons

The Tenniel–Swain style of clear, crisp outlines and sparse backgrounds altered little over the years, and the *Punch* editors quickly warmed to this distinctive mix. Tenniel's solid figures suited the classical allegories and early memorial drawings which were meant to inspire and provoke rather than to be amusing. He first made a substantial mark with the *Punch* obituary cartoons in the early 1850s. The earliest was in homage to the Duke of Wellington (14 September 1852), whose death touched the nation. Tenniel drew a careful, well-finished portrait of the Duke, more suggestive of a painting or a memorial piece of sculpture, with an expertly drawn lion and military symbols. This set the stage for subsequent tributes to national figures: these, according to one enthusiastic critic, "often marked the highest point to which Tenniel's art has reached".

Tenniel's early *Punch* tribute to the Duke of Wellington, who died in 1852

Comedy was another matter. Tenniel's humour was of a dry, restrained intellectual type which took time to appreciate. His *Punch* cartoons are often forced comedies, his figures exaggerated as if they were actors in an amateur dramatics production, their sharp outlines likened by one critic to the bold-faced type on theatrical posters: such was their garish appeal. From Leech he learned subtlety and to use detail and seemingly minor incidents and middle-class foibles to underpin his comedy. Together they led a remorseless campaign against that singular and unfortunate woman's fashion, the bloomer; that "unwomanly" and "hideous deviation" of divided skirt-trouser, a kind of pantaloon-cum-calf-length skirt sponsored by the American Amelia Bloomer *née* Jenks. They showed up its ridiculous aspects, drew women in unflattering situations to play up the hideous nature of the style, and the fashion soon died out; although Leech's popularity was such that some believed he very nearly converted his female readers to turkish trousers instead. The fickle world of fashion was a favourite target for *Punch*, and Tenniel pondered the changes in his drawings of the great cravat and collar question, and the even greater bonnet question – those enormous cloche-like bonnets which totally obscured a woman's head. The rise of the crinoline, again an American invention and antidote to the bloomer, with its voluminous skirts and stiff hooped petticoats (which Leech saw as an iron cage welded together), was ripe for satire. Tenniel used the crinoline fashion when the skirts grew outrageously ornate and voluminous, as an apt symbol of national extravagance in his effective cartoon, "The National Crinoline" of 1863. He had also studied the intricacies of the fashion well enough to use them again in his ill-fated Alice drawing (the crinoline turned to a balloon-tyre skirt) a few years later.

Tenniel shared Leech's conservative view of the world. Both their comic contributions to *Punch* were spiked by a mock outrage at what they saw as the excesses and foibles of their peers. A favourite quip which encompassed two such follies was "A skirt divided against itself cannot stand, it must sit upon a bicycle". Although Tenniel was rarely demonstrative with friends or his public, the bicycle craze brought out the worst in him; as it established itself, his temper flared. From the 1860s through the 1890s he frowned disapprovingly at the contraptions that threatened to replace his beloved horseback riding and clogged the footpaths and country roads. "Can't think how you can let yourselves be seen on the beastly things!" he snapped when a group of *Punch* colleagues pedalled past his horse, his "comically disgusted" tone attempting to hide a true hatred of their bicycles. [6] It was clear by the 1890s that the bicycle was here to stay and, much to his chagrin, Tenniel was asked to incorporate them into his *Punch* cartoons. True to his "no models" dictum, he invented his own "modern roadster", a curiously plausible piece of mechanical invention which relied only upon his memory of the earliest bicycles. *Punch* published it as "A Bicycle Made for Two", which satirized Henry Fowler and the Parish Councils Bill. The reactions were unexpectedly flattering: "The cycling world fluttered in a manner that must have been very encouraging to the artist. His machine, they said, was the most wonderful one ever placed on the market." Only the more mechanically-minded pointed out how his lady cyclist, riding over the front of the cycle frame, would buckle the wheel with her weight, and that his narrow handlebars would be thrown up, not down, and break as she fell. The gears, too, were on only one side of the chain, the sturdy-looking frame " a marvel of ingenuity misapplied!" Irate cyclists eventually wrote to rival papers about Tenniel's dangerous bicycle, condemning it as misleading and inaccurate. Yet they failed even to mention the political point that was being made – such was the influence of Tenniel's drawings over his public.

Railways proved another stumbling block for Tenniel. He preferred to rely upon his memories of those early and long out-moded trains he had studied as a student in London, adding to them what he thought were appropriate new "bits of metal"; as one surprised observer noted, the result was nothing more than "a bit of ironmongery that came into his mind". He was not above using artistic licence at the expense of accuracy to make a comic point. In his "Forlorn Maiden of the Trade" of January 1893 for example, he drew a captive girl, bound and tied across the rails; yet she was so out of logical proportion that she would have had to be at least ten feet tall, according to one shocked observer: "This violated the public conscience even more than the fact that the engine rushes along the inside line of the two sets of rails; and they declared that never before had the maxim *ars longa* been more triumphantly indicated than in the maiden's figure." Tenniel often equated railways with death, as in his chilling *Good Words* illustrations. A telling preliminary drawing survives, "Death and the Railway", in which Tenniel drew a skeleton watching a train approach a broken bridge. [7]

As *Punch*'s chief political cartoonist Tenniel quickly rose to prominence and achieved a unique reputation. His allegorical figures, especially his stern classical Britannia, the robust and stubborn John Bull, and his benevolent Queen Victoria, helped to educate as well as entertain his readers throughout the empire. John Ruskin claimed Tenniel's *Punch* cartoons were a much welcomed change from mindless radicalism because his "grave power brought a steady tone and law of morality into the license of political contention". It is his interpretations of contemporary events which the present-day social historians regard as most representative of middle-class Victorian virtues.

Politically, Tenniel refused publicly to declare his allegiances; he certainly was not as forthcoming as his predecessors. From the start he was told which of the weekly cartoon subjects and settings to draw. Inevitably, he chose subjects which might suit his talent for facial expressions, and ultimately decided how large or what the emphasis was to be. These were the only hints to suggest where his own true political sympathies lay. His friends saw him as an "Old Whig", whose sense of propriety and justice came closest to the Liberal leader Gladstone rather than Disraeli. He leaned further toward the views of his older friends, like Arthur à Beckett, but he was never as right-wing or reactionary as Charles Keene. He remained an idealist with conservative values, especially abhorring the horrors and needless destruction of war. This was a more restrained, more acceptable, less radical approach than that previously taken by *Punch*'s more fiery-tongued reformers, born out of the tradition of Gillray or Hogarth. Tenniel was a direct descendant of the famous "HB", (John Doyle – Richard's father), whose benign approach to political cartoons was later adopted by John Leech. Tenniel followed the news with great care so as not to misunderstand what he was asked to draw, but when pressed for his own views he shook his head and smiled: "As for political opinions, I have none", he proudly explained to his interviewer in 1889, adding, "at least, if I have my own little politics, I keep them to myself, and profess only to those of my paper". Professionalism was his creed and with it he helped to change the face of *Punch*.

THE PATENT SAFETY RAILWAY BUFFER.

Tenniel's hatred of the railways appeared in early *Punch* (18 July 1857) issues

THE "PAS DE DEUX!"

Boyhood dancing lessons inspired political parody as here, with Lords Beaconsfield and Salisbury, *Punch*, 3 August, 1878

> If I have infused any dignity into cartoon-designing, that comes from no particular effort on my part, but solely from the high feeling I have for art. In any case, if I am a "cartoonist" – the accepted term – I am not a caricaturist in any sense of the word.

He was most hurt by critics who thought his cartoons too severe, restrained or grotesque, lacking in the quality of more obvious comedy which the paper's less successful rivals tried to promote.

> My drawings are sometimes grotesque, but that is from a sense of fun and humour. Some people declare that I am no humorist, that I have no sense of fun at all; they deny me everything but severity, "classicality", and dignity.[8]

Even critics today agree that his cartoons often sat too hard on the page to be truly comic in the more obvious style of Leech, Du Maurier or Sambourne. For one whose draughtsmanship was mostly self-taught, he did create some remarkable examples of "poster politicians", and what one recent critic has called "possibly the finest pencil work after Maclise of the Victorian era".[9]

The startling events of over forty years of Queen Victoria's reign gave Tenniel ample opportunity to exploit his talent and interpret public events at home and abroad. One admirer thought he was "the best example of the right man in the right place at the right time". Even before his official appointment as chief cartoonist he occasionally provided stirring versions of tragic events, especially during the early 1850s. The Russo-Turkish war in 1853 inspired "The Bear with a Sore Head" in a July issue. Here Tenniel drew a beehive upset by a Russian bear, howling over the angry stings of the bees, which suggested the outrage of European powers at the Russian invasion of Turkey. He was, even at this early stage, given animal subjects to draw, and he became known for certain formulas – the snarling bears, lions or tigers which symbolized the anger and outrage of the nation. Subtlety surfaced in such satiric anthropomorphic works as "The Eagle in Love" of February 1853, in which the French Emperor Napoleon III, drawn as a fearsome eagle, has his sharp talons trimmed by his domineering and cunning wife Eugenie: it echoed *Punch*'s view that Napoleon III was a treacherous, dangerous neighbour worthy of the closest attention. Tenniel repeated the theme seven years later in "An Unpleasant Neighbour", in which the emperor lights a firework advertisement, "Blaze of Triumph! Roman Candles! Italian Fire!", placed uncomfortably near John Bull's Roast Beef House, and the irate Englishman rushes out in excitement: "Here, have I got to pay double insurance all along for your confounded fireworks!"

The Crimean War and Indian Mutiny provided ample opportunities to perfect Tenniel's animal drawings. The most effective was his snarling British lion sniffing at a doorway, which alluded to the conference which followed the fall of Sebastapol and had the caption: "The British Lion Smells a Rat". His concern for accuracy and his carefully drawn figures dressed in correct military uniforms, were accepted as universal symbols of national pride. In "The United Service" of 10 February 1855, perfectly drawn French and English guardsmen symbolized the new alliance between the two countries and were posed in a friendly contest of measuring their heights. The drawing captured the national sense of a need for unity between two old rivals. In fact it was often reproduced as a reminder of that tenuous possibility, even appearing on the back of playing cards. His most powerful and many believed most successful cartoon, however, was "The British Lion's Vengeance on the Bengal Tiger" (22 August 1857). This was

THE BRITISH LION'S VENGEANCE ON THE BENGAL TIGER.

PUNCH, *August* 22, 1857.

Tenniel's stirring plea for Indian Mutiny revenge, *Punch*, 22 August, 1857

inspired by the horrific reports of a savage massacre of British women and children by Sepoy rebels. British papers were filled with detailed descriptions of the carnage, and even *The Times* led the call for immediate and decisive reprisals:

> The first thing, of course, is to put down force by force . . .. We can only hope that the suppression of the Mutiny will be speedy and decisive . . . to retain power in India we must sweep away every political establishment and every social usage which may prevent our influence from being universal and complete.[10]

Shirley Brooks suggested Tenniel's lion and tiger subject at the weekly editorial meeting, and Tenniel produced a ferocious British lion leaping upon an Indian tiger as it mauled a woman and child. Despite obvious inaccuracies – the lion's stump-like paws, for example – the drawing appeared spread across two pages and powerfully reflected the national sense of outrage and call for revenge. In fact some authorities objected to its sensationalism as it seemed too dangerous in the face of such fervent national emotion: "Vengeance was the cry; and the wise and humane counsels of Lord Canning met only with contempt and anger, and rendered him the most unpopular man of the day." Critics later saw this one Tenniel cartoon as a great example of his supreme power to influence public opinion; "his moral intensity was stamped here", one suggested. Another thought "No one, not Landseer himself, had so translated into line, stone or colour, the grandeur of the lion."[11] At such an early stage in his career, this one drawing helped to secure his reputation as a political artist. One admirer even wrote to him shortly after it was published, to ask for the original drawing. Tenniel wrote back to him that the original was destroyed, since "the drawing in question, like all my drawings for *Punch*, was made at once upon the wood . . ."[12]

So powerful was the sentiment that Tenniel's attacking lion was revived and republished in 1900, to help restore patriotic fervour during the demoralizing counter-offensives of the Boer War.

Attempts to classify and analyse the nearly 2,000 Tenniel cartoons have met with mixed success. His *Times* obituary divided his *Punch* drawings into three categories: the playful, the pathetic, or the terrible, but these were fairly arbitrary groupings. Equally important were his allegorical figures, the national symbols of France, Germany or Italy, as well as animals or classical statues, his political portraits and his "Farmer George" version of John Bull (borrowed from the rotund Mark Lemon), which helped to convince his public of his inventive talents. Those grotesque elements *The Times* found "terrible" surfaced at an early period in dense backgrounds and spectres of social evils: his famous "The Haunted Lady" in July 1863, in which a seamstress is worked to death to complete her mistress's ball gown, gave added bite to the anti-sweatshop campaign. In "The Tempter"(27 November 1886) a macabre shrouded ghost carries the torch of anarchy to entice an unemployed workman: "What! No work! Come and enlist with me, – I'll find work for you!!" Each one was Tenniel's individual way of condemning evil.

A plea for sweat-shop reform in "The Haunted Lady, or 'The Ghost in the Looking-Glass' ", *Punch*, July, 1863

Tenniel's work was recognized but not always liked in the United States. Some of his most powerful condemnations of war were based upon American themes during the War of Secession (Civil War) of 1861–65. For these Tenniel helped to perfect the "Uncle Sam" character into a more flattering successor to the "Brother Jonathan" version of the early days of the War of 1812. A lanky, strapping country bumpkin he was, dressed in stars and stripes, a straw in his mouth, a wide-brimmed hat on his unkempt hair. To Tenniel this supreme American was represented by Abraham Lincoln whom he drew from the early 1860s. Tenniel's Lincoln appeared as a tall, lean, rail-splitter, who openly appealed to the blacks (9 August 1862), and dominated *Punch* cartoons for four years. Indeed, the cigar-chewing upstart Yankee drawn as Uncle Sam by John Leech was easily transposed into Tenniel's Lincoln (the cigar removed) throughout the 1860s. He became a crude, unflattering figure to British readers of *Punch*, placed in compromising situations to comply with the paper's opposition to the North and to Lincoln. As late as 1909 one William S. Walsh was still inflamed over Tenniel's Civil War cartoons, especially the one in which he drew Lincoln as a "freed coon" (frightened raccoon up a tree), and wrote a book denouncing them. Even when Lincoln was assassinated, the familiar Lincoln–Uncle Sam figure emerged in Tenniel's drawing of Andrew Johnson, combined with a Brother Jonathan figure to represent America. This developed into the Uncle Sam of today.[13]

Nevertheless, Tenniel's critical cartoons of the American conflict represented the British view and outraged many Americans. The slavery issue was forced into the open in Tenniel's "Mrs. Carolina asserting her Right to Larrup her Nigger". In "The Sensation Struggle in America" (7 June 1862) the catastrophe of the Civil War was powerfully suggested by two irate backwoodsmen fighting on opposite sides of a treacherous abyss, labelled "Bankruptcy". Reports of massive loss of life and shocking destruction of resources inspired this bitter appeal for an end to the war. In his famous "The American Juggernaut" (3 September 1864), the relentless war machine rolls on through the carnage and smoking rubble. He drew favourite classical allusions to suggest the power struggle: in "Habet", he reversed the familiar historical gladiatorial roles with white gladiators about to perform before Negroes in "Ave Caesar", a drawing many consider one of his finest satires. Then, when Lincoln's assassination was announced in 1865, Tenniel borrowed from his early *Punch* obituary cartoon style to provide a poignant tribute "Abraham Lincoln Foully Assassinated" (14 April 1865). This alone to some degree helped to alter American opinions towards him and brought a more sympathetic view of Mr Punch from across the war-torn Atlantic. At last the paper had softened its prejudiced views and recognized the northern leader as an irreplaceable statesman.

Since Tenniel's weekly "Big Cut" was hotly debated before he received his written orders, the subjects came from a large number of sources. Some were obviously chosen because Tenniel was familiar with the settings, like the theatre and the Shakespearean themes or operatic scenes like "The Incantation" from *Der Freischutz*; or there were also equestrian and hunting subjects like "A Leap in the Dark" (3 August 1867), in which Disraeli as the horse is ridden by Britannia "going blind through the hedge of reform". Popular paintings inspired parodies: in "Who Said Atrocities?" (12 January 1895) a familiar Landseer dog was reworked; in "Uncle Toby and Widow Woodman" (22 April 1893), the genre painter C.R. Leslie was the inspiration; as well as works by Tenniel's more

THE " INCANTATION."

(Scene from the Very Latest Version of " Der Freischütz.")

The operatic themes favoured by Tenniel were also used, here Weber's *Der Freischütz, Punch*, 22 February, 1890

famous friends, Millais's, "The Princes in the Tower" was parodied as "Little Victims" (28 August 1880). Similarly, Tenniel recalled his boyhood dancing and fencing lessons in cartoons like "The Pas de Deux" (3 August 1878) in which Disraeli dances with a Turkish ruler. Literature and literary themes suggested *Punch*'s well-read middle-class audience would understand clever parodies, like that on Dickens's Mrs Gummidge in "The Political Mrs. Gummidge" (2 May 1885), or even variations on Tenniel's famous Alice illustrations. Some cartoons derived from more obscure sources. Tenniel's slavery cartoons, in particular a slave chained to a British ship, were borrowed from Ward Hunt's stirring slavery circular, "Am I not a Man and a Brother?". On the whole Shakespearean themes

LITTLE VICTIMS.

HARE (*terrified*). "WHAT'S THAT?—THE LORDS?"   RABBIT (*shuddering*). "P'R'APS IT'S THE FARMERS!!"
(*With Mr. Punch's apologies to "The Princes in the Tower," by* J. E. MILLAIS, R.A.)

A parody of Millais, *Punch*, 28 August, 1880

were by far the most sympathetically treated and carefully drawn by Tenniel; they were the ideas he had loved as a boy and as he developed his sketching skills had interpreted them during the early *Punch* series "Punch's Illustrations to Shakespeare". Most recently he devised an elaborate homage to this favourite preoccupation in *Punch's Special Shakespearean Number* of 1863. This took the form of an elaborate processional in which Shakespeare's car was drawn by twin-winged horses and driven by Mr Punch, while a motley collection of familiar faces, like Mark Lemon dressed as Prospero, a malignant-looking organ-grinder as Caliban, and portraits of leading statesmen and rulers dressed as Shakespearean characters followed. He re-adopted the intricacies of such an elaborate processional composition years later, in his 1894 almanack drawing "Mr. Punch in Fairyland – a Midsummer Night's Dream" which remains his best Shakespearean tribute and a most uncharacteristic fairyland invention.

His success as a political cartoonist relied to a great degree upon the portraits which he took special care to get right. He refused to exaggerate or distort for the sake of a joke, and would not accept the label caricaturist. Even those politicians most ripe for satirizing, like the fiery rebel Parnell or the free press reformer Charles Bradlaugh, received just and even treatment from Tenniel's pencil. "Caricature is always ugly and often vulgar, and I do not like it", he was fond of saying. It was a high-minded attitude which harkened back to the days of his famous predecessor, "HB", who had built a career upon just such gentle political portrait satires, which he called "Political Sketches". Although Tenniel's colleagues dubbed him a master of burlesque, capable of placing convincing portraits in comic poses, he preferred the more inspired allegories, the tributes and less exaggerated cartoons to enhance his careful portrait drawings. Those *Punch* cartoons which, significantly, he selected for the *Art Journal* tribute number of 1901, were largely of this type. Yet too often a deadline threatened his original plans for accurate and complimentary portraits, especially as he still refused to work from models, and used only the occasional photograph for minor details on uniforms or facial expressions.

> I get a photograph only of the man I want to draw, and seek to get his character. Then, if the photograph is in profile, I have to 'judge' the full face, and *vice versa*; but if I only succeed in getting the character, I seldom go far wrong – a due appreciation is an almost infallible guide.[14]

But the process of getting the character's likeness took time. Tenniel's early versions of the Queen, Gladstone and Disraeli, for example, reveal how variable were the results even after he was satisfied enough to send the drawing off to the *Punch* engraver. In fact, he eventually inspired less talented rivals, like the cartoonist Matt Morgan, who had joined the rival comic paper *Fun* in the 1860s. With little experience of political illustration, Morgan cheerfully admitted to *Punch*'s editor how "he used coolly to take Tenniel's cartoons and literally trace such likenesses as he required of public characters from them. This he showed me himself and called it, 'founding himself on Tenniel'."[15]

The Queen proved Tenniel's most difficult subject, a fact he openly admitted. By the time Tenniel joined *Punch* she had become a stocky, rather plain-looking woman, who taxed even the most accomplished of her portraitists. Tenniel's versions managed to make her either a stern-faced matron or kindly, motherly figure, with thick neck and round face which he quickly agreed was far from flattering. But then Leech and later Linley Sambourne also struggled in their own ways with the Queen's likeness, which must have provided some small comfort to Tenniel. His critics generally agree his best royal portrait was "Queen of the East" (18 March 1876), in which the Queen visits a hospital. She appears here drawn in her role as the wise, consoling matron and matriarch, intent upon comforting the nation's ills. As a royal figure, posed as the new Empress of India in "New Crowns for Old Ones" (15 April 1876), he failed miserably, for he drew her to look more like a servant about to collect a parcel at the door than a monarch about to receive a new crown.

Those politicians with distinctive profiles, like the goatlike features of Disraeli, were easier to master. From his earliest appearances as in "Meeting of Creditors" (10 July 1852), to his unmistakable profile as the goat in Alice,

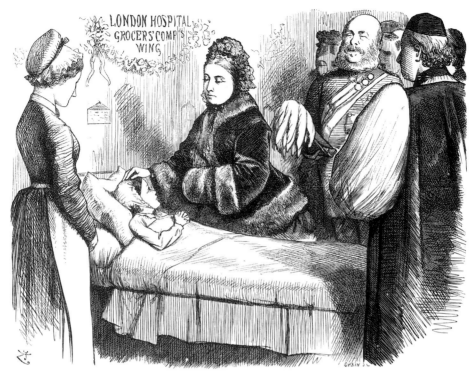

HER BEST TITLE—"QUEEN OF THE EAST."

"MY DARLING, I HOPE YOU WILL BE BETTER NOW!"

[*The New Wing of the London Hospital, given by the Grocers' Company, was opened by Her Majesty in person, March 7th, 1876.*

The matronly Queen preferred by Tenniel, *Punch*, 18 March, 1876

Tenniel's Disraeli was an ideal subject well suited to his cartoonist's talents. His dark, distinctive curls and strip chin whiskers with his protruding nose and underlip could easily be transposed into a variety of comic juxtapositions, as in the face of the Egyptian sphinx in "No Mistake" (25 November 1876). Indeed, the diversity of interpretations of this one politician eventually helped to fill a book of over one hundred *Punch* cartoons by Tenniel and his colleagues, published in 1878 as *Benjamin Disraeli, Earl of Beaconsfield, K.G.*

This book was a companion to Tenniel's own volume of republished *Punch* cartoons of William Gladstone, his favourite statesman, which was also issued in 1878. It seems more care was taken in getting Gladstone's distinctive features right. His unmistakable presence could be felt in some of the most apt images, which saw Gladstone as a lion, as Ajax, as Hercules, as a strong and fearless woodsman, or more comically dressed as a waiter or even a chicken. Over the years Gladstone assumed a Tenniel-like presence, and Tenniel filled his book with a hundred clever yet generally flattering poses, skilfully avoiding ridicule to make political points about his hero. In fact he worried that he might abuse the powers given him, might overstep the mark and offend his favourite politician, as in the case of the famous "The Political Mrs. Gummidge" (2 May 1885). Here he gave Gladstone's features to the gnarled old crone Mrs Gummidge from

Mrs. Gummidge-Gladstone : " I ain't what I could wish myself to be. My troubles has made me contrairy. I feel my troubles, and they make me contrairy. I make the house uncomfortable. I don't wonder at it ! ! ! "
John Peggotty-Bull (deeply sympathising—aside) : " She's been thinking of the old 'un ! "—*David Copperfield.*

"The Political Mrs. Gummidge", *Punch*, 2 May, 1885, used Dickens to parody Gladstone's dilemma over events in Egypt and Russia, having denounced Disraeli over the affair

Dickens's *David Copperfield*, seated at the fireside with her knitting. The idea in fact was proposed by Francis Burnand, and centred around the crisis between Britain and Russia after General Kormaroff advanced into Afghanistan, as well as an equally troubling incident in Egypt (signified by Gladstone's "Egyptian Knitting", which he had dropped). Tenniel's Mrs Gummidge is about to stir her pot of "Russian Stew", watched over by Disraeli's portrait above the mantel and a sympathetic John Peggoty-Bull, while she muses on her inadequacies: "I ain't what I could wish myself to be. My troubles has made me contrary. I feel my troubles, and they make me contrary. I make the house uncomfortable. I don't

wonder at it!!" This extremely personal confession from Mrs Gummidge–
Gladstone worried Tenniel; he felt he might have gone too far and angered his
model, although he had not written the text. Gladstone studied the cartoon
carefully and described it as "a prosperous and successful effort not only to
associate sound art with politics, but also to humanise the warfare connected with
a trying mode of life". Tenniel was still apprehensive, however; whenever he was
required to draw Gladstone, he always treated his subject with characteristic
restraint:

"Mr. Punch's design for a colossal
Statue to Peace", *Punch*, 1862

> I had the opportunity of studying Mr. Gladstone's face carefully when he did me
> the honour of inviting me to dinner at Downing Street, and I have met him since;
> but I fancy, after my "Mrs. Gummidge" and "Janus", I don't deserve to be honoured
> again! His face has much more character and is much stronger than Mr. Bright's
> [John Bright, M.P.]. Mr. Bright had fine eyes and a grand powerful mouth, as well
> as an earnest expression, but a weak nose – artistically speaking, no nose at all –
> still, a very intellectual face indeed.[16]

In the end Gladstone was magnaminous in judging Tenniel's work, and once
expressed his gratitude to *Punch* "for its services in the Liberal cause", although
the paper had not always seen his point of view. He even paid the staff a visit on
7 May 1889, when he attended a weekly editorial dinner in his honour and
entertained them with anecdotes and personal remarks to the delight of Tenniel
and his colleagues. Such gestures only enhanced Tenniel's respect for the man
and in turn inspired such sympathetic cartoons as "Forlorn Hope" of October
1893, in which Gladstone's political aspirations, symbolized by an old fortress
crowning an enormous cliff, were suggested as unattainable, while the warrior
politician dressed in chain-mail travelled unsuccessfully up the steep, slippery
slope: "a hopeless task, eloquent of the courage of despair". This cartoon was
considered by many to be Tenniel's most sympathetic and touching tribute to
Gladstone and the demise of his political influence, second only to the later
cartoon "Dropping the Pilot" for its poignancy.

War was a subject Tenniel learned to interpret over many years, for his *Punch*
career encompassed the periods from the Russo–Turkish and Crimean to the
Boer wars. His most effective device was the allegorical Angel of Peace, usually
a flawless classical maiden in long robes and perfect wings not unlike those he
had studied at the British Museum as an art student. When he drew her seated
upon an enormous cannon in a symbolic anti-war gesture published on 3 May
1862, it was declared suitable for "a design for a colossal statue which ought to
have been placed in the International Exhibition [of 1900]". It was these stirring
juxtapositions which helped to raise Tenniel's political cartoons above the
mundane. The Angel of Peace appeared frequently, as in the touching appeal for
peace across the Channel during the Franco–Prussian War, "For the Sake of
These", in which the angel consoles the 'homeless orphan children of both
countries. Similarly in "The 'Boeuf Gras' for Paris, 1871" (14 March 1871),
Tenniel drew a black shrouded Peace, with her head bowed in sorrow, leading
a sacrificial ox as the symbol of British food sent "with England's aid" to the
starving war victims in Paris. Tenniel's Peace was an idealized symbol which
effectively made his points yet looked humane enough for the critic to admire her
as a "woman with a tender heart". She could be sympathetic and represent the
national feelings for the oppressed and war-torn inhabitants of the world, in strict
contrast to the ferocity and terror of the war he drew around her. Tenniel's
Franco–Prussian War series culminated in just such an image; his "Vae Victis"

Tenniel's *Punch* tribute to the
starving French during the Franco–
Prussian War

(11 March 1871) showed a teutonic victor trampling the crumpled body of Peace as the warrior descended upon Paris. This alone, according to the *Art Journal*, was "a worthy memorial of perhaps the greatest event in modern history, impressive in its pageant, and terrible in its pathos . . . Which of our modern painters can boast so heroic a design?"

*   *   *   *   *

By the late 1870s Tenniel's work began to show serious signs of decline. Disillusioned with wood-engraving following *Through the Looking-Glass*, and weary of over fifteen years of weekly *Punch* cartoons, he longed for greater, more creative challenges. He returned to his painting and rekindled the hope of a subsidiary gallery painting career, which might run alongside *Punch*. He began to accept occasional commissions from friends and admirers for re-worked watercolours and pastels of his favourite *Punch* cartoons or early book illustrations. He attacked such work with characteristic zeal; his letters to friends at this time are filled with polite apologies refusing dinner invitations or visitors to his studio, for he was too busy to interrupt his painting. Even his business letters were written in the familiar "In agony of haste". It is significant that at this period Tenniel missed out his weekly *Punch* cartoon for the third time in his long career, and that the gap was marked not just by one but by four cartoon omissions over the period 1875–78. He clearly had his mind on other, more taxing ventures.

Part of the reason for a falling off in quality of his *Punch* cartoons lay in the turbulent, uncertain state of affairs at the magazine's offices. The era of the boisterous, good natured yet ineffectual editor Shirley Brooks came to an unexpected end at his death on 23 February 1874. Brooks had been largely responsible for the paper's slow but steady slide into mediocrity. His "old generation" confidence had not proved strong enough to combat the need for new blood, and he had appointed only one new artist, Linley Sambourne, during his four-year term as editor. Moreover, the paper lost one of its key journalists, Horace Mayhew, who had died suddenly and who had been responsible for many of its key articles and comic pieces over the years. Tenniel watched with growing concern the abrupt changes and the apparent restlessness of even the more established staff members. George Du Maurier's usual witty social cartoons now turned slipshod and uninspired – more the result of his recent threat of total blindness, but damaging to morale nonetheless. Brooks was followed by the new editor, Tom Taylor, who had an uneventful six-year reign, marked only by further decline and flagging spirits among his confused staff. His *laissez faire* policies did little to boost *Punch*'s fortunes, and the paper reached a low ebb of popularity. He upset his staff by writing illegible instructions or sent unwanted or unexpected advice at the last minute, undermining the little confidence that remained in his abilities as editor. Taylor, like his predecessor, was an old generation figure with valuable and influential friends, a talent for writing plays, but with little organizational skills. He was fastidious and like Tenniel he loved the classics: he was known as "The Professor", having earlier served as Professor of Language and Literature at London University, before turning barrister, then journalist. For the next thirty-six years he contributed to *Punch* with a humourless dry style which failed to inspire: "his hand was heavy, though his heart

Tom Taylor, an endearing *Punch* editor

was kind", according to one critic. And yet he inspired a circle of young talent which assembled at Taylor's Wandsworth cottage, "Lavender Sweep", where this remarkable group, including the artists G.F. Watts and Richard Doyle, fell under the spell of a caring father figure. In the end, Tenniel tactfully accepted his editor's foibles, struggled on with his own increased responsibilities and remained loyal to his old friend until the end of his editorship.

During this period Tenniel's drawings suffered from carelessness and occasional lapses in accuracy. The inevitable last minute rushed deadlines, especially towards the end of the year when the dreaded almanack drawings were due as well as the unexpected double-page cartoon, taxed his patience. Occasionally he was challenged for lapses in his usual performance by more knowledgeable readers: the indefatigable artist and war correspondent George Augustus Sala criticized Tenniel's balloon drawing as inaccurate when it appeared as the frontispiece of *Punch* (Volume 67, 1879). His Indian drawings played an increasingly important role throughout the 1870s, the era of the Prince of Wales's tour in 1875, followed by the Queen's elevation to Empress of India. His tribute to the Prince's visit was a typically curious, rather weak effort, which Taylor stretched across two pages (16 December 1875). Here again Tenniel used the processional device for an elaborately costumed parade of exotic characters, the Prince pulled by Mr Punch in turban, the British Lion and Tiger of India, all set to a triumphant verse from Milton; unfortunately it suffered from weak, uninspired drawing, which is surprising from the artist who had triumphed with *Lalla Rookh*'s superior exoticism years earlier. The more conservative press, like the

Poor draughtsmanship extended over this double-page tribute to the Prince of Wales in India, *Punch's Almanack*, 16 December, 1875

Detail from a double-page cartoon
in which Tenniel's figures are far
from well-drawn

Athenaeum, felt it a duty to criticize such misleading lapses in Tenniel's work at this time. For example, he had drawn the Queen's new Empress of India crown incorrectly; it was not "a four-arched Germanic structure" but in fact a dome, which the *Athenaeum* believed was yet another example of the slovenliness of the paper, "whose artists are always falling into this error in their cartoons of the Empress of India".

Although Tenniel claimed not to have illustrated any further books after the second Alice, by the late 1870s several of his previously published drawings reappeared in new guises. The three illustrations in the anthology, *A Thousand and One Gems of English Poetry*, 1872, were borrowed from his early *Home Affections* volume; those in Thornbury's *Historical Legendary Ballads and Songs*, 1876, reused work from *Once a Week* and *Lalla Rookh*. These were largely the result of enterprising publishers hoping to cash in on Tenniel's name and had little directly to do with the artist himself. One serious exception was the new drawing he produced for his first employer S.C. Hall's bizarre temperance tract, *The Trial of Sir Jasper. A Temperance Tale in Verse*, 1873, written and compiled by Hall himself. It was the work of a devout teetotaller whose message formed the basis of this sixty-four page illustrated verse tale. He convinced the Dalziels to engrave most of the illustrations he commissioned from his now famous artist friends, drawings by E.M. Ward, John Gilbert, George Cruikshank (himself a teetotaller), Birket Foster and the Frenchman Gustave Doré, which appeared alongside Tenniel's one drawing (ironically not engraved by the Dalziels but by Butterworth and Heath, the inferior jobbing engravers). His full-page drawing was a grotesque sketch of "The Aged Drunkard", a withered victim of the evils of drink to which Hall had written the verse:

> See the degraded wretch we picture here:
> He blights the corn before it reaches the ear.
> Yet he was once a gentleman – whose name
> Was heralded among the heirs of fame.
> See him with gin his very soul is stained!

Lewis Carroll gave his permission to re-publish Tenniel's three "Walrus and the Carpenter" Alice illustrations with his own verse in the popular children's anthology, *Mother Goose's Nursery Rhymes*, 1877. They appeared alongside other "Alphabets, Rhymes, Tales and Jingles" illustrated by such recently successful artists as Walter Crane. It was then that Dodgson tried to persuade Tenniel to illustrate yet another book, this time *The Hunting of the Snark*, but with little success. Tenniel had not adequately recovered from the Alice collaborations to consider taking on a new and inevitably prolonged commission for Dodgson. In fact he had witnessed the failure of his new frontispiece design to Dodgson's *Alice Puzzle Book*, a collection of puzzles and riddles, a book which reached the printing stage, but was not published (the text was eventually produced elsewhere, with Gertrude Thomson illustrations). Tenniel instead contented himself with his past success with Dodgson and continued to be proud of his Alice illustrations, sending an original *Through the Looking-Glass* sketch to a friend "With John Tenniel's Kind Regards, Xmas 1875". Dodgson, on the other hand, was left to search elsewhere for an illustrator for *The Hunting of the Snark*. He deeply lamented what he called the "hopelessness of finding an artist worthy to succeed Mr Tenniel", and searched diligently for an artist capable of illustrations of "the same amount of finish as those of Mr Tenniel".[17]

Tenniel preferred to concentrate upon his own "pet projects" during occa-

sional periods of freedom from the pressures of *Punch* and further book publications. He was confident enough in this new ambition by 1877 to refuse a new
offer, because he had "for some time past entirely discontinued making drawings
for book illustrations".[18] This was not altogether true, for he now worked secretly
on illustrations to an edition of Shakespeare which he had long hoped to
complete. Two surviving drawings, engraved by the Dalziels, suggest the care
and finish he put into this favourite project; his scenes from *The Tempest*, *Twelfth
Night* and *The Merchant of Venice* had dense, richer background settings and the
confident Italian figures are among Tenniel's finest. But, despite an offer from
his *Punch* publisher, Bradbury and Evans, to publish the book when he completed it, and with at least two drawings engraved by the Dalziels, the project was
eventually abandoned for want of time.

Tenniel's version of *The Tempest*, a favourite Shakespearean theme

"Malvolio" from Shakespeare's *Twelfth Night* was engraved but unpublished

His gallery ambitions were always overshadowed by the narrow prejudices which infiltrated the art world at the time; the gap between the professional painter and the illustrator was still as wide as ever. Indeed, no *Punch* illustrator ever became or was considered for an associate membership at the prestigious Royal Academy. And, while Tenniel's own watercolours and drawings for *Punch* cartoons were readily accepted there by the hanging committee, they were relegated to the minor watercolour rooms and passed over with little critical notice. It was a disturbing prejudice which plagued the careers and ambitions of his many younger artist colleagues as well; illustrators like Walter Crane, Randolph Caldecott and Kate Greenaway, who painted for the galleries yet failed to elevate their careers into the more prestigious echelons of the profession. So it was that Tenniel joined the second rank of artist–illustrators as a contributor to the New Watercolour Society from 1874, becoming an associate and full member this same year. The Society had an impressive history, however. Originally founded to rival the more prestigious Old Watercolour Society, it had been revived in 1831 and was eventually given royal status, its members styled themselves RI for the Royal Institute of Painters in Watercolour. Most regarded membership here merely as a stop-gap, a minor accolade to be brushed aside when more prestigious avenues were conquered. When Kate Greenaway was asked to join she accepted after unsuccessful bids for RWS and RA status; but she refused to use the inferior RI after her name. Caldecott and Crane were also members, although their more talented associates soon gave up their membership when they were awarded RA or RWS rank. Tenniel was not as fortunate,

Tenniel's watercolour of "Sir Rupert the Fearless", from *The Ingoldsby Legends*, 1864, which he exhibited at the Royal Academy, 1873 (Sotheby's)

Engraved version of *The Ingoldsby Legends*, 1864, p. 141

despite his RA exhibition work: instead he flooded the RI with some twenty-seven watercolours of varying quality. It was a sign of his acceptance of the status quo, and belief that the illustrator had a distinctive role to play, despite the restrictions. His friend the art critic M.H. Spielmann, tactfully explained the dichotomy:

> If the illustrator confine himself to his own particular branch, he must not hope for any prize in the hierarchy of art. The great prizes are not for him! No doubt it will be all the same a hundred years hence – but for this: if he has done his work well, he has faithfully represented the life of his time, he has perpetuated what he has seen with his own bodily eyes; and for that reason alone his unpretending little sketches may, perhaps, have more interest for those who come across them in another hundred years than many an ambitious historical or classical canvas that has cost its painter infinite labour, imagination, and research, and won for him in his own time the highest rewards in money, fame, and Academical distinction. For genius alone can keep such fancy-work as this alive, and the so-called genius of today may be the scapegoat of tomorrow.[19]

Consequently Tenniel chose to submit to the hanging committee of the Royal Academy unashamed versions of past illustrations, newly watercoloured but largely adopted from once published engravings. The first appeared in May 1873: a variation of his ten-year-old *Ingoldsby Legends* illustrations which he called "Sir Rupert the Fearless" and illustrated the lines: "Lurline hung her head, turn'd pale and then red, Growing faint at his sudden proposal to wed." It was rather a dull watercolour, the cavalier Sir Rupert appealing to his lady love is surrounded by an indistinct fantasy of sea creatures in a subterranean landscape. A more successful yet curiously unexhibited watercolour of the period was "Pygmalion and the Statue" of 1878. Here a classical sculptor in his studio stares in wide-eyed disbelief as his model comes to life. It was a variant of an early drawing for "Clytie" in *Historical Ballads*, the dense engraved line here painted in Tenniel's favourite tones of pinks and greys. Other Academy exhibition work included religious subjects, like a chalk and charcoal study based upon a

"Sir Rupert", watercolour version dated 1873, of Tenniel's illustration to *The Ingoldsby Legends*, 1864 (Sotheby's)

Engraved version of "Sir Rupert", from *Ingoldsby Legends*, 1864, p. 135

Tenniel's poignant tribute to womanhood, "Pygmalion and the Statue", 1878, watercolour. 23 x 14³/₈" (Victoria and Albert Museum)

favourite Victorian biblical passage: "Jesus saith unto her, Mary. She turned herself, and saith unto him, Rabboni . . . " There were elaborations on topical *Punch* cartoons, like "Peace" exhibited in 1874, followed by a severe mace-wielder in "Trial by Battle" in 1878. He even returned to an early John Martin theme, reminiscent of his *Paradise Lost* illustrations, and painted "Eve" as a seductive nude with the *Genesis* quotations attached: "And the woman said. 'The serpent beguiled me, I didst eat' ".

Despite his thwarted gallery ambitions, Tenniel was magnanimous enough to acknowledge the success of his painter friends and to help promote the careers of the less fortunate. He sent four guineas to the Artist's General Benevolent Fund "in agony of haste", to help support that worthy charity.[20] He nurtured friendships with those who now rose to prominence as genre painters in the mould he had once set for himself. The enormously successful William Powell Frith, painter of "Ramsgate Sands" and "Derby Day", was a special friend. He and Tenniel had once joined forces on Hall's *Book of British Ballads*, but then had gone their separate ways until recently, when Tenniel became a welcomed guest in the Frith home in nearby St John's Wood. Frith had by then achieved full RA status (as early as 1853) and enjoyed royal patronage; his paintings were engraved and sold in large editions throughout the empire. He gathered together those of his artist friends who wished him well for social evenings. Here they admired his newest works, like the time Tenniel's friend, the medievalist illustrator and bird painter Henry Stacy Marks joined Tenniel for an Easter drink at the Friths', under the delighted gaze of the artist's young wife. In return Tenniel was immortalized in Frith's elaborate group portrait "Royal Academy Private View, 1881", where he was painted alongside thirty-two prominent artistic and political personalities and stood near his hero Gladstone, and Du Maurier, while further off the aging Oscar Wilde held court and Lily Langtry looked suitably demure. More inspiring to the illustrator in Tenniel was the recent elevation to greater artistic circles of the realistic illustrator-turned-painter, Luke Fildes. Tenniel was among the first to send Fildes "my sincere congratulations upon your selection last night" when the painter was elected an associate of the Academy in 1879; it was followed by a similar letter of sincere congratulations in 1887, when Fildes was made full RA. Tenniel's letter was delayed but was still a heartfelt wish for "I only hrd (sic) the news of your 'exaltations' yesterday".[21]

Tenniel, though, was proud of his own insular, carefully maintained life – which by most standards might be called dull. It suited his character to shun excitement and choose his own diversions from precious routine. He walked nearly three miles to the *Punch* offices each Wednesday for the editorial meeting, then returned home to complete his cartoon by Saturday. After this he might take a ride with friends in Hyde Park, or go to a nearby country retreat, since he rarely left the four mile radius around the city. In a curious letter to his friend, the landscape painter George Vicat Cole, Tenniel gives a rare glimpse of this carefully managed if eccentric approach to life: "I propose to leave by the 9.5 train tomorrow morn. due at Reading 10.27 – 'Be in time – be in time' being always my 'Motto'!! Hoping that the weather means to have *no nonsense*. I remain sincerely yours, John Tenniel." He adds ominously, "Barometer awfully *low*". Social occasions were, as always, treated with the respect and politeness due to them – as in the time he accepted the "polite invitation" to dine with the Lord Mayor and Lady Mayoress at the Mansion House, accepting with "much honour".[22] His two previous trips abroad had not inspired him enough to consider lengthy excursions on the Continent and he never took holidays, so it came as a considerable surprise to his friends when in October 1878 he announced a plan to visit Venice. His close friend Henry Lucy, the journalist who was soon to become *Punch*'s parliamentary reporter "Toby M.P.", invited him to join him and his wife for an Italian holiday. Curiously, for one so struck by classical and Renaissance models, Tenniel had never been to Italy. Now, for a variety of reasons, he agreed to the visit: for one, it was a sign of a new, more relaxed attitude toward his *Punch* responsibilities, since he knew Charles Keene could very adequately take over the "Big Cut". When Keene heard the news, he was clearly flattered by the opportunity to diversify his talent, however temporarily: "Tenniel is going away to Venice and he has never had a holiday since he has been on 'Punch', so I have to be in the way", Keene told a friend two month's before Tenniel's departure – clear indication of Tenniel's carefully considered decision to visit Venice. In fact Tenniel enjoyed this, only his third visit abroad, so much he stayed a month and was away most of October. It was long enough for four Keene "Big Cuts" to be published, and Tenniel's familiar cartoons did not reappear in *Punch* until early November. This made a total of thirteen cartoons done by Keene in place of Tenniel over the years.[23]

When Tenniel returned home it was to a household filled with sadness and domestic upheaval. It centred on the death of his devoted housekeeper and companion Mrs Giani, who had served him for twenty-three years. He was left crushed by yet another death; this time that of a woman whom he had regarded as his spiritual anchor and confidante; the person who had helped to restore his broken spirits after the tragic loss of his wife, her daughter. Such was the depth of Tenniel's new grief that his friend Francis Burnand now claimed, "His grief at the decease of this kindly old lady might have proved fatal to his career had it not been for the encouraging presence of his unmarried sister, Miss Tenniel".[24]

Indeed Victoire Tenniel proved a godsend at this painful moment in her brother's life. "Vic", as Tenniel called her, was the archetypal Victorian spinster, a "genial and stately woman" (according to one of Tenniel's friends) who had obviously inherited the family's aristocratic bearing: "she might have been, and quite probably was, the model for one of Leech's portly and handsome *maîtres familiarum*".[25] Competent and understanding, she quickly adjusted to her new duties and ran her brother's large household, saw that his routine was uninterrupted and carefully maintained, guarding him against further domestic upsets, unnecessary and unwanted correspondence and visitors. She carried out her duties with a slight military air which she shared with her brother, and undoubtedly had inherited from their beloved father, who was still alive. Finally it was she who agreed to open Tenniel's weekly *Punch* packet, which gave him his "weekly pang" at first seeing his drawing engraved.

Fortunately Victoire was also there to soften yet another blow to Tenniel's life. This was the death of their father, early in 1879, aged eighty-six. The loss of this inspiring figure who had served as the head of the family for almost sixty years was one neither brother nor sister could reconcile; for they both owed much to their father's firm, virtuous view of the world. Fortunately John Tenniel senior had lived long enough to see his children prosper, especially his namesake John junior, whose artistic career and reputation flourished even now, as he reached his sixtieth birthday. Although Tenniel went into customary mourning for his father, he was revived enough by Derby Day to send light-hearted greetings and a "little Punch drawing" he had been "cooking up" as a birthday present for his proprietor's son, Willie Agnew, which he signed affectionately "Jackides".[26]

The following year marked Tenniel's last appearance at the Royal Academy. This took the appropriate form of a finished *Punch* cartoon, which he called "The White Elephant Turned 'Rogue'". It had been inspired by the book by Sir J. Emerson on the white elephant, the cartoon originally published in *Punch* (8 November 1879). Significantly it remained unsold at the Academy. Tenniel returned to his *Punch* duties with a mixed sense of loss and dedication, having seen his efforts in the galleries come to little real reward. Instead he now relished his role as the senior artistic member of staff to a new generation of *Punch* illustrators and journalists. Some, like the artists Linley Sambourne and Harry Furniss, became close and cherished friends, as did journalist Fred Anstey Guthrie. Of this new generation, most were at least twenty years Tenniel's junior, with that same degree of effusive, refreshing youthfulness, coupled with a genuine talent, and well-trained draughtsmanship which had earlier attracted Tenniel to Du Maurier. When Tom Taylor's *Punch* editorship came to an abrupt end at his death in July 1880, this brought the paper's proprietors and select senior staff members, including Tenniel and writers Arthur à Beckett and Percival Leigh, together to choose a new editor. The frontrunner was Francis Burnand, who was in the end unanimously elected and served as editor until 1906. Unfortunately he failed to provide the dynamic leadership necessary to inspire the newer contributors and prevent *Punch* from a further slide downhill. The result was that Burnand was forced to retire from his editorship, in favour of a more competent and far-sighted man.

Nevertheless Tenniel liked his new editor, and he and Burnand worked closely together for thirty-four years; a period Burnand described "among the most delighted memories of my life". Although seventeen years Tenniel's junior, Burnand shared his friend's courteous approach to a demanding job. They enjoyed riding their horses together when the week's paper had been safely finished and the weekly ride helped to clear the way for the next issue.

> Any number of delightful rides we enjoyed together, one of many and one of the best and longest having been a couple in Epping Forest, when Linley Sambourne, Tenniel, and myself put up our horses at the Forest Inn, Chingford, dined happily, slept well, rose early and rode all day, arriving in London about eight in the evening. A most delightful outing.[27]

Like Tenniel he also loved the theatre, and was a successful dramatist with over 120 plays to his credit. His most successful and popular was "Black-Eyed Susan", which ran for 800 nights in London's Royalty Theatre, Soho, then toured the provinces and America. Tenniel attended one London performance and was fascinated by the exuberant dancing and rousing choruses, especially the virtuoso performance of the show's star, the elderly heroine Dame Hattey, played in drag by the actor Danvers. He stole the show with his amazing dancing, "bounding about like an irrepressible indiarubber rag doll, or a puppet". Afterwards Tenniel sent Burnand a clever sketch drawn from memory of Dame Hattey whirling about the stage, in "feats of legs" he punned, in gratitude "for his Comedie Burlesq-U-E".[28] Tenniel knew his new editor loved puns, and loved to share some of his own more accomplished versions with him. On more serious matters, Burnand tried to be tolerant on religious and political issues but ended up feigning a personal neutrality which earned him the accolade "Commandant of the Household Brigade of British Mirth" from his staff.

Unfortunately Burnand's approach turned *Punch* into an even more uninspired affair, with mediocre illustrations from two distinct quarters. Keene still provided the social satires although he shared the role with Du Maurier, whose earnest parodies of the burgeoning members of the Aesthetic Movement were the best to appear at the time. Secondly, Tenniel, in his own distinctive style, provided the political cartoons, which had become stereotyped and too familiar in their restraint to be fully effective as comic satires, let alone supreme examples

F.C. Burnand, Tenniel's new *Punch* editor

of the "art" his admirers claimed for them. The "Big Cut" offered little real visual humour and only brief inventiveness with clever Disraeli (who died in 1881) or Gladstone portraits. Most cartoons were based upon literary precedents and were still debated and argued over as hotly as ever, despite the bored expressions of the more senior staff members. One observer noted:

> George Du Maurier . . . I learned, had been in the habit, directly the discussion set in, of drawing up another chair for his legs, placing a handkerchief over his face and going to sleep. He woke up once with a start and inquired if the company were still talking about Gladstone and Disraeli, and on hearing that this was the dismal truth, "Good Heavens!" he exclaimed, "why don't you talk about something sensible? Why don't you talk about the beauty of women?" and again passed into oblivion.[29]

Tenniel's dry wit and brief yet perceptive comments were greatly welcomed in such an uninspired atmosphere. If left to his own devices, as in the almanack drawings, he still was capable of creating striking inventions which amused his friends and his readers. One of his own favourites was a pen and ink design for the 1879 almanack, which he eventually hung over his study mantelpiece. It was called "Prometheus Unbound" or "Science in Olympus", and parodied the recent technological advances of the telephone and electricity. There was a strong element of uncertainty and disquiet about these new threats to the future, and Tenniel's design, while humorous, echoed his innate conservatism. He aptly chose classical heroes to pinpoint his worries: a baffled Vulcan scratches his head at the sight of a Nasmyth steam hammer cracking an egg; Mr Punch dazzles Jupiter with the glare from an electric light; Mercury rides aloft on a penny-farthing, while in the foreground Venus is photographed by Father Time, an impish Cupid thumbing his nose at the camera. Tenniel loved to twist familiar

"Prometheus Unbound, or Science in Olympus", original pen drawing for engraving in *Punch's Almanack*, 1879, exhibited at the Fine Art Society, 1895 and which hung over Tenniel's mantelpiece. $10^{1}/_{2}$ x $19^{1}/_{2}$". (Sotheby's)

legends and mythical characters to suit his dry sense of humour; and although one needed to know mythology to appreciate best his inventions, he preferred to challenge rather than "draw down" to his readers. There were also more obvious comic touches, like Bacchus and a satyr sipping coffee to restrain their natural instincts. In the foreground the cartoon's theme is suggested by a messenger boy who speaks into a telephone. The wire stretches off into the clouds while a composer, poet, ballerina and opera singer wait in the wings for their turn to convert culture to the air waves. Tenniel's vision of the future not only threatened but inspired his creative instincts. In another design of a similar subject he proposed a "fantastic future", where Christmas turkeys were hatched by electric heat, bicycles were powered by electricity to enable their riders to read *The Electric Times* while riding without concentrating upon their pedalling. Electric current opened up infinite possibilities for luxury goods, like foreign beef from Australia resuscitated by the current; or an electric balloon shaped like a bird-like fish, complete with wings and a suspended basket for passengers. Tenniel's drawing included a brightly lit electric sign on the balloon which proudly proclaimed the joys of travel by electricity: "London to Paris in two hours" and "No seasickness".

One of Tenniel's newest friends was the ebullient Linley "Sammy" Sambourne, who Tenniel first met at Mark Lemon's funeral. Sambourne was asked to join *Punch* in 1871, where his adaptability and ability to draw well to deadline whatever the subject made him an ideal understudy to Tenniel: eventually he took over the chief political cartoonist post in 1901. Sambourne was one of the liveliest of new faces around the *Punch* table, a delightfully likeable character with a flamboyant taste for good food, fine wines and dinner parties, where he shone as a master of verbal wit, a mixer of metaphors, perfecter of spoonerisms

Tenniel's vision of an electric future, *Punch*, 1882

and expert joke teller. As a *Punch* draughtsman he quickly developed a distinctive, even hard-outlined style not unlike Tenniel's, except that every line, however trivial its effect, was evenly drawn like a grid-work. Moreover, his use of heavy shaded areas of grey linked him to the Sixties School illustrators, while his sinewy experiments in art nouveau free-forms eventually joined him to the Aubrey Beardsley generation. Most important of all, he was adept at drawing accurately on the spot to order: Du Maurier claimed he was the only man in London who could draw a top hat correctly. His output was therefore prodigious, amounting to 4,000 cartoons and drawings – nearly twice as many as Tenniel's. His friendship with Tenniel, who was twenty-four years his senior, took time to develop, but it gradually ripened into a mutual admiration for one another's talents: "What an extraordinary improvement there is in Sambourne's work!" Tenniel then exclaimed.

> Although a little hard and mechanical, it is of absolutely inexhaustible ingenuity and firmness of touch. His diploma for the Fisheries Exhibition almost gave me a headache to look at it – so full, cram-full of suggestion, yet leaving nothing to the imagination, so perfectly and completely drawn, with a certainty of touch which baffles me to understand how he does it.[30]

Part of the key to Sambourne's skill lay in his habit of collecting photographs for models. He owned nearly 10,000 photographs of animals, military uniforms and historical costumes: those items which would have tried the patience of a less-accomplished artist. He even went so far as to press his friends and servants to dress in costumes and pose for his more difficult drawings. Tenniel was aware of this clever use of photography and in fact borrowed from the practice briefly for his difficult portraits. Moreover, there was something about Sambourne's youthful, uninhibited approach to life which secretly appealed to the more staid, regimented element in Tenniel's character. He relished snippets of news of his friend's exciting lifestyle, the seemingly endless round of parties and late nights which he freely admitted amounted to a dangerous "burning of the candle at both ends". In time they rode together frequently, thoroughly enjoying each other's company. Another friend recalled one of their numerous amusing riding incidents together:

> Tenniel, when riding down a lane, had been bitten on the wrist by a fly which had just been feeding on a long-dead rabbit. As a consequence his arm had swollen badly, and, as he told Sammy, he had felt extremely ill for a day or two, after which he recovered. "Ah", said Sammy, "it's lucky that it didn't happen to *me*, or, living as I do, I should have died!"[31]

Another new friend and energetic addition to Tenniel's circle was the artist Harry Furniss. Having grown up in Ireland on a diet of *Punch*, he longed to contribute to the paper at an early age and even produced his own "The Schoolboys' Punch", before coming to London to earn a living as a black and white draughtsman for papers like the *Illustrated London News*. Then in 1888, at the age of twenty-six, he was asked by Burnand to work for *Punch*, not as an official staff member, but as a regular freelance contributor. He joined forces with Henry Lucy, the paper's parliamentary reporter, and created some remarkable if merciless cartoon spoofs on current politicians which outraged as much as entertained – especially the wives of the prominent statesmen who tried in vain to protect their husbands from Furniss's barbed pen. His favourite ruse to obtain his required parliamentary portraits in the House was to tell Politician A that he wanted to draw Politician

Harry Furniss self-caricature

B, if A would keep him talking: while all the time he wanted to draw A instead. His style was quick; impressionistic sketches and lightning versions of faces and poses which earned him the dubious distinction of the fastest worker on *Punch*. Yet he never took over the "Big Cut" from Tenniel, or agreed to a steady salary, being paid instead by the square inch. Eventually he fell out with *Punch* over payment and the copyright of his work and left after fourteen years to start up his own ill-fated comic paper. His influence and friendship with Tenniel was much treasured and he helped to brighten up the uncertainties of the 1880s and early 1890s.

Tenniel at work by Harry Furniss

The two men respected one another's talents from the start. The year before Furniss joined *Punch* he had achieved a remarkable reputation by his exhibition of comic spoofs on the Royal Academy exhibitions. Having worked three years in secret upon the eighty-seven drawings parodying the old guard painters, he eventually exhibited them in Bond Street. Tenniel was among the crowds who flocked to the Gainsborough Gallery where they were shown and the exhibition became the hit of the Season. It was followed by Furniss's book, *How He Did It – Story of the Artistic Joke*, 1888, which Tenniel studied closely before sending his enthusiastic praise to its author, pronouncing it "admirable! reproductions first rate!!"[32] On the other hand, Furniss was quick to notice his friend's distinctive appearance and curious aversion to models. This inspired his satiric caricature "Sir John Tenniel at Work", in which the lean, long-moustached Tenniel leans over his drawing board, behind him a male (nude) model which everyone knew Tenniel still defiantly refused to use.

Tenniel and Furniss also shared a love of horseback riding since it was a necessary release from the pressures of work. Tenniel was the superior horse-man, and the year after Furniss had joined *Punch*, he wrote well-meaning advice to his new friend, recommending horses which might be best for him. He suggested a Mr Walker of Felixstowe for "two cobs, one of which he is sure would suit you". He had just purchased a new horse there but "my little cobbie" at first seemed "rather too small" for his long frame. Only after two weeks breaking it in did he change his opinion and wrote to Furniss:

> I think my own little cobbie will do me very well – there's a good deal [of nervousness] at present, but I believe he'll get over it, in time, he's very nervous, very strong, very fast, & wants to *go* – not a bit the quiet "*old gentlemans*' cob" I imagined him to be when I rode him on trial at Felixstowe.[33]

Finally Furniss shared with Tenniel the common trial of working under the infuriating Lewis Carroll. Despite Tenniel's sincere warning against illustrating for the author ("I'll give you a week old chap; you'll never put up with that fellow a day longer"), Furniss persevered over seven years to produce illustrations for two volumes of *Sylvie and Bruno* published in 1888 and 1894. He was the first, however, to admit Tenniel's warning had been sound advice.

In fact Tenniel broke his own aversion to work again for Dodgson during this period, accepting his subsidiary role now as a matter of course. Dodgson planned an abridged version of Alice for his younger readers, called *The Nursery Alice*, which he hoped to be available by 1889. Again unexpected delays and poor printing plagued the project Dodgson had suggested as early as 1881 – the year a combined *Alice* and *Through the Looking-Glass* edition appeared with Tenniel's name mis-spelt "Tennel" on the green cloth cover. Tenniel then agreed in principle to colour twenty of his original Alice engravings for the nursery edition, to help guide the colour printer Edmund Evans when he mixed his oil-based inks

Gertrude Thomson's Alice
pastiche cover for Carroll's
Nursery Alice

and cut each colour section on wood blocks. As it happened this stage stretched over several years: a bemused Tenniel had to write to Evans as late as the end of 1886 to ask "if anything is being done with the 'Alice' coloured pictures".[34] Another gap of almost three years passed before Dodgson revived the book project in February 1889, then having completely rewritten the text, simplifying and adding more references to Tenniel's pictures. During this time it seems that Dodgson had not bothered to inspect Evans' proofs, so that when the first printed sheets arrived in June, he was horrified: "The pictures are far too bright and gaudy, and vulgarise the whole thing. *None must be sold in England*: to do so would be to sacrifice whatever reputation I now have for giving the public the *best* I can." He rejected the colour engravings and insisted Evans must begin again with Tenniel's coloured originals beside him; then he must see the results before a new edition (of 10,000 copies) could be printed. As for the inferior first printed edition, Dodgson hoped America would again take them: ironically the book was rejected there "as not gaudy enough", while the covers were poorly bound and spines cracked when they were opened. All these delays were infuriating proof that Tenniel's reticence to work again with Dodgson had been well founded. Only by Easter 1890 did the second edition of *The Nursery Alice* appear, with a weak pastiche of Tenniel's style on the cover by Dodgson's new protégée Gertrude Thomson.[35]

Tenniel spent the remainder of 1889 quietly, preoccupied with his weekly *Punch* cartoons and occasional paintings for friends. This year the art editor and critic M.H. Spielmann was given a brief glimpse of Tenniel's routine, as well as some hint of his plans for the future. As he now neared his seventieth birthday, Tenniel told him how his spare moments were filled by reworking old *Punch* sketches from among the "scores of my sketches, of which I have hundreds" for an enthusiastic admirer. Having painted a rare oil self-portrait several years earlier, he now agreed to copy it in pen and ink for use by Spielmann. It remains one of his most characteristic portraits, the long, drooping moustaches, high forehead and piercing eyes (which did not suggest partial blindness) were those of an elegant, dapper gentleman as always immaculately dressed in high starched collar, silk tie and pearl stick-pin. Despite his age, Tenniel continued to take great care with his appearance and prided himself upon his conservative yet well-turned-out public image. His memories of dressing up for the stage in velvet tunics, high boots and wide-brimmed plumed hats were revived when he chose a scene from *Gil Blas* to paint. He called it "How Gil Blas Arrayed Himself in the Blue Velvet" and had painted it in 1881, depicting the self-made Blas vainly admiring his new-found riches before a mirror, his peacock feathered hat and ruffled shirt of the types favoured by the thespian Tenniel.

To his friends and public he possessed the image of the ideal gentleman with a quiet, refined manner and extreme if occasionally deferential sense of courtesy. He was proud of his good health and rarely missed work because of illness. "His upright, lithe figure, his ruddy countenance, his bright and cheery look belied the tale of years. Conjoined with a healthy body was a sunny temper", his friend and Venice travelling companion Henry Lucy recalled of what he concluded was Tenniel's "beautiful nature and perfect manner". This left him uncertain "as to whether he more resembled Don Quixote or Colonel Newcome". But for all of his sixty-nine years he was "in spirit the youngest of the staff".[36] Tenniel stressed his fine health when Spielmann interviewed him, proudly claiming that while he had seen so many of his younger colleagues struck down in middle-age by over-

"How Gil Blas Arrayed Himself in the Blue Velvet", painted by Tenniel in 1881

indulgence and over-work, for almost thirty years he had been uninhibited by illness; "in all that time I have hardly left London for more than a week; yet I enjoy wonderful health, doubtless to be attributed to regular riding".[37]

His insularity made travel of any kind a major upheaval, and for this reason he rarely considered it. An exception was made in May 1889, when he agreed to accompany ten of his *Punch* colleagues to Paris for the International Exhibition. They took the early morning train to the port of Dover and boarded the boat to Calais, where a group photograph was taken on board. In it Tenniel stands out as the most immaculately dressed and handsome of his fellow travellers, despite

The *Punch* staff at the Paris Exhibition, 1889. Tenniel stands third from the right, in derby, George Du Maurier is seated first on the right.

his age. When the high-spirited members of the group arrived in Paris they marched through the city streets to the exhibition grounds, where the Eiffel Tower was scaled only by the adventurous Du Maurier and Fred Anstey, while Tenniel firmly refused to leave the ground. Later he drew the iron tower on the cover of the Special *Punch* Number, which appeared in September, commemorating their journey and the Paris Exhibition.

Apart from *Punch* colleagues and artist friends, Tenniel's social circle was surprisingly small, considering the scale of his public reputation. He avoided politicians – undoubtedly an occupational hazard – and rarely went out as he grew older. Social engagements could prove embarrassing if a well-meaning hostess threatened to lionize him; he would always prefer small, more intimate groups of friends to large gatherings. He was a model of courtesy and correct behaviour, but occasionally he grew impatient with the interruptions, like the time an enthusiastic admirer wrongly claimed they shared a mutual acquaintance and on the strength of this invited Tenniel to lunch. He wrote back a polite but firm refusal, adding "I never eat lunch!" Other letters to doting hostesses seeking his company were short one-page or even one-line replies written in a bold nearly illegible hand, sometimes on violet stationery in purple ink, otherwise on his own embossed stationery. His characteristic response to an invitation, however prestigious the event, was similar to the following he wrote to the Gladstones: "Mr. Tenniel has much honour in accepting Mr. & Mrs. Gladstone's kind invitation to dinner on 11th of June."[38] In public he could be shy and self-effacing: when asked to become a steward at a dinner in honour of the actor Henry Irving, Tenniel provisionally agreed, then wrote a second letter to explain, "if the office involved any special duties I should be a very inefficient steward . . .. I wrote in great haste which probably accounts for the ambiguity of the [first] letter." [39] Eventually he discovered the telegram was more conducive to his needs. It was quick, efficient and, most important of all, required the shortest message. Once when he wanted to accept the Marquis of Fillean's invitation, he realized a telegram was the only way to reach him in time, having taken his horse out on "several attempts to ride over to see you, but the difficulties in these days of rain and darkness and fog – especially *fog!*"[40]

His reserve and tendency towards mock petulance was understood by his friends but could be misinterpreted as rudeness by acquaintances. Such was the case with Mrs Millais, the high-spirited wife of his painter friend, who had seen Tenniel in public but thought she had been snubbed or at least ignored by him. Others may have forgotten the incident, but the easily angered Effie Millais

Sir John Tenniel, oil painting by Frank Holl, 23³/₄ x 18³/₄"

wrote to Tenniel in the strongest reprimand to protest. She received an uncharacteristically gushing letter filled with Tenniel's "two thousand apologies" and the rare confession that he felt "shame and humiliation" at what he called "the absurdity of my mistake . . .. What a wholesome thing it is to have the conceit taken out of one, now and then! At the same time it is a great happiness to know that I am not really in disgrace." He promised as soon as possible to call on her "to *prove my identity*".[41] He clearly felt more at ease in the company of younger, bohemian colleagues, like George Du Maurier, who had recently helped to secure Tenniel's invitation to one of the celebrated "octave dinners" of the notorious surgeon and art collector Sir Henry Thompson at which just eight guests arrived at eight for an eight course dinner. Tenniel acknowledged this coveted invitation "with pleasure". In the case of the hostess Mrs Hunter, he left things rather too late to refuse her invitation to dine, but sent instead his card on the day: "I have already two engagements for this evening and in quite the opposite direction". As he grew older, he relished the attentions of these hostesses or more especially their daughters, and in exchange for their attentions he offered them rare glimpses of his carefully sheltered private life. After one particularly alcoholic evening with friends, Tenniel returned home at 1.00 a.m. to find a note from Miss Chappell asking his preference for wines for his forthcoming visit to her. He replied in a shaky hand that after the evening's revels "my judgement in the matter of 'port-wine' is not profound" but added helpfully "47 Port-51 Port. Happy could I be with either" – a rare glimpse of an inabstenious Tenniel.[42]

It was perhaps inevitable that such a famous, gallant and handsome widower should be taken up by well-meaning hostesses to help fill their drawing rooms and provide necessary prestige on such occasions. In return Tenniel offered small kindnesses, sent autographs to friends of friends and even sent sketches and copies of his books to admirers, however remote their acquaintance. Those hostesses he considered worthy friends received entertaining, longer letters of thanks, like the grateful note he sent Mrs Robb for her gift of pheasant eggs. He assured her every one would be "devoured with the liveliest of satisfaction. But it really seems to me to be almost a wickedness to eat them, so I am thinking of hatching them in the kitchen oven, and starting a 'Pheasant Farm' on the roof of my house."[43] Mrs Skirrow occupied a prominent place in his social life during the early 1880s. She was a redoubtable hostess who collected celebrities and hung their portraits in her "gallery of friends" for all to admire. It seems she was especially taken with Tenniel, sent him an annual birthday and Christmas gift as well as frequent invitations to her home. Obviously flattered by her attentions, Tenniel soon realized there was little he could do to reciprocate since he rarely entertained himself, except take her into his confidence and offer news of his work. A typical letter to her was almost confessional in tone: "Pray forgive this hurried note, being as I am, in the annual agonies of the Punch Almanack which, naturally, becomes more and more difficult & troublesome as the years roll by." In time he sent his favourite photographic portrait to her with a rather coy yet characteristic letter, which ended,

> it only remains for me to request you to add to the obligation, and therefore, in begging the favour of your kind acceptance of the accompanying portrait – the latest taken – I am sure I need hardly assure you that it would make me very happy & very proud, to be allowed a little corner in your 'Gallery' of friends. The likeness is supposed to be a very good one, inclusive of the fact that it is about twenty-five years younger than the original . . .[44]

By the early 1890s his friendship with Mrs Skirrow was challenged by the attentions of a younger, more exciting woman. She also collected celebrities, flirted with them and encouraged long correspondences to bring excitement to her rather dull married life. Her name was Elspeth Grahame, wife of Kenneth Grahame, a bank clerk and eventual author of *The Wind in the Willows*. Elspeth had been taught to regard the famous as fair game for her affections: as a child in Edinburgh and then in London she grew up among the privileged circles of literary, scientific and artistic life collected by her equally gregarious mother. Swinburne, Browning, Oscar Wilde and Lord Leighton had called at her home, and as a schoolgirl, she had toured the London streets with the eccentrically dressed Tennyson, who castigated her for dressing too prominently since he thought it called undue attention to him. More recently she had written the aptly named fantasy novel *Amelia Jane's Ambition*, 1888, and married a middle-aged bank clerk, only to repent her choice and ask Mrs Thomas Hardy for advice on the melancholy business of being a wife – Mrs Hardy being a most unpropitious choice for a confidante. Tenniel met her when she was still an attractive high-spirited thirty-year-old woman. She was intent upon cultivating her own peculiar brand of fairy-tale fantasy, coupled with a headstrong manner which she used to impose her will upon a large and diverse collection of famous correspondents. She could flatter even the most reticent into writing her uncharacteristic letters, filled with artistic turns of phrase like those she received in 1890 from the leader of the Irish Party Justin McCarthy. He wrote lyrically about his love for "Rivers – and poets who love Rivers and painters who gave us pictures of them". So it was that the seventy-two-year-old Tenniel was taken up by Mrs Grahame, and he too wrote a series of unusually long "coyly gallant" letters to her. These were filled with sub-Carrollean fantasies like his favourite invention, the "Furious Flycycle" and brief sketches or elaborate valentines to charm and delight his young admirer.[45]

Tenniel remained devoted to his riding throughout the 1890s, spurred on by his founding membership in the "Two Pins Club". Founded on 25 May 1890 and surviving a brief two years, this group of like-minded horsemen included *Punch* associates Linley Sambourne, Harry Furniss and Francis Burnand, with the Lord Chief-Justice, Sir Charles Russell, as President and Sir Edward Lawson and three others chosen "for social distinction" to make up the nine total members. They met each week on Sundays, for rides in Richmond Park and afterwards lunched along the river. The group was inspired by those two most legendary of horsemen, John Gilpin and Dick Turpin, whose names were the source of the two "pins" in the club's name. Tenniel loved their rides and deeply regretted the end of such a delightful weekend diversion, when the club ceased to meet in 1892.

By this time Tenniel's relationship with *Punch* began to suggest disturbing signs of change. In the past the editor was expected to prevent cartoon subjects being repeated, but with so many changes of editorship over the past few years such continuity proved impossible. Eventually Tenniel, as a senior staff member, was unofficially appointed censor of unoriginal material – another reason for his diligent attendance at the editorial dinners. Indeed, from 1864–94 he rarely missed a Wednesday evening meeting, although he allowed Linley Sambourne to take over the "Big Cut" twice in 1894. Moreover, the staff continued to change. Percival Leigh, one of the longest standing and most talented of *Punch* comic journalists, died in 1889, leaving a considerable gap in humorous talent. His death was followed by an even greater loss to Tenniel, when Charles Keene, his old art student friend and *Punch* colleague of over thirty years, died on 10 January 1891, aged just sixty-eight. His death was a profound reminder of the fallibility of Tenniel's own position on the paper. The old generation now quickly faded to make way for a newer group of talented writers and artists, like the expert draughtsmen Phil May and Bernard Partridge.

Bernard Partridge joined *Punch* in 1891, having been introduced to the paper by Du Maurier and Fred Anstey Guthrie. He quickly established himself as an important staff member and for ten years seated himself alongside Tenniel at the *Punch* table each Wednesday. At first he was intrigued by Tenniel's power over his younger colleagues. By then a thirty-year-old ex-actor, Partridge had produced some striking theatrical caricatures which must have endeared him to Tenniel's own preoccupations with the theatre. Moreover, he was a supremely talented humorist and would eventually become the second *Punch* cartoonist in 1901, and principal from 1909–45. Partridge clearly recalled those early *Punch* meetings, fascinated by the spell Tenniel seemed to have over his younger colleagues. He focused his attention upon the senior staff, especially "the two supremely interesting personalities" Tenniel and Du Maurier, but it was Tenniel's unique presence which coloured his memory of those early days:

> I well remember the impression Tenniel produced on me – an impression of extreme courtliness and suavity. One noticed the tall soldierly figure and the precise neatness of his dress, and then, as he gave one a cordial greeting, the exquisite diction with which it was produced. It was a keen pleasure to listen to his speech. Without a trace of pedantry his enunciation always charmed the ear by the rare purity of the vowel sounds.

The old and new generation *Punch* staff, 1895, from left to right: George Du Maurier, Arthur à Beckett, Linley Sambourne, Tenniel, Francis Burnand, F. Anstey, Henry Lucy, E.T. Reed, Bernard Partridge (pouring), Lawrence Bradbury.

They soon became friends and met outside the office, Partridge occasionally sharing a cab with Tenniel on the way home, when he might be invited in to see his mentor's latest sketches. At the *Punch* meetings he fantasized about Tenniel's obvious power, however benign his manner:

> There he sat, a grave, placid figure, with that dominant note of strong simplicity suffusing every word and action. Reticent he was – not often himself suggesting, but weighing every suggestion of others – impatient of all superfluity, resenting and rejecting anything that would hamper the translation of his theme into the terms of his own forceful austere line. He puffed his churchwarden continuously – one remembers the firm, nervous grip of his fingers on the stem and the vague half-sketched gestures that punctuated his talk; the occasional flashes of fun and the rare liftings of the veil that let his enthusiasms peep out. But always the qualities that radiated from him were those of which his work was compact – strength and reticence. No personality ever reflected more completely the work it projected.[46]

Bernard Partridge self-portrait

Such was the respect and admiration Tenniel received from the younger staff members. "I realised with increasing sureness that the great quality that distinguished the man, as it distinguished his work, was dignity," Bernard Partridge concluded. This attribute dominated the impression formed by another awestruck young addition to the paper, the sporting writer R.C. Lehmann, who first met Tenniel in April 1890.

> I had been brought up on a liberal diet of *Punch* back volumes as well as current numbers, and had learnt a good deal of modern history from Tenniel's glorious cartoons. I felt as if I was about to be introduced to a great historic figure who had somehow survived from the splendid past to our degenerate days.

Indeed, Tenniel's ordered manner and careful consideration of each new idea endeared him to the younger, more effusive, innocent and certainly less experienced staff. Lehmann was most impressed by his almost military-like manner ("he must have been at one time a calvary colonel"). And yet he managed to instil warmth in his colleagues by taking an honest interest in their ideas, charming the "new boys" with his geniality and self-effacing comments. "I am sure that, through all the years of our association, I never lost that early feeling of reverence", Lehmann concluded.[47] So did the *Punch* parodist Fred Anstey Guthrie, who knew Tenniel as "a kind and sympathetic friend; he took an interest in my *Punch* work, and seemed to like to know what I was thinking of doing, and to encourage me in it."[48] This overall feeling of dignified fatherliness is best depicted in a late portrait of Tenniel by the master social-realist painter, Frank Holl.

On 19 July 1891 *Punch* published its one-hundredth volume and a grand celebration dinner was held at "The Ship" in Greenwich. Fifty years had passed since its first number appeared and forty of those had been enjoyed by Tenniel, who remained as strong an influence as ever. At the celebration dinner his colleagues sought to express their gratitude to their most senior staff member and raised their glasses to toast his health as "the great survivor". In a sense it was a salute to bygone days, for *Punch* was no longer the illustrated paper Tenniel had once known and loved. His own very singular approach to his drawings, the meticulous pencil work on box wood, had been supplanted at last by a new technical advance which required only one original pen drawing, photographically reproduced onto the block – but that original had to be perfect in its conception, and in ink – the medium Tenniel found most difficult. No longer were the newer artists allowed to use shorthand to cover up their deficiencies; the paper demanded accurate artistic drawings done from life; "men and women,

Tenniel by Bernard Partridge

horses and dogs, seascapes, landscapes, everything one can make little pictures out of, must be studied from life", Du Maurier noted somewhat sadly after he had left *Punch* in 1894. The era of quick sketches, the "mere dancing upon paper" had passed, replaced by the virtuosity of intricate inked surfaces and elegant, slick artistic effects at the expense of humour. The culprit was, of course, the photo-engraving technique, or "process" as it was known, which *Punch* first used for a Linley Sambourne drawing in the issue of 3 December 1892. Tenniel's eventual process-engraved ink drawings first appeared in the almanacks then as full-page cartoons. He never was comfortable or pleased with the new technique that had threatened and in many cases destroyed the livelihoods of his wood-engravers. Edmund Evans now struggled to keep his wood-engraving business, although he magnanimously acknowledged the benefits of the new process ("What a wonderful advance") which he thought "very fine" for realism and reporting in such social realist papers as the *Graphic* and the *Illustrated London News*. "But it has ruined Punch. J. Tenniel is the only one of their staff that will have his drawings still [wood] engraved by Swain", Evans explained in 1899.

> Punch I believe has done a good work in the world, it never was vulgar, or ridiculed things sacred – but only the follies and pride of *men* – and *women*. It has fallen off, artistically, lately the drawings are very poor, bad now, with an exception now and then.[49]

Tenniel would have agreed with his old engraving colleague. There were, however, more obvious and immediate benefits in using the process technique, as it allowed him to keep the original drawing, thus saving the time and effort of re-working his old sketches when friends asked for the originals – and his *Punch* drawings were now very much in demand. When *Punch* published his poignant tribute to Gladstone and the Duke of Argyll, mounted on horseback hand in hand as mutual "Old Crusaders" (18 May 1895) set against Turkey's recent persecution of Christian Armenia, Tenniel received a telegram from the Marquis of Lorne at Windsor, requesting the original drawing. Unfortunately he no longer owned the finished ink design since a few hours previously he had agreed to present it to Gladstone's son on behalf of his father – such was the impression it made on Tenniel's hero.

Most critics believed there was one Tenniel political cartoon which would remain his masterpiece; according to *The Times* it was "an example of Sir John Tenniel's art that will live long to show how great an artist he was". It was called "Dropping the Pilot" (29 March 1890) and appeared as a vertical double-page wood-engraved tribute to the German Chancellor Bismark, dismissed by the scheming Emperor Wilhelm II. The idea for the cartoon had come from Tenniel's old friend Arthur à Beckett, then too ill to attend the editorial meeting, where it was unanimously accepted – a suitable tribute since à Beckett died shortly after publication. Tenniel drew the weather-beaten old mariner as Bismark as he descended the symbolic ship of Germany, relinquishing his leadership to a benign looking Wilhelm, who watches from the deck above. Here was a chance for Tenniel to offer yet another tribute to the demise of older generation leadership, and his sympathetic portrait of Bismark won him great admiration. It had been expected that Bismark would be retired when it was published but *Punch*'s cartoon was something of a *coup*, for it appeared the day he actually left his official residence. According to *The Times* Bismark had been removed by the scheming German Emperor "simply longing with his whole heart to be rid of me

Tenniel's tribute to Bismark, "Dropping the Pilot", *Punch*, 29 March, 1890

in order that he may govern alone – with his own genius – and be able to cover himself with glory". Tenniel's Bismark was a hunched, broken man, dignified yet clearly unwanted, while the almost non-committal expression of Wilhelm highlighted the well-known bitterness between the two men. When the cartoon appeared, Tenniel's great champion, Lord Rosebery, commissioned him to make a copy (the original was destroyed by the wood-engravers), which he sent to

Bismark as an unofficial tribute. This was acknowledged with Bismark's short cryptic thanks: "It is indeed a fine one".[50] Ironically Tenniel's original version was not quite accurate, and when General Ellis pointed out the emperor's crown was wrong, Tenniel apologized to his editor and agreed to alter the block. It was supremely important "that the mistake in the Bismark cartoon should by all possible means be rectified. Nothing is simpler – the block *plugged*. The crown re-drawn & engraved & there you are!"[51]

Tenniel's political cartoons were not always popular on the Continent. For example, *Punch* was banned at various times throughout France and Austria, while in Germany, where the royal family had subscribed to the paper for nearly forty years, the new Emperor Wilhelm took immediate offence at Tenniel's satiric views of his rule and banned the paper from 1892. *Punch* had perceptively seen him as a threat as early as 1889, when Tenniel drew the boy Wilhelm on an English beach with his grandmother Queen Victoria: "Now, Willie, dear, you've plenty of *soldiers* at home; look at these pretty *ships* – I'm sure you'll be pleased with them!" Three years later, after assuming power, he became "Wilful Willy", the headstrong ruler of all Germany, whom Tenniel drew as the German children's character Strumwelpeter ("Shock-headed Peter") screaming among his favourite military "toys". In Russia too, Tenniel suffered from censorship, as Linley Sambourne reported after a visit to Moscow and St Petersburg. There,

> should it happen that any cartoon or cut at all trespass on Russian subjects, and especially his Majesty the Tsar, the page was either torn out or erased in the blackest manner by the Bear's paw. I have seen some of Mr Tenniel's cartoons so maltreated and have myself been frequently honoured in the same way.[52]

Such was the price of Tenniel's international fame and influence. It allowed one admiring critic to conclude his survey of Tenniel's mastery of line:

> In his erect, agile figure, grey moustache and keen face, there is a stronger sensation of a *beau sabreur* than one of the best draughtsmen in Europe. Long may he be with us to brighten our lives with his pleasant fancies and his genial humour.[53]

6 The Final Years
1893–1914

With the passing years Tenniel retained his self-effacing approach to life, despite his considerable public reputation. Aware of his influence, he preferred to keep in the background, or to use it to help those less fortunate. When friends died, he rallied round to offer comfort, just as he had done in earlier less successful times performing for charity benefits. Although he never had children of his own, he loved his young nieces and especially his nephews, whom he visited in the country or brought to London to entertain. He regarded family loyalty as a great virtue, and was flattered when his servants displayed an affection and willingness to help him through his "golden years". It struck him especially hard when he heard of the plight of penniless widows, or orphaned children. Recently he had learned of the death of an old friend who had spent fifty years toiling away in the Post Office without provision for his three young sons. Tenniel was shocked that they had no means of support, and he wrote to Mrs Furniss for advice, "to ascertain – if possible – to what – if any – the 'Post Office Widow's Orphan's Fund' may be available".[1]

He also found the adulation of his fans an embarrassment. Those long fawning letters, innumerable requests for autographs or photographs as well as original drawings, were an annoyance, however flattering their intent. Although he was always courteous and usually replied to each letter, he could be sarcastic or even petulant, a sense of irritation written between the lines. When the amateur poet Thomas Hutchinson composed and sent some embarrassing verses praising Tenniel, along with a request for his "book-plate", Tenniel brushed the letter aside for some time before eventually answering in tones of mock friendliness which left his admirer as confused as Tenniel undoubtedly had been by the letter:

> Dear Sir,
>
> Pray accept my best thanks for the *admirable* little verses you were so good as to send me, as also for the very flattering compliment they conveyed, whilst at the same time – quite unintentionally I am certain – heaping "coals of fire" upon my head!!! In simple truth, the only apology I can offer for my seeming want of courtesy in not replying to your previous letter is, that, in the first place, you asked for a copy of my *"Book-plate"* – a thing I do not possess – and next, that I entirely failed to gather – from your letter – what it was you wished me to do in regard to the two volumes of "Alice's Adventures". If I had known that it was simply a desire to stick my *"autograph"* in the books – quite a new idea to *me*! – of course there would have been no delay in the matter; as it is, I can only hope to be kindly excused in the circumstances – I have now much pleasure in sending you two "signatures", which may perhaps sufficiently serve the purpose required.[2]

Tenniel's legendary wit remained with him throughout his later years. He loved

"Tenniel the humorist" by Harry Furniss

to poke fun at himself, to turn a seemingly innocent situation into a joke. As he approached his now famous weekly *Punch* cartoon, he found time to shoot off a frantic query to amuse his friends: "My dear T, How do sapling oaks grow? What are they like? I'll be shot if I know! Is a shillalagh (sic) a big stick or a thin one? *RSVP* Haste. Ever JT."[3]

It was typical of Tenniel that he did not adopt the "Sir" of his recent knighthood when he signed his letters, since that honour had proved yet another embarrassment to him. When the news of his nomination came in early June 1893, according to Fred Anstey Guthrie

> he was not only surprised, but strongly inclined to refuse it if he possibly could. However it represented to him that, in the interests of *Punch*, he must accept the honour, and it was that consideration alone which decided Tenniel to do so.[4]

His knighthood was announced publicly on 10 June, and Tenniel wrote in astonishment to Spielmann how he was overwhelmed by well wishers: "I am receiving shoals of letters and telegrams, I suppose you know the reason Y." The papers that day were full of details of his accomplishments, the *Illustrated London News* (whose proprietor was knighted that year) published Tenniel's photograph alongside a brief resumé of his career. Incorrectly giving the date of his joining *Punch* as 1845, the paper explained that in *Punch* alone "his cartoons have been a distinguished and famous feature . . .. To Sir John Tenniel the whole world without distinction of party, offers its heartiest congratulations." Tenniel then joined the seventeen most notable new knights mentioned in the papers (distinguished from the worlds of "art, journalism and medicine") who travelled to Osborne on 11 August to receive their knighthoods from the Queen.[5] Tenniel tried to deflate the growing adulation he experienced over his knighthood by joking. Five days after the honour he received a serious request from an admirer for an interview and list of "favourite things" for which he compiled the following witty retorts, part truthfully, part in jest:

> [Favourites]
>
> King : Richard 3rd
> Queen : Queen Eleanor
> Hero : Buffalo Bill
> Poet : The writer of 'Bab' ballads
> Artist : Vermicelli di Napoli
> Author : Johnsonius Dictionarius
> Virtue : That which meets with more than its *own* reward.
> Colour : Crushed strawberry
> Air [musical] : "Knock'd em in the Old Kent Road!"
> Dish : Sheepshead & Trotters
> Flower : Cauliflower
> Costume : Pyjamas
> Name : Jemimer – auu
> Occupation : Building Castles (in Espagne)
> Amusement : Riding my Gee-gee [hobbyhorse] & other "hobbies!"
> Motto : "Better late than never "
> Dislike : Being "Interviewed"!!!
> Locality : My own "den"!
> Ambition : "Gave it up long ago!!!"[6]

It was widely believed in political circles that Tenniel's knighthood had been long overdue. As early as the 1880s Lord Salisbury was said to have intended to make a recommendation, but the suggestion was delayed and ultimately forgotten. Appropriately it was Tenniel's beloved Gladstone, as Prime Minister, who revived the idea, partly to acknowledge the support he felt *Punch* had given him. The public, however, recognized Tenniel's knighthood as a much deserved non-partisan gesture, for he was "the personification of the good-humoured and loftier side of political life". To his *Punch* colleagues his knighthood represented a welcomed blow against the art world's prejudices surrounding the mere black and white illustrator; it was long over-due recognition that "black and white drawing was the glory of England and Cinderella of the RA" according to one enthusiastic observer. His colleague George Du Maurier was delighted, for he had led the campaign to instate the illustrator-as-artist into more exalted fine art circles. "I can suggest ideas – not about me in particular, or anybody else, but about the noble craft in its infancy which we *petits dessinateurs sur bois* are the humble pioneers", he once told his own champion Henry James.

> The mind of a Thackeray – the pencil of a Menzel – & two pages weekly in *Punch* for say forty years! Tadema, Leighton, Burne-Jones, hide your diminished heads – Wattses, take a back seat – Poynters and Albert Moores, put your heads in a bag! You will never near Phideas & Titian & Raphael, & if you did, you wouldn't be popular.[7]

He and his colleagues believed a *Punch* artist was a member of a valuable profession, the supreme social observer who could interpret the world pictorially just as a novelist chose words to do so. Therefore Tenniel's knighthood was a significant step; a black and white illustrator had at last been recognized throughout the Empire. A celebration banquet was staged in his honour by his *Punch* colleagues at his favourite haunt, The Mitre, along the river at Hampton Court. At this, " The last state event in the world of Punch-politico-rejoicings", according to the *Punch* historian, his publisher and friend William Agnew rose to toast the health of Jackides, "the Grand Old Man of *Punch* for whom not one member of the staff but entertains an affection of the warmest and the most cordial character ". Later his artist colleagues joined together at the Arts Club for yet another tribute dinner on 20 November, when an agitated and extremely nervous Du Maurier rose to propose a toast to "dear old John Tenniel".

It was inevitable that as Tenniel reached his mid-seventies, his weekly cartoons should show signs of strain and weakness. In 1895 twice he missed his "Big Cut" and Linley Sambourne willingly took over for him. He preferred to take greater care with his pen-work surfaces. This took valuable time working under pressure of the strict deadlines and proved very wearing. The almanack design for 1894, "Mr Punch in Fairyland–A Midsummer Night's Dream" was one such intricate, elaborately conceived pen design. Based upon a line from his beloved Shakespeare, "Weaving spiders, come not here; Beetles black, approach not near", it was a rare example of Tenniel's ability to parody his predecessor Richard Doyle (now dead for over ten years) and pointed out that he still had the ability to fill a double page with a remarkable selection of diverse figures, if given the time.

On the whole the 1890s were a time for reflection rather than achievement. He politely acknowledged the presentation copy of the second volume of *Sylvie and Bruno* sent to him by Dodgson and illustrated by his beleaguered friend Furniss, but he offered no critical comments on the book he had once been asked to illustrate. He was also kept informed of the continued popularity of the Alice books, even now after nearly thirty years since their first publication. Dodgson, too, continued to bask in the fame that these two small volumes brought him. He agreed to supervise a dramatization of the first book, staged at Worcester College, Oxford with costumes designed after Tenniel's now classic illustrations. Tenniel continued to receive the occasional letter or request for Alice originals from his doting fans, and he took a special interest in the whereabouts of his original drawings long after they had left his studio. He presented signed copies of the books when asked, and even had a special mounting box constructed for one collector, while one of his nephews agreed to rebind a presentation edition for an especially earnest collector. He sent an enthusiastic American collector one of his most successful later Alice drawings of Alice upsetting the jury box, and wrote to reassure him: "I am very happy and proud that the little drawing should be in your possession." New editions of both books continued to appear, and Dodgson sought his invaluable advice on their printing; as in the case of a re-issue of both books in 1897, when Dodgson noted with relief that "Sir John Tenniel thinks them fully equal to the original issue".[8]

Similarly, he looked through those *Punch* drawings now saved from destruction by process-engraving, as well as older pencil sketches for book illustrations, to see which were worth reworking. This was a habit he enjoyed throughout his later years. He would readily take his *Punch* engravings and trace over the figures in pencil for admirers; or he used pastel, chalk or even watercolour to finish or revise past work. It allowed him to "keep his hand in", and exercised those painting skills which otherwise might be neglected. He chose the strongest compositions for pastels, like the poignant reminder of his impending retirement, done the year of his knighthood as a competent if dull pastel, based upon Milton's line from *Il Penseroso*: "And add to these retired leisure / That in trim gardens takes pleasure". He chose a garden setting in his favourite Cromwellian days, and an ageing cavalier ready for a relaxing game of skittles at the "Britannia Tea Gardens, proprietor T. Trim". Such work was generally weak and more a private exercise than preparation for public exhibition. Others were more successful and eventually were exhibited, although they rarely found public favour: they were too far removed from the sharp, even clarity of wood-engraved line which his *Punch* public expected from him. Even the watercolour versions of *Punch* cartoons were weak, usually painted in favourite tones of grey and pink to emulate the engraver's tonal range, and they lacked clarity of interest without their captions or topical political associations. Indeed, his *Punch* cartoons remained the most successful contribution to his later career, and a last collection was again issued as the fourth volume of the series, *Cartoons from Punch by Sir John Tenniel*, which were re-issued designs to cover the period 1882–91.

Eventually Tenniel joined together a number of his more successful *Punch* drawings for his first one-man exhibition at the prestigious Fine Art Society in London in March 1895. It was called simply "A Collection of Drawings for *Punch* Cartoons &c", and all 177 exhibits were for sale ("prices on application"). The catalogue essay was written by his *Punch* colleague E.J. Milliken, who had written so many of the cartoon captions in *Punch*. The collection was largely of those recent drawings saved from destruction by process-engraving, although a few earlier preliminary pencil sketches had been reworked and finished to emphasize the variety of Tenniel's talent. These included "The Red Monkana" of 3 June 1871 and the now famous "Vae Victus" of 11 March 1871. In addition twenty original sketches for Alice were scattered throughout the gallery, as well

Original pen design for process engraving in *Punch*, 1893. 7 x 5¼" (Victoria and Albert Museum)

"Bumble at Home, or The Winter of our Discontent", a watercolour in favourite pink and grey colours, one of several Tenniel painted from published *Punch* cartoons (10 January, 1891). (Huntington Art Gallery)

as his own favourite ink drawing "Prometheus Unbound" (which failed to sell), and "Mr Punch in Fairyland". It was on the whole a diverse and rather confusing exhibition, the catalogue entries lacking any explanation of the context so vital to understand the now ephemeral nature of his political jokes. (A complete list of exhibits is given in Appendix III.) But it was a prestigious event. Over the years the Fine Art Society had initiated a popular series of more established illustrators' exhibitions and most recently had featured work by Kate Greenaway and George Du Maurier's own *Punch* drawings. Tenniel's exhibition had a greater purpose as well: not to earn needed money – as in the case of Greenaway – but to present his original drawings for the first time for public scrutiny. Following a year after his knighthood, it was hoped they would help to explain why he had achieved this singular honour. Milliken's catalogue essay stressed the inimitable restrained, classical qualities of Tenniel's draughtsmanship and his matchless sense of invention, which made him "unique to British caricature":

> That no one else could have done exactly his work is certain; whether he could have done another, or perhaps even greater, work is less certain . . .. As a political cartoonist, his leading quality is loftiness and poetic dignity of conception. Through all his talent gleams a high and magnanimous spirit, the spirit of *noblesse oblige*. He never stoops to the gutter. Its stones and mud are no missiles for him. He strikes, but does not bespatter; he pierces, but does not poison. He is ever a knightly adversary.

Five years later Tenniel was persuaded to repeat the publicity exercise, and he staged a second Fine Art Society exhibition in May 1900. This time he selected just 161 drawings – again from *Punch*, but those mostly published after the first exhibition – as well as a few original drawings from *Ingoldsby Legends* for contrast. Among the more significant *Punch* cartoons was a series of war themes which fitted the current mood of the country, now in the throes of the Boer War.

Although Tenniel was optimistic about the sale of his work, his hopes were disappointed by a public which demanded little of him during this period in his career. They simply did not want to see new aspects of the famous *Punch* illustrator's talent. In the end Tenniel gave way to public opinion and refused to exhibit again. He did not stop working, however, and continued to produce watercolours and draw in pastel for his own amusement throughout the last years of his life. The prejudices he had encountered in the galleries had plagued the last days of his friend George Du Maurier as well. When he recently tried to re-establish himself as a painter, he too met with failure before turning to literature and writing the pair of best-selling novels *Trilby* and *Peter Ibbetson* which surprised his friends and delighted his public. His death in October 1896 brought an end to yet another of Tenniel's most cherished and inspired friendships. It was significant that his funeral was attended by just two *Punch* colleagues – Tenniel and Francis Burnand – representatives from among the survivors of *Punch* in its heyday.

The older generation of artists and writers were fast disappearing and this greatly saddened Tenniel. Recently he had sent his sincerest congratulations to his old friend Millais to acknowledge his election as president of the Royal Academy in March 1896 – what Tenniel called "obviously a foregone conclusion".[9] Less than six months later Millais too was dead from throat cancer; his death was not only a tragic loss to the art world but also to Tenniel's gradually dwindling circle of friends. Those ageing colleagues who managed to survive as artists found they had to diversify to thrive. Harry Furniss was one whose indefatigable energies and talent as a comic draughtsman helped him explore the potential of artistic performances: he devised a series of entertainments and sketched before an audience, his famous "shows" punctuated by jokes and anecdotes which delighted Tenniel when he once attended. Later the enterprising Furniss appeared in his own propaganda films as a bombastic patriot with a rotund, jovial presence who danced about the stage, arms waving over a blackboard and chalk as he delighted yet exhausted his audiences. Tenniel was clearly reluctant to accept such drastic changes in his profession. After attending one of Furniss's shows, he wrote back cautiously to thank his friend "for the opportunity you kindly gave me to see the 'show', which I enjoyed immensely. It is very amusing, very interesting, altogether excellent, & bound to be a big success, anyhow."[10] The "artist as showman" remained an alarming prospect – to him at least.

In most respects Tenniel was too old to change his attitudes and habits. The invitations continued to arrive and were treated with the utmost courtesy, as he wrote to apologise for not realizing he had "double booked" one evening: "Pray forgive my non-appearance at your 'reception' last night. I am indeed sorry but had to struggle – *somehow* – through a big dinner party, and then collapsed *utterly*!! With kindest regards and a thousand apologies – I remain very sincerely yours."[11] He still, despite his considerable reputation, submitted work for exhibition with a timid, courteous covering letter, like the time he sent along "a

Tenniel's last *Punch* cartoon was an appeal for world peace – "Time's Appeal", 1901

list of 19 drawings which I venture to offer for the acceptance of the committee".[12] He refused to accede to the exuberant new generation of art nouveau
decadents, and he doggedly retained his now unfashionably classical line, with
its sense of good-mannered restraint and old-fashioned ideals, which the *Art
Journal* thought a brave attitude to take during the decadent 1890s: "Such a
capacity was once considered as a test of a great artist, and we may hope that
before very long it will be so considered again." Characteristically he had poured
a great deal of effort and time into preparing for his Fine Art Society exhibitions,
fitting in the drawing and arrangements between weekly *Punch* commitments.
He devised a rigid work schedule which did not include unexpected visits from
colleagues, and just before his Fine Art Society exhibition he declined all
invitations or visitors because he was "awfully busy". Similarly he refused to
contribute to the prestigious British section of the Paris International Exhibition
in 1900 because he was too busy preparing his second Fine Art Society
exhibition, which inevitably used up his stock of "best drawings".[13]

It was with deep regret, although almost inevitable, that Tenniel should think
of retiring. He had reached his eightieth birthday in 1901 and had served *Punch*
for almost half a century. In the end he chose the year of Queen Victoria's death
to announce his retirement from *Punch* – an appropriate choice for one so long
associated with Victorian virtue and old world values, now that era was about to
close. His last *Punch* cartoon appeared on 2 January 1901. It was a farewell wish
for Peace which he called "Time's Appeal", where a troubled Father Time and
his famous Angel of Peace attempt to stop the chariots of war. It was a poignant
reminder that Tenniel had seen too many wars and so much suffering. He left
Punch with a final appeal for humane values and common sense in the world:
"This is my last," he explained when it appeared, "but not, I think, my worst."

The announcement of his retirement caused a considerable stir, especially
among publishers anxious to be the first to launch tributes to his long career. His
Punch publisher produced *Cartoons Selected from the Pages of Punch* in March

1901, which was followed by a special Easter Number of the *Art Journal* entirely devoted to his career, with the illustrations all chosen by Tenniel. For the first time his early paintings, book illustrations and *Punch* work were discussed together in an albeit cursory manner, although the emphasis was still on the *Punch* cartoons,

> for though there are doubtless as good fish in the sea as any that have come out of it, and many able designers on the present staff of Mr. Punch, it will be a long time before we can become quite used to his successor, however able he may be . . .. At the same time we may hope that faculties still so clear, and skill still so unimpaired as those of the designer of this cartoon will not remain idle.

Only his closest colleagues were told the real reason for his retirement at this time: Tenniel discovered the sight of his one good eye now began to fail. When William Agnew proposed a toast in his honour at his last *Punch* editorial dinner, he remained seated, half-dazed and puzzled, yet in the end mildly amused by the gesture. "I suppose I must reply. But you haven't drunk my health yet!" he pointed out poignantly. He paused, then rose to make one of the short, painful speeches he so hated, mumbling how he "felt it better to retire before he was obliged", then ended with "Well – we won't prolong the agony; thank you all very much" and sat down. Francis Burnand was quickly invited to fill the unexpected silence, but he flatly refused, because he felt that anything he said of his old friend then would be an anti-climax.[14]

Thus began a round of embarrassing tributes to his long career. Tenniel endured these politely but always found the well-wishers, the speeches, the letters and the lavish banquets a painful reminder of his failures. He suffered a sense of inadequacy at so much attention over what he felt had been so little real work. Although eighty, he was still in remarkably good health, despite his poor eyesight, and had only reluctantly given up riding two years previously. His cartoons in *Punch* had been admired by an older generation of politicians, royalty, playwrights and fellow artists, as well as the most noted new talents of the day. This fact was highlighted by an announcement in *The Times* on 18 April, that a public dinner in his honour was planned, initiated by Lord Rosebery and set for the Whitehall Rooms of the Hotel Metropole on Wednesday, 12 June. Among the "noblemen and gentlemen organizing committee", chaired by the future Prime Minister Arthur Balfour, were the Dukes of Norfolk, Devonshire, Bedford and Argyll, numerous contemporary politicians of all parties, fellow knights, and artists like Sir Edward Poynter, PRA. The world of the theatre was represented by Sir Henry Irving, Herbert Beerbohm Tree, W.S. Gilbert, A.W. Pinero, and George Grossmith; the world of recent literature by George Meredith and Arthur Conan Doyle, as well as his *Punch* colleagues and publishers. In all some two hundred guests arrived on the night to pay tribute to him; the artist contingent alone was an overwhelming display of the giants of his profession: John Sargent RA, Hubert Herkomer, Val Prinsep, Luke Fildes, Frank Dicksee RA, the Hon. John Collier, Sir James Linton – all establishment figures with daunting reputations. Among the literary figures were J.M. Barrie and Bram Stoker, author of *Dracula*. Unfortunately Lord Rosebery was unable to attend, due to "domestic sorrow" according to *The Times*, as were the Dukes of Norfolk, Marlborough, Bedford and Argyll and the Lord Chief Justice and the Speaker of the House, who sent letters of apology; a special apologetic telegram arrived from Sir Henry Irving as well. The evening was a tremendous success, filled with much laughter, long toasts and even longer speeches and much cheering.

Afterwards *The Times* devoted two and a half full columns to its report, printing Arthur Balfour's long speech in full. It seemed an appropriate tribute to the paper's long-standing protégé, and recalled the days when *The Times* had lavished such extravagant praises on Tenniel's *Lalla Rookh*.

Tenniel found the entire evening almost overwhelming. He sat on the rostrum, entirely subdued by the seemingly unending expressions of admiration from such a vast and distinguished group. Arthur Balfour spoke extravagantly of Tenniel's long career, concluding that he "is known in every part of the universe where *Punch* has access", which brought cheers of approval. He also claimed Tenniel was "in some respects one of the most successful illustrators of books that I think we have ever seen". He praised his perseverance and restraint in the face of terrible world events:

Tenniel's retirement photograph inscribed "With much love J.T. 1901"

> the whole tone of public life, irrespective of politics or creed, is the better for such a sweetening influence . . .. Think of the Ministries which he has seen rise up, culminate, and decay; think of the revolutions abroad which he has witnessed . . .. Therefore it is that in my judgement our guest of this evening is destined to be for the historian of the future one of the great sources from which to judge of the trend and character of English thought and life in the latter half of the nineteenth century.

Balfour then offered a toast to "a great artist and a great gentleman" and the toastmaster responded: "My Lord Duke, Your Excellency, My Lords and Gentlemen – pray silence for Our Guest". Tenniel then rose to make his carefully prepared reply; he did not at first appear nervous, although he had a horror of speeches and was usually daunted by the prospect of public speaking to large groups – a curious attitude if one recalls his thespian performances. In the next few minutes he experienced one of the most traumatic embarrassments of his life, which would leave him "appalled and miserable and haunted by the incident" until his death, shattered even by the memory of what he remembered of "that horrible dinner ". He started his speech well enough, adopting the mock petulant tone familiar to his friends:

> If any answer were needed or example, I should say, to prove the truth of the old adage that some have greatness thrust upon them, none I think could be more convincing than that which my presence at this particular time affords, and which the tremendous reception which has just been accorded me so unmistakably confirms. [Cheers] What I have done that this amazing honour should be thrust upon me, and why I should be here at all, altogether passes my feeble imagination to discover. Unhappily I have no gift for words; I have never addressed, or attempted to address . . .

At this point, as *The Times* later reported, "Sir John paused for a few moments, exhibiting signs of strong emotion, and this little interval of silence was received with every mark of sympathy by his audience, who renewed the cheers with which they had greeted his rising". Valiantly he tried to regain his composure and proceed with his speech, and even briefly resumed: "Anything that I might attempt to say would not in the least degree express my heartfelt thanks". After further loud cheers, he faltered yet again. His friend Fred Anstey Guthrie recalled what happened next:

> There was a long silence, followed by encouraging applause, after which he tried again, and for the first time showed nervousness. Once more he came to a stop; there was a longer and more painful silence, and then he said in an audible aside to the chairman, "It's no use, I can't go on"; and sat down.

The stunned audience eventually gave three cheers then broke into "For he's a jolly good fellow", but even this encouragement failed to hide Tenniel's acute embarrassment and shame. Afterwards his friends flocked round to congratulate him for such an uncharacteristic yet poignant display of strong emotion. It seemed so well-timed, like a performance by the actor they knew him to be; but he only shrugged. Augustus Birrell tactfully insisted his speech "made one in love with silence". Anstey Guthrie was soon made aware of the deeper damage that had been done:

> Nevertheless I am afraid that to the end of his life Tenniel was not free from disturbing memories of that evening, even though it did him nothing but honour. But to impose upon an exceptionally modest man, who had probably never made a speech in public before in his life, the duty of replying to the most well-deserved compliment was, I cannot help thinking, mistaken kindness.

To Tenniel he had publicly displayed a most ungentlemanly weakness. His sister and Mrs Lucy found this highly amusing from their seats in the gallery. They chided him afterward for so skilfully avoiding his duty, and although said in jest, Tenniel was greatly hurt by their comments, his sense of pride damaged by even the slightest suggestion of cowardice. "Oh, no," he tried to assure them, "I had a beautiful speech, but I couldn't say another word of it."[15]

The evening ended with an American tribute from their Ambassador, Mr Choate. It was a clever speech which incorporated familiar references to the characters in Alice drawn by Tenniel, to point out universal truths about human nature, especially among English politicians: "The gentlemen of England love to sit upon benches great and small. What lessons did they not learn from the Caterpillar?" He thought Tenniel's politicians were not only respectable, dignified statesmen but humorous objects of public affection thus skilfully pointing out "that there was but one step from the sublime to the ridiculous". The speech was hailed as "the American tribute" and was much appreciated across the Atlantic, where *The Times'* special correspondent noted the following day:

> To him is due in great measure the great American popularity of *Punch*. If Americans sometimes thought Sir John Tenniel drew Brother Jonathan [Uncle Sam] in harsh lines, they never disputed his honest intention, still less his wonderful gifts of imaginative insight into great affairs. The Press extols him today *a propos* of yesterday's dinner in London, the *New York Evening Post* discusses his remarkable career, his kindliness, *distinction*, and effectiveness.[16]

*   *   *   *   *

Retirement proved a challenge to Tenniel's resourcefulness after so many years employed on *Punch*. Typically he continued to keep busy painting and re-drawing his old work. He proposed a scheme to trace and colour his best *Punch* cartoons and work began in earnest until his poor eyesight prevented its completion. He experimented with oil painting and retouched his early "St Cecilia" fresco study; he practised watercolour washes by colouring his collection of old theatrical photographs. The few new paintings he worked on were of various subjects with no particular scheme in mind. He painted "Griselda being parted from her child", watercolour versions of St George and the Dragon and even returned briefly to his ill-fated Shakespeare illustrations. All this work was sadly hindered by his poor eyesight, the once tight, meticulously coloured stipple

Tenniel presented this study from "The Sinking Ship", *Punch*, 19 September, 1900, to his friends the Lucys. It depicts a Boer farmer escaping from the sinking Transvaal. 6¹/₂ x 7¹/₈". (Victoria and Albert Museum)

washes giving way to more easily accomplished sweeps of uneven, flat colour. Nevertheless he was proud of his accomplishments, and when old friends and colleagues called occasionally to enquire about his health, he eagerly took them to inspect his favourite study where he now worked on these new paintings, surrounded by the memorabilia of his past. Once he was asked whether he was preparing for another exhibition, but he replied wistfully, "No, I shan't send them to be exhibited anywhere. What's the use? They don't care for my work except in connection with *Punch*. Besides, I'm tired – I can't take the trouble." He also busied himself with tracings and placed buff-coloured paper over his engraved designs to reproduce the barest outline of his more successful *Punch* compositions. These he presented to those friends he knew would appreciate them. Recently he had given his skilful spontaneous early study for " The Sinking Ship" to the Lucys, knowing they would like to have one of his last studies for a *Punch* cartoon.[17]

He now lived in relative isolation and relished visits from his few devoted friends. Mrs Fred Burnand, wife of *Punch's* editor, had asked for Tenniel-drawn heraldry and eventually she received news of the project, written in a blotched and shaky handwriting:

Tenniel occupied many retirement hours making tracings of published cartoons

No need to tell you that I have had great pleasure in trying to help you with the 'Beasties' and I am sending you *3* in the hope that *perhaps one* of them may be of some use to you – Unluckily, I am no good at Heraldry and therefore must pray & beseech you not to "*give me away*" by telling any one that the ridiculous things were *done* by *me*. Trusting I haven't kept you waiting very long – failing sight – a shaky hand – and visitors in the house being my only apology for *such* . . . [18]

He earnestly followed his successors' careers and took a lively interest in *Punch* and its new draughtsmen. Phil May had replaced Charles Keene as the paper's social cartoonist and Tenniel had just had time enough to work alongside that raffish bohemian to admire his comic skills, which caused an immediate hit with *Punch* readers. May's sudden death of cirrhosis of the liver and tuberculosis in

1903, aged just thirty-nine, was especially upsetting news to Tenniel, who sent a contribution to the artist's widow's fund, saddened as he was by such a tragic death.[19] At home he was a cordial host to visitors but now declined invitations to dine out. He found London's streets increasingly dangerous, and he disliked the new motor-cars which he begged his friends to avoid. He still read the papers and followed current affairs so that he could understand and criticize his successor Linley Sambourne's weekly "Big Cut", and he discussed the latest news with his visitors. When a guest arrived he would greet them on the first-floor landing, then usher them into his coveted study to talk over "old times". Whatever the weather or his state of health he always insisted upon seeing his guests out: "Of *course* I shall come!" he told them in mock petulance, "I'm not so feeble as all that!" Then he would stand at the doorway, thank them for coming and assure them poignantly that he was always glad to see them: "You *know* that's true, don't you?" His most frequent and devoted visitor was Fred Anstey Guthrie, who left a vivid record of his visits during the last years of Tenniel's life. Their friendship remained a cherished memory to them both: "And one left his gate with a deeper reverence and affection for him than ever, and a stronger sense of the dignity and beauty that attend the old age of a great and good man."[20]

Fred Anstey Guthrie was a devoted visitor to Tenniel

Tenniel's poor eyesight was partially helped first by his wearing a green eyeshade then strong spectacles to help him work. The King's oculist, Dr George Critchett, who was among his most prestigious friends, tried to help but it soon became clear there was little that could be done for his one good eye.[21] Characteristically, Tenniel refused to give in to this most serious weakness. His eighty-seventh birthday was marked by the press reports of "A Venerable Artist" and a brief reminder of his past prominence.[22] His greatest ambition was still to revisit the *Punch* offices and shake hands with old friends as he explained it, to experience "the happiness of meeting the dear clever boys again, and, on the earliest Wednesday I can manage, shake hands". He was prevented from this by a four-week-long bout of influenza which left him weak and dazed. Nevertheless *Punch* would remain his primary preoccupation until the end; the reverential hold Mr Punch had over him never truly eased up. Letters from eager collectors, historians and admirers enquiring about aspects of his career continued to arrive, and he took especial care over those who asked about the origins of his *Punch* cartoons. Again he was courteous in his replies, despite the obvious hardship of writing letters now. He studied each weekly issue of *Punch* to try to understand his artist successors' work, and once sent a warm letter to the *Punch* parodist E.J. Reed, congratulating him on his merciless parody of the recent spate of new Alice illustrators which had caused such an unpleasant stir among purists and the press.

Tenniel reached his ninetieth birthday on 28 February 1909. It was an event marked by a new domestic upset, one from which he would never recover. His devoted sister Victoria, still his housekeeper and nurse, suffered a fall which injured her hip and made the task of climbing stairs in his large house impossible. No longer could she watch over and nurse him, and yet his failing eyesight demanded constant attention. It was decided, reluctantly, to sell his house in Maida Vale and move to a more suitable ground-floor flat. This decision was a considerable emotional wrench for Tenniel, for he loved the large house he and his wife had shared so happily together and which over the years he had filled with his collection of medieval furniture, weaponry, suits of armour and favourite sculpture. Only "with some indignation" did he agree to the move, and eventually chose a prestigious new block of purpose-built flats recently opened in Fitzgeorge Avenue, West London, in the area today known as West Kensington. Although a pleasant enough new development of six five-storey mock Queen Anne blocks in red brick and stone, with high windows and leafy courtyard entrances, the surrounding area was less auspicious, bordering on the busy commercial Cromwell and Hammersmith Roads and the railway to Earl's Court. Today the blocks remain a tiny oasis among even larger towers, noisy traffic and rows of decaying terraced artisan houses. It was certainly not the spacious genteel, suburban atmosphere in which Tenniel had lived most of his adult life: "When I first came in I could just make out a corridor painted white with a lot of doors on each side, and I said, 'Good God! It's like a prison!' " Above all he objected to the noise, especially the sound of coal being taken up the service lift next to his bedroom. Flat-living was not to his taste, especially since it proved claustrophobic, in contrast with the large rooms he had enjoyed in his old house: when this was sold it proved large enough to be converted into an art school for women. "I suppose they would call it 'The Tenniel Studio'", Guthrie joked. Tenniel looked up, shocked, "They'd better not!"[23] His one real consolation now was that his beloved sister seemed to thrive in the new flat and, although still unable to walk, she cheerfully manoeuvred through the streets in a bath chair.

His original indignation at the move brought on a severe attack of illness which some believed might prove fatal. However he eventually recovered well enough to enjoy the glimmer of limelight that his ninetieth birthday brought him. His old friend Henry Silver wrote to *The Times* to announce the momentous event in an attempt to revive interest in Tenniel's work and pointed out how his *Punch* cartoons continued to be relevant:

> Were some of Sir John's drawings seen in certain of our Board schools, they might help to save our small boys from becoming "Little Englanders". And if the cartoons which did good service in the [Indian] Mutiny were seen now in Calcutta and Bombay, they might check the scheming baboos and their allies here in St. Stephen's.[24]

In a similar manner, the *Daily News* praised the dignity of his work. It was the result of an "erect, and quiet personality, in the avoidance of all publicity and display in his simple, secluded life, in the refusal to grasp at money . . . " This same year Tenniel's first published *Punch* design attracted considerable attention when it was exhibited at the "Mr Punch's Pageant" exhibition at the Leicester Galleries in London.

Despite her handicap, Tenniel's sister continued to assist her brother in answering difficult or insistent correspondence. She watched over his health and protected him from unnecessary upsets and strain, and his favourite nephews offered encouragement. One now worked as a book-binder and another, Major Bernard Green, helped with the persistent queries of one of Tenniel's greatest American admirers, Harcourt Amory, and helped his uncle to authenticate the Alice drawings and tracings Amory had collected (which are now at Harvard University). Tenniel could still use a pen, though, if he were so inclined. The news of his successor Linley Sambourne's tragic death in 1910, after a long and valiant battle with illness, inspired Tenniel's poignant tribute to his old friend: a brief pen portrait of Sambourne as a fearless crusader, dressed in chain mail, his sword at the ready.[25] Then, in the middle of 1911, Tenniel's beloved sister and companion died, leaving him crushed by this supreme loss. Fortunately he could rely upon his faithful and devoted servant Miss Inez Juster – aptly named to remind him of his "Fair Inez" of previous years – and she now proved a godsend. She read to him all day, watched over his sleepless nights and helped him through the giddy spells which now seemed to increase. It was characteristic of Tenniel that he left his new "Fair Inez" £250 in his will, which he stipulated she should receive only if she was "still in his service". The giddy spells made all thoughts of going out impossible now, and Tenniel resigned himself to his new life. His blindness made him a prisoner to his thoughts, comforted only by pleasant memories of friends in the past. The flat continued to annoy him; it was "a mere makeshift of a house. Everything cramped into the smallest space", he complained. When his eyesight weakened further, he entertained himself by watching the blurred shadows on his walls, which sent his still vivid imagination soaring:

> Sometimes it's a troop of cavalry riding by and I see every man and horse distinctly and even hear the clinking of their bits, or else it's a row of very serious persons dressed like judges and holding some important trial; it amuses me as a rule, but it gets to worry me at times – they're mere fancies, of course.[26]

His ninety-third year was plagued by another severe bout of influenza, from which he did not expect to recover. By now his beard had grown full, a silvery complement to his snowy white hair which still marked him out as a distinguished elderly gentleman. The influenza kept him bed-ridden, but he refused to turn visitors away: "It's a great compliment when my old friends come to see me", he explained to his most frequent visitor, Fred Anstey Guthrie, who left his bedside with Tenniel whispering the poignant verse: "If we do meet again, why, we shall smile; If not, why, this parting was well made." Yet he recovered from this new bout of 'flu and, although now totally blind, he was well enough to sit among his favourite pictures and books, to feel his treasured old oak chest stuffed full of drawings and the fine Jacobean cabinet and suit of armour he defiantly stood in the cramped hallway. When Anstey Guthrie arrived in August the summer days reminded him of rowing and those long-awaited annual outings on the river with his close friends. "All that is over for me", he mumbled wistfully, "I forget names and everything now." His mind was clear enough though, to teach Guthrie the finer points of social etiquette as he understood them. When Guthrie explained about an unwelcomed invitation he had received, he was surprised at Tenniel's receptive response: "I gave him my reasons for not attending a certain function, on which he said, 'Well, of course, if you feel like that – but the fact is, you don't *want* to go!' which was in truth the case."[27]

Guthrie called again, early in February 1914, and was told Tenniel had rapidly failed since New Year's Eve. His mind wandered now, yet he mumbled clear enough for Miss Juster to understand how he criticized imaginary *Punch* drawings and pointed out the serious faults in the lions and tigers which were once his exclusive domain. Such a store of resilience surprised his nurse who, when she asked Tenniel to put out his tongue, received the petulant reply: "Yes – and look like a fool!" When the doctor examined him, he reported reassuringly that for a man of ninety-three his heart and lungs were perfectly sound.

Nevertheless Tenniel was dying from old age, and might have had a greater chance of survival if his blindness had not destroyed his will. He had lived all his life dependent upon his eyesight and without sight it was too easy to give in to his weakness. When Guthrie called on 1 February, he found Tenniel asleep: "I was allowed to go into his bedroom for what I then thought would be my last sight of him, and he lay looking very much as Colonel Newcome must have looked on *his* death-bed." Yet a fortnight later he returned to find Tenniel recovered enough to recognize his favourite visitor.

> His ramblings, I was told, still took the same form. " That lion's all wrong!" he would say, "And *that* isn't Britannia!" When someone asked if he was looking at a drawing of Bernard Partridge's he understood in some way and replied indignantly, "No–no–he's a *draughtsman* – he wouldn't draw like that!'"[28]

Such were the touching last remarks of the artist who had spent his entire working life devoted to Mr Punch. By some inspired act of fate, Sir John Tenniel died on his favourite night of the week – on Wednesday 25 February 1914, the day his beloved *Punch* colleagues were gathered for their weekly editorial dinner; in fact "just at the hour when we were talking over the subject of the week at this Round Table that he loved so well", one later recalled. He was a few days short of his ninety-fourth birthday.[29]

Although Tenniel left the relatively substantial sum of £10,500 in his will to friends and relatives, his final wish was for a funeral "as simple and inexpensive as possible". Following the rather unusual funeral practice for the time, set down by his colleague Du Maurier, he was cremated at the Golder's Green Crematorium in North London, attended by his favourite nephews, a few close friends and, of course, his *Punch* colleagues. Sadly, his longest surviving *Punch* colleague, Francis Burnand, was too ill to attend, but he sent a wreath to commemorate their friendship. Two days later Tenniel's ashes were buried in Kensal Green Cemetery, that favourite burial ground of prominent Victorians, where his fellow *Punch* men, John Leech, Thackeray and Richard Doyle now lay.

One of the first of several substantial obituaries appeared in *The Times* (27 February 1914). It claimed Tenniel had "revolutionized the art of political caricature in this country", and went on at considerable length to quote tributes from surviving friends and give extracts from the speeches at his retirement banquet. Here too it was announced that *Punch* planned a special supplement devoted entirely to Tenniel the following week; "a memorial to Tenniel's great art and his sweet and simple nature" to be illustrated with nearly fifty of Tenniel's "masterpieces", selected "with the view to giving a fair representation of his work during his fifty years of active service". Among the numerous other tributes, *The Connoisseur* perceptively selected his "Dropping the Pilot" cartoon as their memorial. It was a significant gesture in the face of the impending First World War, which they felt, with Tenniel's death, marked the end of an era: "The Victorian era can boast of few living men of fame in this age of unrest and modernism, and the world of art has just recorded another death in the famous *Punch* cartoonist . . . "[30]

Most important of all, Tenniel left a legacy of some thirty-eight illustrated books, numerous magazine illustrations, almost 2,000 *Punch* cartoons, and two small but undoubtedly unique classics – the Alice books. His *Punch* colleagues offered their own poignant verse tribute, written by Owen Seaman:

In Memoriam – John Tenniel

Now he whose gallant heart so lightly bore
So long the burden of the years' increase
Passes at length toward the silent shore,
From peace to deeper peace.

And we, his honoured comrades, by whose side
His haunting spirit keeps its ancient spell,
We bring our tribute, woven of love and pride,
And say a last farewell.

Yet not farewell; because eternal youth
Still crowns the craftsmanship whose hand and eye
Saw and interpreted the soul of Truth,
Letting the rest go by.

Thus for his pictured pageant, gay or grave,
He seized and fixed the moving hour's event,
Maker of history by the life he gave.
To fact with fancy blent.

So lives the Artist in the work he wrought;
Yet Nature dowered the Man with gifts more dear –
A chivalrous true knight in deed and thought,
Without reproach or fear.[31]

Epilogue: Sir John Tenniel and the Critics

Tenniel was fortunate in receiving favourable critical attention at an early stage in his career; it was a valuable asset which helped spur him on to greater artistic achievements. As early as 1848 Nagler's *Künstler Lexikon* included him as a young (then twenty-eight) painter "of fortunate talent" – the judgement largely the result of his Westminster Hall fresco designs. Throughout the 1850s, when he found himself torn between a career as a painter or as a black and white illustrator on *Punch*, whenever his various minor book and magazine commissions were published, his name featured prominently upon the title-page, often alongside such impressive collaborators as Millais or Holman Hunt.

By the 1860s – that golden period of wood-engraved book illustration – Tenniel ironically was often categorized with the movement's precursors; the older generation artists like Cruikshank, Phiz or Leech, who relied upon a sketchy, uncertain style rather than the dense, well-drawn, shaded details so characteristic of the giants of the so-called Sixties School – Houghton, Pinwell, Millais or Walker. Tenniel was considered a minor illustrator, his classical, outline style and sparse use of shading forced him into the unfashionable historical or gift-book illustrator category. Worse still he was linked with those minor illustrators of weak fillers in over-produced gift-books, draughtsmen of grey, inconsequential engravings like Birket Foster, Samuel Read, or even John Gilbert. Such was the case when he appeared in Bohn's appendix to the pioneering Chatto and Jackson *Treatise on Wood Engraving* in 1861. Here Tenniel was listed among "Artists and Engravers of the Present Day", yet as a mere "successful illustrator of historical subjects, and ballad poetry"; the point pressed home by reproducing his illustrations from *Lalla Rookh* and Barry Cornwall's *Dramatic Scenes*. And yet only with his *Lalla Rookh* illustrations did he receive the critical attention suited to a major illustrator.

By the 1870s, when his reputation was enhanced by the two Alice books, Tenniel was at last taken seriously by critics. John Ruskin, that supreme art critic of the period, declared Tenniel a major force in the world of wood-engraved illustration and broke his Oxford lecture on engraving techniques to declare "had Tenniel been rightly trained, there might have been the making of a Holbein, or nearly a Holbein, in him".[1] The point was further enhanced when a Tenniel entry appeared in the important new reference book, Clement and Hutton's *Artists of the Nineteenth Century*, 1879.

John Ruskin's praise of Tenniel helped to a great extent to elevate and establish him as a serious illustrator. By the 1880s, as Slade Professor of Fine Art at Oxford, Ruskin included Tenniel in his series of eclectic lectures, "The Art of

England", and devoted his "Artists of the Fireside" lecture to the influence of *Punch* artists John Leech and John Tenniel. He claimed these two artists alone were "the real founders of *Punch*, both in force of art and range of thought". It was typical of Ruskin's approach that he should castigate his audiences for overlooking such accessible talent, and he implored them to reconsider the seemingly ephemeral nature of the weekly comic cartoonist. Tenniel clearly had the ability to create more significant works; Ruskin unashamedly compared him with his beloved Italians, then went on to claim:

> On the contrary, Tenniel has much of the largeness and symbolic mystery of classical art: in the shadowy masses and sweeping lines of his great compositions, there are tendencies which might have won his adoption into the school of Tintoret, and his scorn of whatever seems to him dishonest or contemptable in religion, would have translated itself into awe in the presence of its vital power.

But there was much wasted energy and misplaced direction in Tenniel's work, according to Ruskin. At one point he calculated in a certain Tenniel *Punch* cartoon of his mid-career (published in 1863), that there were a staggering 1,050 "intersections" (lines to be chipped out by his engraver) in a space of just two inches of shadow. He called this "wanton and gratuitous":

> For indeed, in many a past year, it has every now and then been a subject of recurring thought to me, what such a genius as that of Tenniel would have done for us, had we asked the best of it, and had the feeling of the nation respecting the arts, as a record of its honour, been like that of the Italians in their proud days.[2]

It was only in the 1890s, the decade of Tenniel's knighthood, that his critics began seriously to assess the importance of his work as a draughtsman and illustrator, as well as a political cartoonist. Many marvelled at his longevity on *Punch*. A chapter was devoted to him in the aptly named anthology *Toilers in Art*, 1891, where he joined the most famous and neglected artists and engravers of the past. In time his true critics had a chance to assess his influence upon newer generations of artist illustrators, which led to more cautious, carefully considered judgements. The first true critical study of Tenniel as a political cartoonist appeared in Graham Everitt's pioneering *English Caricaturists and Graphic Humourists of the Nineteenth Century*, which reached its second edition in 1893. Everitt included Tenniel in his chapter on Leech and Doyle, and perceptively compared his predecessors' work with his own. The result was that Leech came out best as "a delineator of English habits, manners, eccentricities, and peculiarities . . . as a political satirist Tenniel was the best of the two". He traced Tenniel's early "Big Cuts" up to the 1860s, and concluded,

> In all these and a host of other admirable satires, the superior art training of Mr Tenniel is seconded by his strong dramatic power, and above all by his unquestionable genius . . . His failings when they do occur, are perhaps more noticeable on account of his style and the mode in which he drapes his figures.

By this time his fellow illustrators recognized his achievements as well. Walter Crane had become a distinguished illustrator–designer by the 1890s and he included a brief mention of Tenniel in his influential survey, *Of the Decorative Illustration of Books Old and New*, 1896. It was a minor compliment, however, for he lumped Tenniel together with the early draughtsmen like Birket Foster and John Gilbert; artists of "that form of luxury known as the modern gift-book, which, in the course of the twenty years following 1850, often took the shape of selections from or editions of the poets plentifully sprinkled with little pictorial

BEFORE THE TOURNAMENT.

A typical Tenniel-styled *Punch* cartoon, based on his favourite chivalric theme, *Punch*, November, 1868

vignettes engraved on wood". On the other hand, the brilliant pen draughtsman and critic Joseph Pennell recommended Tenniel's draughtsmanship to his student readers; he wrote in *Pen Drawing and Pen Draughtsmanship in England*, 1889:

> The attempt at so-called freedom, which on the part of the student is nothing but carelessness, is often sure to be his ruin . . .. Far better would it be for the student to follow the painstaking, careful lines of Tenniel in such work as *Alice in Wonderland*, for though the drawings may have been made in line with a hard lead pencil, and the student will probably not keep for long to Tenniel's methods, he will at least learn from them that pen drawing is not the easy slip-shod art he is pleased to think it.

Inevitably it was as the political cartoonist of *Punch*'s "Big Cut" that Tenniel achieved his greatest critical reputation. When Pennell included an Alice-styled illustration from his work for Mrs Gatty's *Parables from Nature* in his survey of *Modern Illustration*, 1895, he noted:

> Sir John Tenniel is the legitimate successor of the old political cartoonist, but, luckily for him, his reputation rests not upon his portrayal of the events of the moment, but upon his marvelous "Alice in Wonderland" and his classical illustrations to the "Legendary Ballads". Political caricature rarely, however, has an exponent like Tenniel . . .

That same year Tenniel's friend, the art critic M.H. Spielmann, completed his monumental *History of Punch*, in which he reproduced Tenniel's ink self-portrait, several original pencil sketches for *Punch* cartoons, and the rare interview on his working methods. They featured in a book which was more hagiography than history. He concluded, somewhat astonishingly, that Tenniel's contribution to *Punch* alone made him "the greatest cartoonist the world has produced". It was left to fellow critic and journalist Gleeson White to temper such enthusiasm with more carefully considered opinion. Writing in his influential survey, *English Illustration, The Sixties,* 1897, White pointed out that Tenniel may be considered a sixties figure, both chronologically and because "he represents the survival of an academic type in sharply accentuated distinction to the Pre-Raphaelism of one group or to the romantic naturalism of a still larger section". In his role as art editor and book reviewer of the *Studio,* White had a considerable knowledge of publishing and book illustration, which undoubtedly coloured his conclusion on Tenniel's career:

> Sir John Tenniel, however, more than any other of the *Punch* staff, seems never thoroughly at home outside its pages. The very idea of a Tenniel drawing has become a synonym for a political cartoon; so that now you cannot avoid feeling that all his illustrations to poetry, fiction, and fairy-tale must have some satirical motive undergoing their apparent purpose.[3]

When Tenniel announced his retirement, the *Art Journal* published Cosmo Monkhouse's lightweight survey of Tenniel's career, which was long on illustrations and short on critical comment. Yet Tenniel had selected the illustrations himself as those he considered most successful throughout his career. As such the article has some merit, and it remained the first substantial monograph published for almost half a century. Similarly the *Punch Supplement* of 1914 is the most substantial survey of the *Punch* aspect of his career and reproduces his most famous *Punch* cartoons, as well as invaluable biographical detail and comments by his friends and *Punch* colleagues. The only further monograph, which used illustration material now in national collections, was Frances Sarzano's study *Sir John Tenniel,* in the Art and Technics series of "English Masters of Black and White" published in 1948.

*   *   *   *   *

The argument whether Tenniel was in fact the most successful and influential political cartoonist of his day continued into the twentieth century. James Thorpe in *English Illustration: The Nineties,* 1935, claimed Tenniel's successor Linley Sambourne was far superior during the 1890s. He had taken over from Tenniel at an appropriate time since Tenniel's work was " by this time weak in drawing with an unpleasant angularity and lacked the strength and invention of Sambourne's work". More significantly, Percy Muir in *Victorian Illustrated Books,* 1971, states that Tenniel's cartoons

> were frequently very funny, usually very well drawn, and nearly always in the best of good taste – this final ingredient being inimical if not fatal to greatness . . .. But Tenniel was a fine old English gentleman, lacking in the depth of scorn and the fire of indignation essential to the really great cartoonist.

Another basis of argument was whether Tenniel was a true Sixties School artist. Gleeson White was the first to claim Tenniel was a member of that select group and linked him in the public's mind with Millais, Walker, Pinwell and Houghton as superior draughtsmen on wood. Yet Forrest Reid disagreed, devoting four pages to Tenniel in his *Illustrators of the Eighteen Sixties,* 1928; he placed him "third on our list of precursors", despite the fact that chronologically his *Lalla Rookh* and first Alice book fall within the period. Reid argued that Tenniel "never exercised the slightest influence on his contemporaries"; his style was too individual, and once formed, he never deviated from it. One may add that though admirably adopted to his work as *Punch* cartoonist, for serious illustration, and above all for the illustration of the tales of modern life [in *Once a Week*, *Good Words*] it was an unsympathetic and unsuitable style.

As a book illustrator, only Tenniel's *Alice* and *Ingoldsby Legends* came near enough to be of influence, apart from which

> Tenniel never got a text that suited him . . .. He was essentially a humorous draughtsman: that is to say, taken by themselves, without any printed joke attached to them, his drawings are funny enough to make us laugh. Also he could draw animals with great skill and understanding.[4]

The growing number of book collectors associated Tenniel with his fellow Sixties School artists of that heyday of black and white illustration. By the turn of the century Harold Hartley had amassed a considerable collection of Tenniel and other Sixties School drawings, which he lent to the "Modern Illustration" exhibition at the Victoria and Albert Museum in 1901, and later to Forrest Reid for use in his book. Hartley was convinced of Tenniel's prominence in the movement, and by the 1920s he toured his collection throughout the country, at the Tate, Royal Academy, Whitechapel, Manchester and Glasgow galleries, where visitors were convinced that Tenniel was indeed a major artist of the period. If this Sixties School label applies to him, it is surely because of his associations with the period's major wood-engravers, the Dalziel brothers. When they published their history of the firm, *The Dalziel Brothers – a Record of Fifty Years*, 1901, they devoted several pages to Tenniel's illustrations and their relationship with him, proudly concluding "outside his *Punch* work, we believe nearly all Tenniel's work for wood engraving was executed by us". Most recently, the printing historian Geoffrey Wakeman concluded the Sixties School distinction was more confused than valuable:

> It is difficult to define exactly what is meant by a "Sixties" book but it seems to be one that is imaginative, in verse or prose, with illustrations by a Victorian artist reproduced by competent often unexciting wood engraving. The great exceptions are Tenniel's illustrations to the Alice books, where the text and illustrations harmonize remarkably well for their period. It is perhaps significant that these are the only noteworthy illustrations Tenniel ever made.[5]

Opinions also differed as to which of Tenniel's thirty-eight illustrated books was his finest. The earliest book, the *Aesop Fables*, which helped secure his post on *Punch*, ironically received a mixed critical reception in later years. Gleeson White linked the book with his illustrated *Undine* as two typical examples of uninspired grey-engraved 1840s gift-books, which "deserve bare attention". Forrest Reid later agreed. The Aesop alone was "much better, though still obviously belonging to the pre-sixty period". Only Percy Muir objected to this rather prejudiced view, when he claimed "we may temper with mercy Forrest Reid's rather harsh, if on the whole just estimate of it" and called the book a mixed production with some good, while "some of the illustrations are quite appallingly feeble and even inaccurate". Only the later revised edition contained a few "outstandingly good" cuts, namely "The Herdsman and the Bull" (No.88), "The Charger and the Ass" (No.183) and "Hercules and the Waggoner" (No.67).[6]

Lalla Rookh was even more difficult to assess. The Dalziels agreed whole-heartedly with the extravagant praises in *The Times*, that it was Tenniel's crowning achievement: "If Tenniel had never done any other work than 'Lalla

"Smuggler's Leap" from *The Ingoldsby Legends*, 1864

Rookh' that alone would have been sufficient to immortalise him" – a comment
no doubt coloured by working with Tenniel on what they termed "fine examples
of his varied powers of design and delicate manipulation – such as gave us great
pleasure in the rendering".[7] Gleeson White was more cautious:

> If to-day you hardly feel inclined to indorse the verdict of *The Times* critic, who
> declared it to be "the greatest illustrative achievement of any single hand", it shows
> not few of those qualities which have won well-merited fame for our oldest
> cartoonist, even if it shows also the limitations which just alienate one's complete

"The Alchemist's Workroom" from *The Ingoldsby Legends*, 1864

sympathy. Yet those who saw an exhibition of Sir John Tenniel's drawings at the Fine Art Society galleries will be less ready to blame the published designs for a certain hardness of style, due in part (one fancies) to their engraver.

Nevertheless by the turn of the century, *Lalla Rookh* had been sufficiently neglected to provoke the *Art Journal*'s lament that it was a mere "tomb for the burial of beautiful works of art". Even Forrest Reid conceded its merits were "several notable designs" (see pp.46, 149), although the *Gordian Knot* illustrations were far superior simply because "Lalla Rookh was hardly the kind of poem likely to inspire Tenniel's best work, and did not in fact do so".[8] Similarly David Bland in *A History of Book Illustration*, 1958, discussed why the book

> showed what depths of sentimentality he could descend to when his text gave him no scope for humour . . .. There is something about his style and he was happiest in farce, as no one can doubt who examines his *Punch* drawings. It was this that fitted him so admirably as an illustrator for [Lewis] Carroll . . .[9]

The one book on which critics were unanimous was *Alice in Wonderland*. As Percy Muir perhaps unfairly notes, "it is almost a case of Alice first and the rest nowhere". Apart from the Dalziels' *Arabian Nights* illustrations, he concluded there is little else that would have been remarked as book illustration were it not for the two Alice books, than which few books in our period have been better illustrated . . .. There can be no disagreement with Forrest Reid's view of Tenniel as virtually a one-book man, considering the two Alice volumes as a unit.[10]

This was a view shared by Tenniel's contemporaries as well. Gleeson White first declared the Alice "an epoch-making book . . . [which] needs only bare mention for who does not know it intimately?" Then in his *Studio* Special Number, "Children's Books and their Illustrators", which surveyed the history of the genre to 1897, he concluded that while Tenniel has illustrated several children's books (sic), only with the two Alice books do

we touch *the* two most notable children's books of the century. To say less would be inadequate and to say more needless for one knows the incomparable inventions "Lewis Carroll" imagined and Sir John Tenniel depicted. They are veritable classics, of which, as it is too late to praise them, no more need be said.[11]

By the turn of the century, the *Art Journal* offered a little more judgement, that Tenniel's Alice was "a thing of beauty and joy for ever". Only Forrest Reid looked more critically at the Alice books to conclude where Tenniel's true strengths lay:

There is more charm in the picture of the black kitten at the end of *Through the Looking Glass* than in any of the pictures of Alice herself, pleasant little girl as she is. One has an idea that the black kitten actually sat for its portrait, but the portraits of Alice seem now and then slightly out of drawing, the head just a shade too large for the trim little body.

The re-united lovers Azim and Zelica in *Lalla Rookh*, 1860

Rackham's version of Alice was attacked by critics

Even Reid concluded, "Never was a text more completely grasped, expanded, and illuminated. Picture and text are indeed so entirely in harmony that one marvels and resents that any later artist should have re-attempted a re-illustration."[12]

Eventually there were new attempts to illustrate Alice by artists who floundered under Tenniel's acknowledged supremacy. His reputation was secure with the Alice books alone and they had won him a devoted following long after publication. His old champion *The Times* jealously guarded over his reputation, and lashed out at the foolhardiness of those misguided souls who tried to better his Alice. At least seven new editions appeared in 1907, the year the book's copyright expired, and among them was the ill-fated Arthur Rackham edition. *The Times* savaged this enough to leave the artist downhearted and unable to attempt the Alice sequel. The paper's critic measured Rackham against Tenniel and noted while Rackham "feels his privilege and his responsibilities", his drawings were not amusing because the humour was "forced and derivative" and showed "few signs of true imaginative instinct". *Punch* too sought to protect its beloved cartoonist's reputation by publishing E.T. Read's parody of the spate of Alices, which Tenniel greatly enjoyed and about which he wrote to congratulate the clever humorist. Rackham was left to ponder his failure over Alice, heartened to a small degree by a kind letter from his fellow illustrator, H.M. Brock, who had been incensed by the tasteless and disgusting *Punch* parody of his Alice.

> It seems to me like a piece of exceedingly bad taste, to say nothing of its unfairness . . .. Of course, you were prepared for everyone to say that no one could ever approach Tenniel etc. – They always do in such a case – but it seems to me that if comparisons – always "odorous" – must be drawn, they might be done decently. I should like to say how much I personally like your drawings. I would not have missed them, in spite of all that Tenniel has had to say on the subject . . .'[3] I should like to say how much I personally like your drawings. I would not have missed them, in spite of all that Tenniel has had to say on the subject . . ."[13]

Tenniel's reputation and work spread to the Continent and to America largely through the success of his Alice and *Punch* cartoons so it was appropriate that his retirement and death was given substantial coverage in the foreign press. In America his photograph was engraved to accompany an analysis of his long career; he featured prominently in two issues of the conservative New York literary paper the *Critic*, as well as in the *North American Review*, *Boston Evening Transcript* and the *Nation*, where his death notice was followed by more substantial obituaries.[14] Although he never visited the country, America knew of Tenniel; his *Punch* cartoons were studied and accepted as valuable glimpses of British life and attitudes, while his Alice drawings were first substantially collected there and America remains the major source of Tenniel material outside London. In the end, his critics seemed overwhelmed by his public reputation. Unable to look clearly at his weaknesses, they saw only the enormous popularity of this supreme ambassador of gentlemanly virtues: "Through an exceptionally long life, in which he came into contact with all sorts and conditions of men, it is safe to say that he never made an enemy, while few men had more friends."[15]

Notes

Chapter 1

1 According to a copy in the British Library, the treatise was by I. (sic) B.Tenniel, F.S.A., privately printed at Hackney, dated 1845, priced 6d.

2 Tenniel's birthdate varies: Bénézit and Thieme-Becker give 27 February; Tenniel gives 28 – see Tenniel to R.T. Pritchett, 27 February 1900 (Huntington Library).

3 Dr Gideon Mantell in *Wonders of Geology*, 1838, which Martin helped to illustrate.

4 Thomas Balston, *John Martin*, 1947, p.164; Balston notes most of these evenings occurred during 1825–35 when Tenniel was just fifteen, and that it seems probable they continued later, but without record.

5 The *Art Union*, September 1839, p.130.

6 William Holman Hunt, *Pre-Raphaelitism and the PRB*, 1909, Volume II, p.39.

7 M.H. Spielmann, *The History of Punch*, 1895, p.461.

8 H.S. Marks, *Pen and Pencil Sketches*, 1894, Volume I, p.136.

9 The sketchbooks are now in the Huntington Art Gallery (nos.70.58 and 70.59). He may have visited Shanklin with the Dalziel brothers, who were often there in the 1850s, since Tenniel's drawings are dated 1853.

10 Spielmann, *op.cit.*, pp.472–73.

11 See R.H. Griffith, editor, *Selections from the bouts-rimés of John Tenniel*, privately printed, Texas, 1933.

12 Spielmann, *op.cit.*, p.467.

13 The book was done about 1846. Two drawings are in the Victoria and Albert Museum; a third, "Scene from the Opera of Maritana: 'Ah he slumbers how serenely'", depicting a boy pointing to a man on a settee, appeared recently at Sotheby's (1 May 1980, no.627).

14 Spielmann, *op.cit.*, p.467.

15 William Bell Scott quoted by Patricia Allderidge in *Richard Dadd*, Tate Gallery catalogue, 1974, p.15.

16 G.S. Layard, *Life and Letters of C.S. Keene*, 1892, p.38.

17 J.C. Trewin, editor, *The Journal of William Charles Macready*, 1967, p.199.

18 S.C. Hall, *Retrospect of a Long Life*, 1883, pp.328–29.

19 H.T. Hyde, *Illustrations of the New Palace of Westminster*, 1849, p.57; see also D. Robertson, *Sir Charles Eastlake*, 1978, pp.65f.

20 Tenniel to Charles Eastlake, undated [c.30 June 1845] (Victoria and Albert Museum).

21 Spielmann, *op.cit.*, p.461.

22 See John Ruskin, *Ariadne Florentina*, 1872.

Chapter 2

1 *Punch Supplement*, 4 March 1914, p.9. Tenniel eventually painted figures in "The Entrance of Queen Victoria into Queenstown Harbour" for a Lloyd Brothers engraving.

2 *Ibid.*, p.16; Spielmann, *op.cit.*, p.425.

3 For a complete discussion of the Doyle resignation see Rodney Engen's *Richard Doyle*, Catalpa Press, 1984.

4 Quoted in *The Times*, 3 March 1914.

5 Spielmann, *op.cit.*, p.466.

6 *Punch Supplement* 1914, p.2.

7 Spielmann, *op.cit.*, p.470.

8 The work was re-exhibited at the Royal Academy, Handley Reade Collection Exhibition, 1972, no. A 48.

9 There is a discrepancy in addresses: Graves lists 23 Newton Street (1851 RA listing) which is near Holborn and the Punch offices; then later entries at 24 Newman Street, near the Clipstone, but other sources list only Newman Street, which is probably correct.

10 Quoted by Edgar Johnson in *Charles Dickens*, 1977 edn, p.277.

11 *Ibid.*, p.380.

12 *Athenaeum*, 7, 28 May 1853, pp.556–67, 654; also *Art Journal* 1853, p.150.

13 Tenniel to F.M. Evans, 25 August 1854 (Author's collection); Marks, *op.cit.*, Volume I, p.136.

14 Julia Tenniel's death certificate gives "wife of John Tenniel", who died of "phthisis certified". Tenniel's friend Fred Anstey Guthrie recalled of Tenniel: "He was a widower, and I believe, though I never heard him say so, had lost his wife not long after their marriage." (F. Anstey, *A Long Retrospect*, 1936, p.160).

15 See Engen *op.cit.*, pp.142, 150, 180, for a discussion of this.

16 The Dalziel Brothers, *A Record of Work 1840–1890*, 1901, pp.130, 132. Tenniel also noted in his refusal, "I am doing some work for the Queen, as it is wanted as soon as possible, all things else must wait till it is finished."

17 S. Houfe, *Dictionary of British Book Illustrators and Caricaturists 1800–1914*, 1978, p.119.

18 Forrest Reid, *Illustrators of the Sixties*, 1975 edn, p.26.

19 *Ibid.*

20 Quoted by Ruari McLean in *Victorian Book Design*, 1972 edn, p.26.

21 Tenniel to Mr Stonehurst, 8 July 1901 (Pierpoint Morgan Library). Tenniel discusses the sale of his original sketches for the book which he inscribed "Original Sketch Copy John Tenniel 1861. This copy received from printers in loose sheets with spaces left for illustrations and sketches are original designs preparatory to making finished drawings on wood blocks by me."

22 *Art Journal*, 8 December 1860, pp.379–80.

Chapter 3

1 Spielmann, *op.cit.*, pp.432, 470.

2 Quoted in Layard, *op.cit.*, p.251.

3   The drawing is now in the British Museum.

4   Henry Silver's diary is in the *Punch* offices, excerpts quoted by Leonee Ormand, *George Du Maurier*, 1969, p.163.

5   Daphne Du Maurier, editor, *The Young George Du Maurier*, 1951, pp.247–48.

6   Anstey, *op.cit.*, p.158.

7   Quoted in *Punch Supplement* 1914, p.14.

8   Henry Silver in *Punch Supplement* 1914, p.11.

9   Frances Sarzano, *Sir John Tenniel*, Art & Technics, 1948, pp.31–32.

10   Anstey, *op.cit.*, p.159.

11   *Punch Supplement* 1914, p.14.

12   Shirley Brooks's diary quoted by Graham Everitt in *English Caricaturists and Graphic Humorists of the Nineteenth Century*, 1893, p.332.

13   *Ibid.*, p.332.

14   Henry Silver's diary entries dated 29 June 1865 (quoted by Sarzano, p.35); also 30 July [1865?] (quoted in *Punch Supplement* 1914, p.11).

15   Du Maurier, *op.cit.*, p.262.

16   Du Maurier, *op.cit.*, pp.41–42.

17   Du Maurier, *op.cit.*, p.50.

18   Layard, *op.cit.*, p.223.

19   Du Maurier, *op.cit.*, p.253.

20   *An Evening with Punch*, 1900, p.168.

21   Reproduced as endpapers of F.C. Burnand's *Reminiscences*, Volume II, 1904.

22   Spielmann, *op.cit.*, pp.520–21.

23   Item no.8 in the National Portrait Gallery exhibition, May 1984; see also Jeremy Maas, *The Victorian Art World in Photographs*, 1984.

24   Spielmann, *op.cit.*, p.423.

25   Quoted in Wilfrid Blunt's *G.F. Watts, England's Michelangelo*, 1975, pp.117–18.

26   W. W. Fenn in *Chamber's Journal*, Volume 80, 14 November 1903, p.792.

27   Roger Lancelyn Green, *Diaries of Lewis Carroll*, 1953, p.259.

28   Layard, *op.cit.*, p.297.

29   Sarzano, *op.cit.*, p.36.

30   Tenniel to John Eliot Hodgkin, 20 April 1861 (Victoria and Albert Museum).

31   Tenniel to Reverend E. Walford, 11 April 1867 (Huntington Library).

32   See *Boston Museum Bulletin*, Volume 71, No.360, 1973, p.64.

33   Dalziels, *op.cit.*, p.130

34   Proofs marked with Tenniel's comments are now in the Victoria and Albert Museum.

35   Tenniel to ? [John C. Hotten (publisher)], 9 January 1861 (Berg Collection, New York Public Library).

36   *Art Journal*, August 1861, p.224; also *Athenaeum*, 15 June 1861.

37   Gleeson White, *English Illustration. The Sixties*, 1970 edn, pp.140–41.

38   Tenniel to George Bentley, 1 May 1862 (Berg Collection, New York Public Library); proofs are now in the Victoria and Albert Museum.

39   Gleeson White. *op.cit.*, p.172; White added the series was "a National Gallery that suffices to uphold the glory of 'the golden decade', and can only be supplemented but not surpassed by the addition of all others".

40 *Athenaeum*, 12 November 1864, p.641.

41 Ruari McLean, *Victorian Book Design*, 1972, pp.140–41.

Chapter 4

1 Dodgson to Tom Taylor, 20 December 1863 (Andrews Clark Library, University of California).

2 Lewis Carroll, "Alice on the Stage", *Theatre*, April 1887.

3 Green, *op.cit.*, p.326.

4 Green, *op.cit.*, p.210; Anne Clark, *Lewis Carroll*, 1979, p.133. Dodgson's diary for 5 April noted: "Heard from Tenniel that he consents to draw the pictures." (Green, *op.cit.*, p.212.)

5 Tenniel to R.T. Prichett, 22 September 1864 (Private Collection).

6 *Theatre*, *op. cit.*

7 In 1977 the British Museum removed this photograph to reveal Dodgson's drawing, the only surviving portrait of Dodgson's heroine by him; see Clark, *op.cit.*, p.132; reproduction in J. Pudney, *Lewis Carroll and his World*, 1976, p.9.

8 Green, *op.cit.*; also *Tenniel's Alice*, Harvard University catalogue, 1978, p.19.

9 Clark, *op.cit.*, p.135.

10 Dodgson to Alexander Macmillan, 20 November 1864 (Rosenbach Foundation, Philadelphia).

11 Dodgson bought Arthur Hughes's painting "The Lady with the Lilacs" in October 1863 while he worked on Alice and hung it over his mantelpiece; see Jeffrey Stern in *Lewis Carroll Observed*, New York, 1976.

12 Marguerite Mespoulet, *Creators of Wonderland*, 1934, pp.60–61, 65.

13 Quoted by Florence Becker Lennon, *Victoria through the Looking-Glass*, 1945; also by Reid, *op.cit.*, p.26.

14 See Sidney Williams, Falconer Madan and R.L. Green, *The Lewis Carroll Handbook*, revised edn 1979 (ed. Denis Crutch), plate x.

15 Quoted by Michael Hearn in *American Book Collector*, No.3, 1983, p.14.

16 For comparison of Tenniel's preliminary drawings with engravings see *Tenniel's Alice*, Harvard University catalogue, 1978; other drawings and proofs are in the Victoria and Albert Museum. For a discussion of Tenniel's engravings see Muir, *op.cit.*, p.110. A checklist of Tenniel's Alice drawings by Justin Schiller was published in 1990 (see the Bibliography).

17 Hearn, *op.cit.*, p.18.

18 Copies of "Happy Families. A new and diverting game for juveniles", Tenniel's card game designs are in the Victoria and Albert Museum and University of California Library.

19 Originally in *Theatre*, April 1887, quoted by Martin Gardner, editor, *The Annotated Alice*, 1970, p.37.

20 Compare Grandville's "Hand Dropping a Pear" from *Le Charivari* with Dodgson's and Tenniel's versions, reproduced in Mespoulet, *op.cit.*, p.61. The sketchbook is now in the Huntington Art Gallery.

21 See W.A. Baillie-Grohman, "A Portrait of the Ugliest Princess in History", *Burlington Magazine*, April 1921.

22 *Theatre*, *op. cit.*

23 Lewis Carroll in *The Profits of Authorship*, 1884.

24 Derek Hudson, *Lewis Carroll*, revised edn 1976, p.136.

25 Williams, Madan and Green, *op.cit.*, p.28.

26 Hudson, *op.cit.*, p.137.

27 Green, *op.cit.*, p.234.

28 See W.H. Bond, "The Publication of Alice's Adventures in Wonderland", *Harvard Library Bulletin*, Volume X, 1956, pp.306–24; also Warren Weaver, "The First Edition of Alice's Adventures in Wonderland: A Census", *The Papers of the Bibliographical Society of America*, Volume LXV, 1st Quarter, 1971, pp.1–40.

29 Tenniel to the Dalziels, undated ("Thursday") (Huntington Library).

30 See *Tenniel's Alice*, 1978, pp.44–46 for a comparison of Tenniel's spacings. Alice [Liddell] wrote to Macmillan after Dodgson's death in 1898, asking to buy Tenniel's original wood block illustrations. They told her, in a needless untruth, that the drawings had been "inevitably destroyed" in the process of engraving. "What, then, shall I have as my legacy?" wrote Alice to Reginald (quoted in Colin Gordon, *Beyond the Looking-Glass*, London 1982, p.231). In 1981 Macmillan "re-discovered" the Alice blocks in a London bank vault see *The Times,* 18 October 1985, p.32.

31 Dodgson to Tom Taylor, 3 August 1865 (Berg Collection, New York Public Library); Dodgson's calendar in Green, *op.cit.*, p.72.; also Green, *op.cit.*, p.236.

32 *Athenaeum*, 16 December 1865, p.844.

33 *The Times*, 26 December 1865; for a list of reviews which Dodgson kept, see Flora V. Livingston, *Harcourt Amory Collection Catalogue*, Harvard University, 1932, pp.16–17.

34 Quoted in Walter de la Mare, *Lewis Carroll*, 1932.

35 Tenniel to Charles Kent, undated [c.2 November 1867] (Huntington Library).

36 The watercolour is now in the Victoria and Albert Museum, 1866, stamped "No 30 '68".

37 See Engen, *op.cit.*, p.140.

38 Dodgson to Mrs G. Macdonald, 19 May 1868 (Yale University).

39 Green, *op.cit.*, quoted by Williams, Madan and Green, *op.cit.*, p.66.

40 Green, *op.cit.*, p.275; M.L. Cohen, *Letters of Lewis Carroll*, 1979, p.124.

41 Dalziels, *op.cit.*, p.128.

42 Cohen, *op.cit.*, pp.148–49.

43 The trial title-page is now in the Harvard Library.

44 Quoted by Gardner, *op.cit.*, p.221; the deleted passage was first published in the *Sunday Telegraph Magazine*, 4 September 1977. See also "A suppressed adventure 'Alice' surfaces after 107 years", *Smithsonian Magazine*, December 1977, pp.50–56.

45 Dodgson to Edward Dalziel, undated [27 December 1870] (Harvard Library).

46 The full text is printed in Williams, Madan and Green, *op.cit.*, p.61.

47 Green, *op.cit.*, p.305.

48 See Mavis Batey, "Alice and her Wonderland Gardens", *Country Life*, 29 October 1981, pp.1456–57.

49 *Tenniel's Alice*, *op.cit.*, plate 74.

50 See J. Maas, *Victorian Painters*, 1969, p.104; also Gardner, *op.cit.*, p.128.

51 Gardner, *op.cit.*, pp.252, 279.
52 Spielmann, *op.cit.*, p.329.
53 Tenniel to George Bentley, 6 November 1871 (New York Public Library), written on black-bordered mauve paper.
54 Hudson, *op.cit.*, pp.180–81.
55 Quoted by Clark, *op.cit.*, p.169.
56 Harry Furniss, *Some Victorian Men*, 1924, p.77; Cohen *op.cit.*, p.754; L.V. Fildes, *Luke Fildes*, 1968, pp.43–44.
57 Sarzano, *op.cit.*, p.63; the inscribed book is now in the University of London Library.
58 Sarzano, *op.cit.*, pp.16, 18–19.

Chapter 5

1   Spielmann, *op.cit.*, p.81.
2   Spielmann, *op.cit.*, pp.463–64.
3   Tenniel to E.J. Milliken, n.d. ("Monday P.M.") (Author's Collection)
4   *Punch Supplement* 1914, p.10.
5   See Sarah Hamilton Phelps, "The Hartley Collection", *Boston Museum Bulletin*, Volume LXXI, 1973, p.64.
6   Anstey, *op.cit.*, p.268.
7   Spielmann, *op.cit.*, pp.471–72. I am grateful to Lady Elton for pointing this drawing out from Sir Arthur Elton's collection (now at Ironbridge).
8   Spielmann, *op.cit.*, p.463.
9   Houfe, *op.cit.*, p.65.
10 *The Times*, 29 June 1857.
11 Spielmann, *op.cit.*, p.177; also *Punch Supplement* 1914, p.8.
12 Tenniel to George Hodder, undated [c.August 1857] (Berg Collection, New York Public Library).
13 See William S. Walsh, *Abraham Lincoln and the London Punch*, New York, 1909.
14 Spielmann, *op.cit.*, p.466.
15 Burnand, *op. cit.*, Vol. I, p.228.
16 Spielmann, *op.cit.*, p.466.
17 Fildes, *op.cit.*, pp.43–44.
18 Tenniel to unnamed correspondent, 22 September 1877 (Private Collection)
19 Spielmann, *op.cit.*, p.128.
20 Tenniel to T. Agnew, 11 May 1877 (Huntington Library).
21 Tenniel to Luke Fildes, 23 January 1879, 14 March 1887 (Victoria and Albert Museum).
22 Tenniel to George Vicat Cole, 10 October 1885 (Author's Collection); Tenniel to Lord Mayor, 29 May 1876 (Author's Collection).
23 Layard, *op.cit.*, p.277; Keene's *Punch* cartoons appeared in 5, 12, 26, October and 2 November issues.
24 *Punch Supplement*, 1914, p.10.
25 Anstey, *op.cit.*, p.160.
26 Tenniel to T. Agnew, Derby Day 1879 (Private Collection).
27 Burnand, *op.cit.*, Vol. II, p.43.

28   Burnand, *op.cit.*, Vol. II, p.35.

29   E.V. Lucas, *Reading, Writing and Remembering*, 1932, p.317.

30   Spielmann, *op.cit.*, p.535.

31   Anstey, *op.cit.*, p.165.

32   Tenniel to Furniss, 15 September 1888 (University of California Library).

33   Tenniel to Furniss, 30 July, 13 August 1889 (University of California Library).

34   Tenniel to Edmund Evans, 6 December 1886 (University of California Library).

35   Clark, *op.cit.*, pp.231–32; Charles Morgan, *The House of Macmillan*, 1943, p.112.

36   *Punch Supplement* 1914, p.12.

37   Spielmann, *op.cit.*, p.463.

38   Tenniel to Gladstone, 5 June 1884 (British Library).

39   Tenniel to Mr Pinches, 16 May 1883 (Private Collection).

40   Tenniel to H. Fillean, 26 November 1889 (Private Collection).

41   Tenniel to Mrs Millais, 8 June 1881 (Pierpont Morgan Library).

42   Tenniel to Mrs Hunter, 2 April 1887 (Private Collection); Tenniel to Miss Chappell, 8 December 1887 (Private Collection).

43   Tenniel to Mrs Robb, 25 June 1888 (Private Collection).

44   Tenniel to Mrs Skirrow, 2 March 1886 (Private Collection).

45   The Tenniel–Grahame correspondence is now in the Bodleian Library and dated 1892–1907; see also references in Peter Green, *Kenneth Grahame*, 1959, pp.202–3.

46   *Punch Supplement* 1914, p.15.

47   *Ibid.*, p.13.

48   Anstey, *op.cit.*, p.160.

49   Edmund Evans to Thomas Jones, 9 September 1899 (University of California Library).

50   From *The Times* report, "Bismark, Some Secret Pages of His History", 1890; also *Art Journal*, 1901, p.7.

51   Tenniel to F.C.B. [urnand], 5 April 1890 (University of California Library).

52   Spielmann, *op.cit.*, p.194.

53   Henry C. Ewart, editor, *Toilers in Art*, London, n.d., p.38.

Chapter 6

1   Tenniel to Mrs Furniss, 14 November 1892 (University of California).

2   Tenniel to Thomas Hutchinson, 30 April 1894 (Victoria and Albert Museum).

3   Tenniel to unknown correspondent [" T "], Wednesday, n.d. (Author's Collection).

4   Anstey, *op.cit.*, pp.160–61.

5   *Illustrated London News*, 10 June 1893, p.689. Tenniel was one of just a few cartoonists knighted, including Leslie Ward ("Spy"), F. Carruthers Gould, Bernard Partridge and David Low.

6   List dated 16 August 1893, signed and initialled (Author's Collection).

7   Du Maurier to Henry James, 27 September 1888 (Harvard University, Houghton Library).

8   Tenniel to Lewis Carroll, 29 January 1894; Tenniel to Ernest Hart, 18 January 1896 (both in Harcourt Amory Collection, Harvard); see also Cohen, *op.cit.*, p.1149.

9   Tenniel to Millais, 8 March 1896 (New York Public Library).

10 Tenniel to Harry Furniss, 18 February 1896 (University of California).

11 Tenniel to Edward Reed, 18 July 1900 (Author's Collection).

12 Tenniel to Walter Horsley, 9 May 1897 (Private Collection).

13 Tenniel to Isidore Spielmann, 9 January 1900 (Victoria and Albert Museum).

14 Anstey, *op.cit.*, p.245.

15 *Ibid.*, pp.160–61; also *Punch Supplement* 1914, p.7.

16 *The Times*, 14 June 1901.

17 The *Punch* drawing published 19 September 1900 is now in the Victoria and Albert Museum.

18 Tenniel to Mrs Fred [Burnand], 21 March 1906 (Author's Collection).

19 Tenniel to Walter J. Payne, 25 August 1903 (Private Collection).

20 *Punch Supplement* 1914, p.16.

21 Tenniel to Mrs Harley, 21 May 1893 (Private Collection); Tenniel attended Mrs Critchett's evening party which he called "far from the *madding* crowd of the Imperial Institute".

22 Clipping from unidentified paper, dated 28 February 1907 (Columbia University).

23 The flats were designed by Delissa Joseph and opened by Frank Green, Lord Mayor of London, on 16 January 1901; see Anstey, *op.cit.*, p.319.

24 *The Times*, 27 February 1909.

25 The drawing of "the late Linley Sambourne" is now in New York Public Library.

26 Anstey, *op.cit.*, p.330.

27 Anstey, *op.cit.*, p.336.

28 Anstey, *op.cit.*, p.340-41.

29 *Punch Supplement* 1914, p.16.

30 *The Connoisseur*, Volume 38, 1914, p.259.

31 *Punch*, 4 March 1914, p.162.

Epilogue

1   See John Ruskin, *Ariadne Florentina*, 1872.

2   Ruskin's "The Artists of the Fireside" lecture was delivered at Oxford on 2 and 10 November 1883, and thereafter published as *The Art of England*, 1884.

3   White, *op.cit.*, p.22.

4   Reid, *op.cit.*, pp.26–27.

5   Geoffrey Wakeman, *Victorian Book Illustration: The Technical Revolution*, 1974, p.72.

6   Muir, *op.cit.*, p.111.

7   Dalziels, *op.cit.*, pp.124–25.

8   White, *op.cit.*, p.112; Reid, *op.cit.*, p.27.

9   David Bland, *A History of Book Illustration*, 1958, pp.265–66.

10 Muir, *op.cit.*, p.111.

11   White, *op. cit.*, p. 127; also in *Studio,* Special Number, Winter 1897–98, p.40.

12   Reid, *op.cit.,* pp. 27–29.

13   Quoted in Derek Hudson, *Arthur Rackham,* 1974 ed, p.74.

14   See French obituary, *Chronicle des arts,* 1914, p.86; American articles include: *Critic* (New York), Volume 33, November 1898, p.316; Volume 38, 1901, p.141. "Tenniel and Punch", *North American Review,* Volume 99, April 1914, pp. 504–7; "The Passing of John Tenniel", *Boston Evening Transcript,* 26 February 1914; and "Sir John Tenniel" by Edmund L. Pearson, *Nation,* 1914.

15   *Dictionary of National Biography,* 1912–1921, p.526; Tenniel's entry by Henry William Lumsden.

Select Bibliography

The following list of references relates to Tenniel's life and career. Background material is also listed in the Notes section. Among the collections of Tenniel material invaluable to the student are: British Museum Print Room (proofs and drawings), British Library (MS material and books), National Portrait Gallery (watercolour and oil portraits, pen sketches of Tenniel at work), Punch offices (MS material and Henry Silver's diary), Bodleian Library (MS material). In the United States Tenniel material may be found in various public collections including New York Public Library (Berg collection, print room and MS department), Pierpont Morgan Library (MS material), Harvard University Library (Harcourt Amory collection of Alice material), Columbia University (MS material), Boston Museum (Harold Hartley collection of over 100 Tenniel pencil drawings, proofs for Alice), University of Texas (MS material), University of California, Los Angeles (MS material), Huntington Art Gallery and Library (MS material and early watercolours).

American Book Collector, No. 3, 1983, pp.11–20. (discusses Tenniel's Alice work in a pioneering article by Michael Hearn)

Anstey, Fred, *A Long Retrospect*, 1936. (account of Tenniel's last days)

Art Journal, 1882, pp. 13–16. (article by Tenniel's friend Arthur à Beckett); 1901 Easter Number by Cosmo Monkhouse (surveys Tenniel's career)

Art News, Volume 24, No. 7, 1925–26, p.7. (note on Tenniel)

Balston, Thomas, *John Martin*, 1947. (gives an account of Tenniel's early London social life)

Bénézit, *Dictionaire des Peintres, Sculpteurs*, 1910, revised 1966. (entry for Tenniel with paintings sold)

Bland, David, *A History of Book Illustration*, 1958. (discusses Tenniel's importance)

Boston Evening Transcript, 26 February 1914. (obituary)

Boston Museum Bulletin, Volume 71, 1973, pp.52–67. (account of the Hartley collection of wood-engravings)

Buday, George, *The History of the Christmas Card*, 1954, pp.130, 134. (discusses Tenniel's comic inventions in *Punch*)

Burlington Magazine, Volume 30, 1917, pp.31,123.

Burnand, F.C., *Reminiscences*, 1904. (account of his friendship with Tenniel)

Chronicle des arts, 1914, p.86. (foreign obituary)

Clark, Anne, *Lewis Carroll*, 1979. (most recent biography with an account of Tenniel's Alice career)

Clement & Hutton, *Artists of the Nineteenth Century*, 1879, 1893. (entry for Tenniel)

Cohen, Norton (editor), *The Letters of Lewis Carroll*, 1979. (notes give Tenniel's influence on Carroll)

Connoisseur, Volume 38, 1914, p.259f.; Volume 40,1914, p.173. (obituary tributes)

Crane, Walter, *Of the Decorative Illustration of Books Old and New*, 1896, reprinted 1972.(assessesTenniel's importance)

(The) *Critic*, (New York), Volume 33, 1898, p.316; Volume 38, 1901, p.141. (American tributes to Tenniel)

Crutch, Denis (editor), *The Lewis Carroll Handbook*, revised 1979 edition of Williams, Madan and Green *(op. cit.)*

Cultura moderne, Volume 1, 1913/14, p.569f. (discusses Tenniel)

Dalziel Brothers, *A Record of Work, 1840–1890*, 1901. (record of engraving Tenniel's work)

Dayot, A., *La peintre anglais*, 1908, p.327, plate 336. (brief mention of Tenniel)

Dictionary of National Biography, 1912–21, pp.524–26. (Tenniel's entry by Henry William Lumsden)

Du Maurier, Daphne (editor), *The Young George Du Maurier*, 1951. (letters by Tenniel's *Punch* associate as useful background)·

Engen, Rodney, *Richard Doyle*, 1984. (full-scale biography and account of Tenniel's *Punch* predecessor)

"The Early Career of Sir John Tenniel", *Country Life*, 28 October 1982, pp. 1306–1308.

Dictionary of Victorian Wood Engravers, 1985. (lists Tenniel and his engravers' careers and works)

Everitt, Graham, *English Caricaturists and Graphic Humorists of the Nineteenth Century*, 1893 edition. (critical account of Tenniel's early cartoons)

Ewart, Henry C., *Toilers in Art*, Isbister & Co., n.d. (contains illustrated chapter on Tenniel by Robert Walker)

Fildes, L.V., *Luke Fildes*, 1968. (discusses Fildes as Dodgson's illustrator, successor to Tenniel)

Forrer, *Biographical Dictionary of Medallists*, Volume 6, 1916. (entry on Tenniel)

Furniss, Harry, *Confessions of a Caricaturist*, 1901. (autobiography by Tenniel's later *Punch* associate)

Some Victorian Men, 1924. (discusses Tenniel)

Harry Furniss, 1984. (National Portrait Gallery exhibition catalogue, lists Tenniel portraits by Furniss)

Gardner, Martin (editor), *The Annotated Alice* , 1970. (notes Tenniel's inspiration on Alice)

Graves, Algernon, *Royal Academy Exhibitors 1769–1904*, 1906, Volume 7. (lists Tenniel's exhibited work)

A Century of Loan Exhibitions, 1914, Volume 4. (lists Tenniel's exhibited work)

Green, Roger Lancelyn (editor), *Diaries of Lewis Carroll*, 1953. (references to work with Tenniel)

Griffith, R.H. (editor), *Selections from the bouts-rimés of John Tenniel*, 1933. (facsimile of Tenniel's early poetry sketches)

Hake, Henry M., *Catalogue of Engraved British Portraits in the British Museum*, Volume 3, 1912, p.47; Volume 4, 1914, p.432. (single and group portraits)

Hall, S.C., *Retrospect of a Long Life*, 1883. (autobiography by Tenniel's first book patron)

Hancher, Michael, *The Tenniel Illustrations to the 'Alice' Books*, 1986. (analyses

Tenniel's sources for the Alice illustrations)

Harvard University, *Tenniel's Alice*, 1978. (exhibition catalogue of a primary Alice collection)

Hodnett, Edward, *Image and Text*. Studies in the Illustration of English Literature, 1983. (contains an essay on Tenniel as illustrator)

Houfe, Simon, *Dictionary of British Book Illustrators and Caricaturists 1800–1914*, 1978. (entry and discussion of Tenniel)

Hudson, Derek, *Lewis Carroll*, 1954, revised 1976. (Carroll–Tenniel background in this illustrated biography)

    Arthur Rackham, 1974, p.74 (refers to Tenniel's Alice)

Johnson, Edgar, *Charles Dickens*, 1977 edition. (section on Tenniel's acting career)

Kunstchronicle, Volume 10, 1875, p.231; Volume 11, 1900, p.440; Volume 25, 1914, p.387.

Layard, G.S., *Life and Letters of Charles Keene*, 1892. (life of Tenniel's art student friend)

Lucas, E.V., *Reading, Writing and Remembering*, 1932.

Maas, Jeremy, *The Victorian Art World in Photographs*, 1984. (account of early Tenniel photographs, some reproduced)

Mackenzie, Norman and Jeanne, *Dickens. A Life*, 1979. (biographical associations)

Marks, Henry Stacy, *Pen and Pencil Sketches*, 1894. (impressions of Tenniel by his artist friend)

McLean, Ruari, *Victorian Book Design and Colour Printing*, 1972. (refers to early Tenniel books)

Mespoulet, Marguerite, *Creators of Wonderland*, 1934. (argues Grandville's influence on Alice)

Muir, Percy, *Victorian Illustrated Books, 1971*. (surveys Tenniel's work)

Müller, H.A., *Biographical Kunstler-Lexikon*, 1879. (Tenniel entry)

Nagler, *Kunstler-Lexikon*, 1848, Volume 18.

    Die Monogrammisten, 1879, Volume 5.

    (Both give entries on Tenniel)

(The) *Nation*, 1914. (obituary tribute to "Sir John Tenniel" by E.L. Pearson)

National Portrait Gallery, *Harry Furniss*, 1984. (exhibition catalogue, lists Tenniel portraits by Furniss).

North American Review, Volume 99, April 1914, pp.504–7. (obituary article "Tenniel and Punch")

Ormond, Leonee, *George Du Maurier*, 1969. (recalls Tenniel's early *Punch* days)

Pennell, Joseph, *Pen Drawing and Pen Draughtsmanship in England, 1889*. (recommends Tenniel's Alice drawings to students)

    Modern Illustration, 1895. (includes Tenniel's work)

Press, Charles, *The Political Cartoon*, 1981. (discusses Tenniel's role in reporting the American Civil War for *Punch*)

Price, R.G.G., *A History of Punch*, 1957.

Punch Supplement, 4 March 1914. (illustrated tribute to Tenniel)

Reid, Forrest, *Illustrators of the Sixties*, 1928, reprint 1975. (surveys Tenniel's career)

Robertson, David, *Sir Charles Eastlake*, 1978. (on Tenniel's Westminster frescoes)

Rumann, A., *Das illustriert Buch der 19 Jahrhunderts*, 1930. (mention of Tenniel's books)

Ruskin, John, *Ariadne Florentina*, 1872. (includes comments on Tenniel as a draughtsman on wood)

The Art of England, 1884. (Oxford lecture "The Artists of the Fireside" on Tenniel and Leech)

Sarzano, Frances, *Sir John Tenniel*, Art & Technics, 1948. (first biographical survey)

Schiller, Justin and Selwyn H. Goodacre, *Alice's Adventures in Wonderland. An 1865 printing re-described*, 1990. (a list of Tenniel's preliminary drawings to *Alice* and *Looking Glass*)

Sketchley, R.E.D., *English Book Illustration of Today*, 1903. (discusses Tenniel)

Spielmann, M.H., *The History of Punch*, 1895. (account of Tenniel's working methods, early *Punch* sketches, an interview with the author)

The First 50 Years of Punch, 1900. (selection of Tenniel cartoons)

(The) *Studio* – Tenniel's work appeared in the following issues:

"Children's Books and their Illustrators", Special Number, Winter 1897–98, p.40.

"Graphic Arts of Great Britain", Special Number 1917, p.6, plate 24.

"Drawings in Pen", Spring Number 1922, p.128.

"British Book Illustration", Winter Number 1923–24, p.30, plate 95.

Thieme-Becker, *Algemeines Lexikon der Bildenden Künstler*, 1927. (Tenniel entry with bibliography)

The Times, 6 December 1900; 1 January 1901; 18 April 1901; 13, 14 June 1901; 27 February 1914; 3, 5, 20 March 1914; 4 May 1914

Trewin, J.C. (editor), *The Journal of William Macready*, 1967. (Tenniel's visit recorded here)

Wakeman, Geoffrey, *Victorian Book Illustration*, 1973. (discusses Tenniel as wood draughtsman)

White, Gleeson, *English Illustration: The Sixties*, 1897, reprint 1970. (discusses Tenniel's illustrations)

"Children's Books and their Illustrators", *Studio*, Special Number, Winter 1897–98.

Who was Who, 1897–1915. (entry for Tenniel)

Appendices

The following abbreviations are incorporated into the appendices:

BM	British Library
BM stamp	Date stamped on receipt of book
BMP	British Museum Print Room
Boston	Boston Museum of Fine Arts
BR	Book review
Crutch	Denis Crutch, editor, *The Lewis Carroll Handbook*, revised 1979
Dalziel Record	The Dalziel Brothers, *A Record of Work 1840–1890*, 1901
ENG	English National Catalogue
McLean	Ruari McLean, *Victorian Book Design and Colour Printing*, 1972
Muir	Percy Muir, *Victorian Illustrated Books*, 1971
n.d.	undated
NU	National Union Catalogue
Reid	Forrest Reid, *Illustrators of the Sixties*, 1928, reprinted 1975 as *Illustrators of the 1860s*
Sarzano	Frances Sarzano, *Sir John Tenniel*, Art & Technics, 1948
TB	Thieme-Becker, *Algemeines Lexikon der Bildenden Künstler*, 1927
UCLA	University of California, Los Angeles, Library
VAM	Victoria and Albert Museum
White	Gleeson White, *English Illustration: The Sixties*, 1897, reprint 1970

Appendix I
Books illustrated by Tenniel

Entries are chronological by publication date, giving title, author, publisher, date discrepancies in illustrations, binding, editions, size. Dates in square brackets – e.g. [ ] indicate approximate dating.

1842

The Book of British Ballads. Edited by S.C. (Samuel Carter) Hall, Esquire, FSA.
London: Jeremiah How 1842 (series 1), 1844 (series 2) (BM)
10 Tenniel illustrations engraved on wood by J. Bastin, printed by Vizetelly Bros; others by Kenny Meadows, Richard Dadd, F. R. Pickersgill, W. Bell Scott, J. H. Paton, J. Franklin, W.P. Frith, J. Gilbert, A. Crowquill, engraved on wood by J. Linton, Edmund Evans, H. Dalziel, W.T. Green.
1842 (folio); 1844 bound in 1 volume, decorated gilt vellum; 1853 edition (BM)
London: Henry G. Bohn (8°); 1879 [1878] edition (BM) (8°).

1845

Undine. A romance from the German of De la Motte Fouque. A new translation with eleven illustrations, designs by Tenniel, engraved by [J] Bastin.
London: James Burns [1845] (BM) 1846 (title-page date) (White) (Muir)
11 full-page illustrations with borders by Tenniel, engraved on wood by J. Bastin, and one by G. Gray.
1845 edition (8°); 1855 edition, London: Edward Lumley; story later included in *The Four Seasons* anthology [1855?] (8°) (proofs in BMP).

1845–6

Poems and Pictures: The Children in the Wood
London: James Burns 1846 (Sarzano) 1845 (McLean)
Tenniel frontispiece design to the third volume in the series (reproduced *Osborne Collection Catalogue*, 1958, facing p.38) coloured covers printed by Gregory, Collins & Reynolds.
1860 edition (VAM) (4to).

1848

L' Allegro and Il Penseroso. By John Milton.
London: The Art Union of London 1848 (BM)
30 full-page illustrations, 1 by Tenniel, others by G. Scharf, H. O'Neil, W.E. Frost, J. Absolon, F. Goodall, E.H. Corbould, K. Meadows, R. Doyle, J. Gilbert, D. Roberts, J.D. Harding, W.P. Leitch, H.C. Selous, engraved on wood by the Dalziels, H.D. & W.J. Linton, H. Vizetelly.
1st edition 30pp. and plates, bound in full brown calf gilt (folio) (Tenniel proof in VAM).

1848

The Juvenile Verse and Picture Book
London: James Burns 1848 (White) (Sarzano)
Illustrations by Tenniel, C.H. Weigall, W.B. Scott, R. Cruikshank, engraved on wood by C.Gray, W.J. Linton.
1866 edition (BM) (VAM) London: Frederick Warne & Co., bound in green cloth gilt (4to); 1868 edition (White) a re-issue as *Gems of National Poetry*, London: Frederick Warne.

1848

The Haunted Man and The Ghost's Bargain. A Fancy for Christmastime. By Charles Dickens.
London: Bradbury & Evans 1848 (BM) (published 19 December) (BR).
5 Tenniel Illustrations, others by C. Stanfield, F. Stone, J. Leech, wood engraved by Martin & Corbould.
1st edition red cloth gilt title; 2nd issue (London: Chapman & Hall), same as above but bound in yellow glazed boards, front cover with title in red and black (probably sold by W.H. Smith railway shops); collected in 1869 edition of *The Christmas Books* (8°) (see separate entry below); later edition London: Chapman & Hall Ltd, New York: C. Scribners Sons 1910 (NU).
Reviewed in *Athenaeum* (London) 1848, no. 1107, p. 1291f.

1848

Aesop's Fables. A New Version, chiefly from original sources by The Reverend Thomas James, M.A., with more than a hundred illustrations designed by John Tenniel.
London: John Murray 1848 (BM) (BM stamp 30 Feb. 48)
106 illustrations by Tenniel, engraved on wood by Leopold Martin, printed by Bradbury & Evans, each surrounded by full-page border (8°).
2nd edition 1851 (BM) with over 20 new drawings by Joseph Wolf, others redrawn by Tenniel ("The Old Woman and the Wine Jar", "Hercules and the Waggoner", "The Bundle of Sticks", "The Trumpeter Taken Prisoner"); other editions 1852,1858 (BM) (both 8°); 1882 (Muir, p.127 "far superior").

1854

Proverbial Philosophy. By Martin F. Tupper, D.C.L., F.R.S., of Christchurch, Oxford
London: Thomas Hatchard 1854 (BM) (BM stamp 25 Jan. 54)
17 illustrations by Tenniel including title and preface vignette; others by J. Gilbert, T. Dalziel, E.H. Corbould, C.W. Cope, J. Godwin, H.N. Humphreys, J. Severn, F.R. Pickersgill, engraved on wood by the Dalziels and Vizetelly.
(Text from the original 1838 edition, London: J. Rickerby)
New edition (1 & 2 series) London [1866] 1867 (BM), with 65 illustrations by Tenniel, G. Doré, H.N. Humphreys, J. Gilbert, M.F. Tupper, B. Foster, T. Dalziel, E.H. Corbould, F.R. Pickersgill; Another edition, London: Cassell & Co. [1881] (BM).

1855

Thirty Illustrations of Childe Harold. The original drawings produced expressly for London: The Art Union of London 1855
2 Tenniel full-page illustrations of a total of 30, others by J. Godwin, T. Faed, J. Gilbert, R. Ansdell, H.C. Selous, E.H. Corbould, all engraved on wood by the Dalziels.
Bound in yellow card covers (folio).

1857

The Course of Time. A poem by Robert Pollok, A.M.
Edinburgh & London: Blackwood & Sons 1857 (BM) (BM stamp 8 June 58)
10 illustrations by Tenniel of 50 total; others by B. Foster, J.R. Clayton, engraved on wood by E. Evans, Dalziels, J. Green, H.N. Woods
(illustrated edition of 1827 poem in its 20th edition)
Bound in orange cloth gilt (8°).

1857

Dramatic Scenes, with other poems now first printed. By Barry Cornwall [B.W. Proctor]
London: Chapman & Hall [1856] 1857 (BM) (BM stamp 8 June 58)
7 Tenniel illustrations; others by B. Foster, J.R. Clayton, T. Dalziel, W. Harvey, J. Godwin, E.H. Corbould, Harrison Weir, E. Dalziel, all engraved on wood by the Dalziels.
(3 Tenniel illustrations re-used in Longfellow's *Tales of a Wayside Inn*, cf. 1867 entry)
404 pages of text (8°); (3 Tenniel proof engravings in VAM).

1857

The Poets of the Nineteenth Century. Selected and edited by Reverend Robert Aris Willmott.
London: George Routledge & Co. 1857 (Sarzano, White) (BM stamp 17 March 57, introduction date 2 Oct)
6 Tenniel illustrations, of a total of 100; others by B. Foster, W. Harvey, J. Gilbert, J.R. Clayton, T. Dalziel, J. Godwin, E.H. Corbould, D. Edwards, E. Duncan, A. Hughes, W.P. Leitch, F.M. Brown, E.A. Goodall, T.D. Hardy, F.R. Pickersgill, Harrison Weir, J. Millais, all engraved on wood by the Dalziels.
1st edition bound in blue morocco-grain cloth, gilt, rear cover design by John Sleigh; Deluxe edition (n.d.) in red morocco gilt.

1857–58

Poems. By William Cullen Bryant. Collected and Arranged by the Author.
London: Sampson Low, Son & Co. 1858 (BM, Sarzano) [1857] (NU) (BM stamp 20 Nov. 57)
3 Tenniel illustrations of a total of 71; others by E. & T. Dalziel, B. Foster, F.R. Pickersgill, Harrison Weir, all engraved on wood by the Dalziels.
(original edition 1846)
American edition, New York: Appleton [1857] (NU).

1857–58

The Poetical Works of Edgar Allan Poe, with an original memoir.
London: Sampson Low, Son & Co. 1857 (White) 1858 (Sarzano)
3 full-page and 1 half-page Tenniel illustrations of a total of 53, others by F.R. Pickersgill, B. Foster, Felix Darley, Jasper Cropsey, P. Duggan, P. Skelton, A.M. Madot, engraved on wood by W.J. Linton, E. Evans, J. Cooper.
American edition, New York: J.S. Redfield 1858 (NU);
Re-issued new illustrated editions – London: Ward Lock (c.1865); London: Sampson Low, Son & Marston 1866 (BM) (BM stamp 3 Jan. 1866), both bound in brown cloth, gilt with green oval overlay, produced under the superintendance of Joseph Cundall, (8°); another edition [1871] (BM) (8°).

1858

The Grave. A Poem by Robert Blair. With a preface by the Reverend F.W. Farrar, M.A.
Edinburgh: A. & C. Black 1858 (BM stamp 29 Dec. 58)
4 Tenniel illustrations, others by B. Foster, J.R. Clayton, J. Godwin, T. Dalziel, engraved on wood by the Dalziels and E. Evans.
Bound in dark green cloth, gilt embossed (8°).

1858

The Home Affections Portrayed by the Poets. Selected and Edited by Charles Mackay.
London & New York: George Routledge & Co. 1858 (BM) (BM stamp 9 Jan. 58)
2 Tenniel illustrations of 100 total, others by J. Gilbert, B. Foster, Harrison Weir, J. Absolon, T. Dalziel, F.R. Pickersgill, J.E. Millais, J.R. Clayton, S. Read, J. Abner, J. Godwin, J. Sleigh, engraved on wood by the Dalziels.
Bound in red cloth gilt (8°); new edition London: George Routledge & Sons 1866, bound in green cloth gilt;
(Tenniel drawings re-issued in *A Thousand and One Gems of English Poetry*, see 1872 entry below.)

1858

Lays of the Holy Land from Ancient and Modern Poets.
London: R. Nisbet 1858 (Sarzano) (not traced)

1858

Passages from the Poems of Thomas Hood. Illustrated by the Junior Etching Club. 1858 (Sarzano)
Tenniel illustrations include "War and Glory" to S.T. Coleridge's verse, "The Battlefield" by T. Penrose.
Smaller edition 1862 (VAM), plates lettered "London: Day & Son, lithographer to Queen, 1 December 1862"; (proofs for etched plates in VAM); re-issued Tenniel illustration "War and Glory" in *Passages from Modern English Poets* (see entry below).

The Mirage of Life, 1859 see 1867 entry below.

1858–60

The Gordian Knot by Shirley Brooks.
London: R. Bentley 1860 (Sarzano, NU) (1858) (BM)
22 Tenniel illustrations as full-page etchings on steel, first issued in monthly parts from 1858, drawings dated 1858 (Reid);
(original pencil drawings and corrected proofs in VAM.)

1860

The Silver Cord by Shirley Brooks.
Tenniel illustrations to 97 chapters originally published in *Once a Week* 1860–61 (see Appendix II).

1860–61

Lalla Rookh. An Oriental Romance by Thomas Moore.
London: Longman, Green, Longman & Roberts 1861 (BM) (BM stamp 17 Nov. 60)
69 illustrations by Tenniel, engraved on wood by the Dalziels, 5 ornamental pages (1 in colour and gold) "of foreign design" by T. Sulman, engraved on wood by H.N. Woods (4to).
American edition, New York: Hurd & Houghton 1867 (NU);
New edition, London: Longmans, Green 1880, bound in red cloth gilt, black decoration (proofs in VAM, also BMP).

1861

Parables from Nature by Mrs. Gatty.
London: Bell & Daldy 1861 (White, Sarzano)
Illustrations by Tenniel, Holman Hunt, M.R. Edwards, W. Millais, Otto Speckter, F. Keyl, L. Fröhlich, Harrison Weir.
New edition 1867 (White) adds work by Burne-Jones ("Nativity"); also 1873 edition; "New and Complete Edition", London: George Bell & Sons 1880 (BM) (BM stamp 17 Feb. 80) contains one Tenniel illustration of two men on a beach (4to).

1861

Puck on Pegasus by H. Cholmondeley-Pennell.
London: John Camden Hotton 1861 (BR) (Sarzano)
4 Tenniel illustrations to "Lord Jollygreen's Courtship" engraved on wood by the Dalziels, others include frontispiece by G. Cruikshank, work by Leech, Phiz, Portch, engraved by Swain, the Dalziels, E. Evans.
1862 edition London: George Routledge; 1869 edition (new and revised of 1862 edition) (BM) (BM stamp 11 Dec. 68), London: John Camden Hotten, with additional illustrations by R. Doyle ("A Tailpiece"), Millais, N. Paton, M.E. Edwards, bound in dark green cloth, gilt (4to); 1874 edition bound in coloured boards, cover illustration not in book, text in sepia ink.
Reviewed in *Athenaeum* (London) 15 June, 1861, no. 1755, pp.794–95.

1862

Passages from Modern English Poets. Illustrated by the Junior Etching Club.
London: Day & Son [1862] (Sarzano)
Tenniel etching "War and Glory" (reused from *Passages from T. Hood*, see 1858 entry), others by Millais, Whistler, H. Moore, M.J. Lawless, H.S. Marks, C. Keene. C. Rossiter, F. Smallfield, Viscount Bury, G. Fitzgerald, J.W. Oaks, A.J. Lewis, F. Powell, J. Sleigh, H.C. Whaite, W. Severn, W. Gale, J. Clark.
Bound in large 8° edition; 1876 edition (large 4to) the etchings transferred to stone and printed as lithographs published by William Tegg (White); (proofs in VAM).

1862

No Church by Frederick William Robinson.
London: Hurst & Blackett 1862 (Sarzano), 1861 (BM)
1 Tenniel design steel-engraved as frontispiece; (the book in the "Standard Library" series, cf. *Grandmother's Money* 1862, *A Noble Life* see [1869] entry below)

1862

Grandmother's Money by Frederick William Robinson.
London: Hurst & Blackett 1862 (BM, Sarzano) (BM stamp 4 July 62)
1 Tenniel design steel-engraved by John Sadler as frontispiece.
(from the original 1860 edition, here issued in the "Standard Library" series; Sadler engraving exhibited at the RA, 1863).

1864

The Ingoldsby Legends by R.H. Barham.
London: R. Bentley [1863] 1864 (BM, NU) 1864 (VAM)
Tenniel illustrations included in 60 total, others by Leech and G. Cruikshank (4to) (from original 1841 edition in 3 volumes), also 3rd series with memoir by R.H. Barham, illustrated by Cruikshank and Leech only, London: R. Bentley, 1840–47 (BM) (12°); new edition [1864] 1865 (BM) (4to); another edition 1866 (BM); 1870 edition (BM) (with variant frontispiece from 1864 edition); 1874 edition (4to); selected legends in "People's Edition", London: R. Bentley 1881, re-issued 1882 (BM); 88th edition in 3 volumes 1864 (BM); (original drawings exhibited Fine Art Society 1900, nos 27, 112, cf. Appendix III; proofs with corrections in VAM, also proofs in BMP).

1864

English Sacred Poetry of the Olden Time
London: Religious Tract Society 1864 (White, Sarzano)
Tenniel illustrations included with those by P. Skelton, G. Du Maurier, J.W. North, F. Walker, C. Green, J.D. Watson, all wood engraved by Whymper. (Original 1862 edition revised.)

1864–65

Dalziel's Illustrated Arabian Nights' Entertainments
London: Ward, Lock & Tyler, 1864-65 (White), 1865 (Sarzano) (published Oct. 1864, dated 1865)
8 Tenniel illustrations, 87 by A.B. Houghton, 89 by T. Dalziel, others by Millais, G.J. Pinwell, T. Morten, J.D. Watson, E. Dalziel all engraved on wood by the Dalziels.

First issued in weekly parts, later issued in 2 volumes October 1864 (dated 1865). [Not to be confused with London: F. Warne, 1866 (BM stamp 9 Jan. 67) edition, revised by G.F. Townsend, with 16 illustrations, none by Tenniel.] Reissued c.1870 bound from original parts, 822 pages red cloth gilt (corrected proof for "Prince Assad" vol. I, p.357 in VAM). Reviewed in *Athenaeum* (London), 12 November 1864 (no. 1933) p.641.

1865

The following list of editions of *Alice in Wonderland* relates only to those published to 1910, or during Tenniel's lifetime.
Alice's Adventures in Wonderland by Lewis Carroll
London: Macmillan and Co. 1865
42 illustrations by Tenniel, engraved on wood by the Dalziels (original sketches exhibited at the Fine Art Society 1895, cf. Appendix III).
First (recalled) issue of First Edition, red cloth, gilt (7 1/2 x 5") (title on spine, cover picture of Alice holding the pig: back cover same except holding Cheshire Cat); 2,000 copies printed at the Clarendon Press, Oxford, all but 10 copies retained by Carroll, having sent out 46 and retained 2 himself. He also sent 34 to hospitals where all but one copy perished. Edition with inverted 's' in the last line of Table of Contents (cf. W. Weaver, *Papers of the Bibliographical Society of America*, lxv, 1971, pp.1–40; also W.H. Bond in *Harvard Library Bulletin*, x, pp.306–24, 1956; Crutch, pp.29–32).
Second (American) issue of the First Edition, New York: D. Appleton and Co., 1866; Bound in red cloth gilt, covers designed as above (8°); issued in 1,000 copies, new title-page printed at Clarendon Press, Oxford, bound in England.
Third (American) issue of First Edition, New York: D. Appleton and Co. 1866; remaining 952 copies shipped to New York in sheets, bound with new title-page printed in America; binding same as above
Second (First Published) Edition, London: Macmillan and Co. 1866 (BM stamp 14 Nov. 65); bound in red cloth gilt, dark green or pale blue endpapers (8°), cover same as 1865 above First Edition, re-set by Clay from copy no. 42, issued in 2,000 or 4,000 copies.
Reviewed in *Athenaeum* (London), 16 December 1865, no. 1990, p.844.

Additional "ordinary" (i.e. red cloth 8°) *editions* issued during Carroll's lifetime:

> Third edition 1867 (5th–7th thousand) (published Dec. 1866)
> Fourth edition 1867 (8th–9th thousand)
> Fifth edition 1868 (10th–11th thousand) (published February, some copies dated 1867)
> Sixth edition 1868 (commencing 12th thousand) (published October 1868, first electrotype edition, used for subsequent editions until ninth edition)
> New Edition 1870 (25th thousand) (post 8°) (VAM)
> "Hospital edition" c.December 1877 (300 copies)
> Seventh edition 1886 (commencing 79th thousand)
> Eighth edition 1891 (commencing 84th thousand) (reset "Mouse's Tail" p.37 and illustration p.91)
> Ninth edition 1879 (86th thousand) (Carroll's final revised edition, answers

Mad Hatter' riddle p.97, notes whole book was re-set in new type and electrotypes from original woodcuts)
Sixpenny edition 1898 (issued December by Macmillan), also 1899, 1900, 1901, 1902, 1903, 1905, 1906, etc.

Vaudeville Theatre Edition
London, New York: Macmillan & Co. 1899. ("One Hundred Thousand"), bound in cloth (as imitation leather) embossed and gilt stamped.

People's Edition
London, New York: Macmillan and Co. 1887 (issued December 1887, printed from electrotypes), olive green cloth, cover illustration from p.171 in black and red, white endpapers (8°) (price half-crown); reprinted 1888, 1889, etc. (at 2s 6d).

People's Edition: combined version of *Alice* and *Through the Looking-Glass*: First issued in January 1888 (dated 1887) (at 4s 6d); frequent editions thereafter.

American Editions (in Carroll's lifetime)
  Alice partly pirated in *Merryman's Monthly*, 1866–67 (see Crutch p.37)
  New York: D. Appleton 1866 (see entry above)
  Boston: Lee and Sheppard 1869 (second American edition) (8°); also 1870, 1871 editions
  New York: Macmillan 1877 (8°)
  New York: Munro 1885 (8°)
  New York: Lovell 1885 (8°)
  New York: Burt [188 –?] (274 + pages) (12°); also 1896 (274 pages) (12°)
  Chicago: Donohue [188 –?] (16°); also [189 –?] (12°)
  New York: Worthington 1890
  Chicago: Belford 1890 (168 pages) (8°)
  New York: Cromwell [1893] (218 + pages); also 1894
  New York: Macmillan 1895 (12°)
  New York: Hurst 1896 (16°)
  New York: Macmillan 1897 (12°) (reprinted 1898, 1899, 1900, 1901, 1902, 1903, 1904, 1905, 1906, 1908, 1909, 1910)
  Philadelphia: Altemus 1897 (sq. 16°) (184 pages)
  Boston: Lothrop 1898
  Boston : De Wolfe 1898
  (For illustrations by artists other than Tenniel see Crutch p.243)

Alice and *Through the Looking-Glass* combined editions:
  New York: Macmillan 1881 (12°), 1885
  Philadelphia: Altemus 1895 (8°) (347 + pages)
  Boston: Caldwell 1896 (12°) (2 issues)
          Lothrop 1898

Abridged Dutch Edition
Lize's Advonturen in't Wonderland
(Nijmegen): [1874 ?] (Crutch)
Abridged Dutch edition, issued in grey paper case, with 3 pages of enlarged Tenniel illustrations colour lithographed.

German Edition
Alice's Abenteuer im Wunderland von Lewis Carroll. Uebersetzt von Antonie Zimmermann. Mit zweiundvierzig illustrationen von John Tenniel.
London: Macmillan und Comp. 1869
Bound in green cloth gilt (8°); second issue Leipzig: Johann Fredrich Hartknoch 1869 (same binding, 8°); reprinted in facsimile, New York: Dover Publications 1974.

French Edition
Adventures D'Alice au Pays des Merveilles. Par Lewis Carroll. Traduit de l'Anglais par Henri Bue. Ouvrage Illustré de 42 Vignettes par Jon Tenniel.
Londres: Macmillan and Co. 1869
Bound in blue cloth gilt (8°), brown endpapers; 1870 edition Paris: Messrs Hatchette; facsimile reprint, New York: Dover Publications 1972.

Italian Edition
Le Avventure d'Alice nel Paese delle Meraviglie. Per Lewis Carroll. Tradotte dall'Inglese da T. Pietrocola-Rossetti. Con 42 Vignette di Giovanni Tenniel
Londra: Macmillan and Co. 1872
First Italian Edition, first issue bound in orange cloth gilt (8°); also smooth red cloth edition, top edges only gilt (see Crutch p.69)
First Edition, Second issue, Torino: Ermanno Loescher, identical to above, dark blue end-papers.

The Nursery "Alice" Containing Twenty Coloured Enlargements From Tenniel's Illustrations to "Alice's Adventures in Wonderland" With Text Adapted to Nursery Readers By Lewis Carroll.
London: Macmillan and Co. 1889
Tenniel's illustrations wood-engraved and printed by Edmund Evans, cover designed and coloured by E. Gertrude Thomson;
bound in cream-coloured glazed-paper boards, cream cloth, unlettered spine (4to); originally 10,000 sheets printed by Evans but rejected by Carroll, then reprinted as the pictures were "far too bright and gaudy"; 12 copies specially bound with unpriced titles as samples for the American market were received 29 Oct. 1889; 14 uncoloured copies specially bound for presentation in 1889.

Second American issue, New York: Macmillan & Co. 1890 (4,000 copies of rejected sheets sent to America, title dated 1890).
Third (People's Edition) [1891] (6,000 of rejected sheets made up with heading "PEOPLE'S EDITION PRICE TWO SHILLINGS", orange end-papers; by 1896 these were withdrawn from sale and offered to hospitals).
Fourth (cheap) issue [1897] remaining sets of sheets made-up with priced titles, overprinted "PRICE ONE SHILLING", white end-papers.
Second (First published) Edition 1890 (same as first edition except 10,000 copies on white paper, unglazed white paper boards, white cloth spine, white end-papers) (priced 4 shillings).
Second (cheap) issue [1896] (re-issue of People's Edition, with new "PRICE ONE SHILLING") buff pictorial boards, cover with Tenniel's Alice and card shower and title; facsimile, New York: Dover Publications 1966.

See Morton N. Cohen, "Another Wonderland: Lewis Carroll's *The Nursery 'Alice'*", in *The Lion and the Unicorn*, Vol. 7/8, 1983–84, pp.120–26.

1865

Ballads and Songs of Brittany, translated by Tom Taylor from Viscount T.C.A. Hersart de la Villemarque.
London: Macmillan 1865 (BM)
Illustrations by Tenniel ("Nomenoe"); also by Tissot, Millais, C. Keene, engraved on steel, most originally published in *Once a Week* (8°) (see Appendix II).

1866

Legends and Lyrics by Adelaide Anne Proctor. With an introduction by Charles Dickens.
New (tenth) edition with additions, London: Bell & Daldy 1866 (BM) (BM stamp 19 Jan. 66)
19 illustrations including one by Tenniel ("A Legend of Bregenz"), others by W.T.C. Dobson, S. Palmer, G.H. Thomas, L. Fröhlich, W.H. Millais, G. Du Maurier, W.P. Burton, J.D. Watson, J.M. Carrick, M.E. Edwards, T. Morten, all engraved on wood by Horace Harral.
Bound in dark red morocco, gilt (4to).

1866

Touches of Nature by Eminent Artists
London: A. Strahan 1866 (Sarzano) (not traced)

1867

The Mirage of Life by W.H. Miller.
London: Religious Tract Society 1867 (BM, Sarzano) (BM stamp 30 Aug. 1859)
29 Tenniel illustrations engraved on wood by Butterworth & Heath, including 14 full-page and 15 half-page (small square 16°).
Later edition (1884) (8°) (BM , NU).

1867

Tales of a Wayside Inn by Henry Wadsworth Longfellow.
London: Bell & Daldy 1867 (BM) (BM stamp 2 March 67)
3 Tenniel illustrations reused from 1857 edition *Dramatic Scenes* (see 1857 entry) to illustrate "The Falcon of Ser Federigo", total of 15 illustrations by B. Foster, J.R Clayton, T. Dalziel, engraved by the Dalziels, also extra plate by M.E. Edwards.
Bound in brown cloth, gilt stamped (8°).

1868

Gems of National Poetry
London: Frederick Warne 1868
A reissue with altered text of *Juvenile Verse and Picture Book*, 1848 (see 1848 entry).

[1869]

A Noble Life by Dinah Mulock.
London: Hurst & Blackett [1869] (Sarzano, White)
1 Tenniel illustration steel-engraved as frontispiece, in the "Standard Library" series with *No Church* 1862, *Grandmother's Money* 1862, (see 1862 entries) (early 1866 edition un-illustrated in 2 volumes).

1869

Christmas Books by Charles Dickens.
London: Chapman & Hall 1869 (BM) (BM stamp 7 Dec. 1870)
5 Tenniel illustrations from *The Haunted Man* (cf.1848 entry), total of 65 illustrations including work by E. Landseer, D. Maclise, C. Stanfield, F. Stone, R. Doyle, J. Leech.
Bound originally in green cloth gilt; also in red cloth with cover of gilt lettering, black holly interlace design (8°);
Later edition London: Chapman & Hall, New York: Scribner's Sons 1910 (NU).

[1871] 1872

Through the Looking-Glass, And What Alice Found There. By Lewis Carroll, Author of "Alice's Adventures in Wonderland".
London: Macmillan & Co. 1872.
50 illustrations by Tenniel, engraved on wood by the Dalziels, dark green endpapers, red cloth gilt (cover design with Red Queen front, White Queen back) (8°).
Edition uniform with *Alice* (with 'Wade' on p.21); issued in an edition of 9,000 copies on December 1871 (title dated 1872); (Artist's corrected proofs in VAM).

Ordinary (i.e. red cloth, 8°) *Editions:*
   1872 (25th thousand) (omits the "Kings in Chess" diagram, altered in the 1878 edition – see below).
   Hospital edition 1877 (300 copies for distribution to hospitals).
   Second edition 1878 (commencing 45th thousand) (used electrotypes of first edition, rest of the chess diagram correcting 1872 omission – see above).
   Third edition 1887 (commencing 57th thousand) (last printing – 60th thousand – withdrawn by Carroll for inferior quality of illustrations; see S.H. Goodacre, *Book Collector*, Vol. 24, No.2, Summer 1975, pp.251–56)
   Fourth edition 1897 (commencing with 61st thousand) (entirely revised and

re-set, new preface dated 1896; although further re-setting after 1898, this remained the standard edition until the 1940s) (for these see Crutch p.251).
Sixpenny edition 1898.

People's Edition
London, New York: Macmillan & Co. 1887 (issued January 1888, reset and revised)
Olive green cloth (8°), cover reproduces illustration p.109 in black and red, price half-crown; many times reprinted and today regarded as the standard edition.

People's Edition (combined volume with *Alice*): see separate entry under *Alice* above.

American editions (in Carroll's lifetime):
   New York: Macmillan 1872
   Boston: Lee & Sheppard 1872 (first American edition, XII + 224 pages, 8°)
   London: Lee 1872 (second issue of above with error, "wade" for "wabe" in
      Jabberwocky – corrected, but London not Boston imprint, 8°)
   New York: Lowell 1885 (224+ pages, 8°)
   New York: Munro 1886 (230 pages, 8°)
   New York: R. Worthington 1890? (224 pages, 8°)
   New York: Crowell 1893 (230+ pages, 12°)
   New York: Burt 1896 (12°)
   New York: Macmillan 1896 (224+ pages, 12°); also 1898, 1899, 1901, 1902,
      1907, 1910, 1924
   New York: Hurst 1898 (12°)

Combined Facsimile Edition
Recent facsimiles of *Alice* and *Looking-Glass* first editions, with introductory pamphlet by Professor of English, University of Minnesota, London: Macmillan, 1985.

1872

A Thousand and One Gems of English Poetry, Selected and Arranged by Charles Mackay, L.L.D.
London, New York: George Routledge & Sons 1872 (BM) (BM stamp 6 Dec. 71)
3 Tenniel illustrations originally published in *The Home Affections* 1858 (see 1858 entry), others by J.E. Millais, J. Gilbert, B. Foster, and others.

[1873]

The Trial of Sir Jasper. A Temperance Tale in Verse by S.C. Hall.
London: Virtue, Spalding & Daldy 1873 (BM) (BM stamp 1 Nov. 73) [1873] (Sarzano)
1 full-page Tenniel illustration engraved on wood by Butterworth & Heath, others by E.M. Ward, N. Paton, J. Gilbert, G. Cruikshank, B. Foster, G. Doré, engraved by the Dalziels.
First illustrated edition bound in blue 'leaf' grain cloth gilt, 64 pages.

1876

Historical and Legendary Ballads & Songs by Walter Thornbury.
London: Chatto & Windus 1876 (BM) (BM stamp 18 Nov. 75) (preface dated
Oct. 1875)
3 re-published illustrations by Tenniel ("Bacchus and the Water Thieves";
"Zelica dying" from *Lalla Rookh* on p.120: and "Clyte"), engraved by Swain and
the Dalziels; others by Whistler, F. Walker, J.D. Watson, W. Small, F. Sandys,
G.F. Pinwell, T. Morten, M.J. Lawless, A.B. Houghton, E. Poynter.
Printed by Camden Press, (4to).

1877

Mother Goose's Nursery Rhymes. A Collection of Alphabets, Rhymes, Tales
and Jingles.
London, New York: George Routledge & Sons 1877 (BM stamp 20 Sept. 76)
3 Tenniel illustrations from "The Walrus and the Carpenter", in *Through the
Looking-Glass*; compilation of over 300 illustrations, others by J. Gilbert,
Harrison Weir, Walter Crane, W. McConnell, J.B. Zwecker and others.
Another edition 1878 (BM) (8°); also 1879 (BM) (8°) (see next entry).

1878

Mother Goose's Melodies
London, New York: George Routledge & Sons 1878 (BM) (BM stamp 13 Aug.
77)
Another edition of *Mother Goose's Nursery Rhymes*, 1877 (see above) with 150
illustrations, 3 by Tenniel from *Through the Looking-Glass*.

[1878]

Illustrated Works of Shakespeare by John Tenniel.
Unfinished book proposed by Bradbury & Evans, with illustrations engraved on
wood by the Dalziels (proofs now in BMP and Hartley Collection, Boston
Museum of Fine Arts) At least 2 engravings were completed: see Dalziel Record
p.130, "Malvolio" reproduced in Reid op. p.26; discussed p.28)

[1880]

*Jewels Gathered from Painter & Poet: A Selection of Poems Illustrated by the
First Artist.*
London: Cassell n.d. [c.1880]
Tenniel illustrations included with 31 total, others by C.W. Cope, J.C. Horsley,
E. Corbould, W. Dyce, F. Pickersgill, C.H. Weigall, engraved on wood by W.J.
Linton, G. Dalziel, C. Gray.
Bound in green cloth, red, black and gilt design on cover, 87 pages, each one with
rustic-style borders in style of H.N. Humphreys (8 x 6").

1889

The Nursery Alice, 1889, see end of *Alice* 1865 entry above

[1891]

Toilers in Art edited by Henry C. Ewart.
Isbister & Co. n.d. [1891]
80 illustrations in this compilation of essays on various artists, the Tenniel essay
by R. Walker.
Bound in green cloth gilt.

1901

The Life and Works of Sir John Tenniel. By W. Cosmo Monkhouse.
London: H. Virtue & Co. 1901 (BM)
4 full-page plates of previously unpublished paintings and drawings, many text
illustrations from books and *Punch*, all by Tenniel.
A Special "Easter Art Annual" of the *Art Journal*; 32 pages, bound in white
wrappers, yellow and brown decorated cover design (folio).

1906

Royal Institute of Painters in Watercolour, edited by Charles Holme.
Special *Studio* Number 1906
Contains watercolours by Tenniel, Caldecott, Greenaway, etc.

POSTHUMOUSLY PUBLISHED WORK

1917

The Graphic Arts of Great Britain by Malcolm C. Salaman, edited by Charles
Holme.
Special *Studio* Number 1917
Contains Tenniel engravings, pp.6,24; work also by Burne-Jones, Sickert,
Pinwell, Bewick, Calvert, etc.

1922

Drawings in Pen
Special Spring *Studio* Number 1922
Contains work by Tenniel, p.128

1923

British Book Illustration Yesterday and Today by Malcolm Salaman, edited by Charles Holme.
Special Winter *Studio* Number 1923-24.
Tenniel drawings (p.30, plate 95), also work by Doyle, Greenaway, Pissarro, Whistler, Rossetti, etc.

1933

Selections from the bouts-rimés of John Tenniel, from the Library of Miriam Lutcher; introduced by Reginald Harvey Griffith.
[Orange, Texas ?] Privately printed 1933 (NU)
9 facsimile leaves of 5 early Tenniel sketches and verses.

Pencillings in the pit. A.D. 1835
Copy in Harvard Library attributed to Tenniel, (ob.16°), n.d. (not examined)

Appendix II
Periodicals Illustrated by Tenniel

Punch
Single, double-page cartoons, initial letters, humorous "social" illustrations –
Vol.19, 1850 – 2 January 1901 (over 2,000 works total) (proofs, pencil drawings
in VAM, BMP, Boston).

Punch's Pocket Books
Tenniel drew 250 designs for this series of elaborate illustrated volumes issued
1843–81, a counterpart to *Punch's Almanack* (see below); bound in morocco
(priced one half-crown)

> 1st series 1846–53 illustrated with vignettes by Tenniel and Doyle, coloured
> frontispiece fold-out by Leech.
> 2nd series 1854–64 illustrated by Leech, Tenniel.
> [American variant: *Punch's Pocket-Book of Fun*. Being cuts and cuttings
> from the wit and wisdom of 25 volumes of *Punch*. Illustrated by 75
> engravings of S.P. Avery after drawings by Tenniel, Leech, Doyle,
> Cruikshank and others. New York: D. Appleton & Co. 1857 NU].
> 3rd series 1865–81, 17 volumes illustrated by Tenniel, C. Keene, L.
> Sambourne, G. Du Maurier, each with long folding frontispiece, title-page
> coloured by hand (Reid) (proofs in BMP).
> New series 1872–79 as an almanack and variety of useful business informa-
> tion, calendar, cash account and diary (UCLA) (see below).

Punch's Almanacks
Eventually replaced *Punch's Pocket Books* (see above), format was generally a
full-page monthly calendar with jokes, less general information than predecessors. Tenniel took over from Doyle with full-page title-calendar border designs
mainly of astrological and monthly themes.

Punch Special Numbers
> *Records of the Great Exhibition*, 4 October 1851, with 9 previously published
> Tenniel, Leech cartoons, many small cuts, (double-folio) (price 6d).
> *Shakespeare Tercentenary Number*, 1863–64, with Tenniel double-page car-
> toon of Mr Punch in Shakespearean procession; others by C. Keene, G. Du
> Maurier, A.R. Fairfield.
> *Mr. Punch in Paris*
> The Paris International Exhibition, 2 September 1889 (BM), with Tenniel
> cover design of Punch in a balloon, brown on light blue paper, others by Du
> Maurier, Sambourne, Furniss.

Cartoons from Punch by John Tenniel
London: Bradbury, Agnew & Co.
    1st Series   1 – 1864 (BR) 100 plates in 1 volume (4to) (ENG) (VAM selection
                    1853–62)
                   2 – 1864–70 (BM) second volume (21 shillings each)
    2nd Series 3 – 1871–81 (BM)
                   4 – 1882–91 (BM) second volume, both issued December 1894
                   (4to) (BM) (42 shillings each)

Cartoons Selected from the Pages of 'Punch' [by Sir John Tenniel]
London: Bradbury, Agnew & Co. 1901 ('March', BM)
Issued in 2 editions (5 shillings or 2 shillings and 6d) (folio).

The Rt. Hon. W.E. Gladstone, from Cartoons by Tenniel.
London: Punch Office 1878 (BM)
Compilation from drawings originally in *Punch* as weekly political cartoons,
(4to).

Benjamin Disraeli, Earl of Beaconsfield, K.G.. In upwards of 100 cartoons from
the Collection of Mr. Punch.
London: Punch Office 1878 (BM)
Compilation volume like Gladstone above, from portrait drawings by Tenniel,
Doyle, Leech, as political cartoons originally appearing in weekly numbers of
Punch (4to).

Mr. Punch Afloat; the humours of boating and sailing, as pictures by Sir John
Tenniel and others.
London: Amalgamated Press [1898?] (NU).

The Queen and Mr. Punch. The Story of a Reign told by Toby, M.P. Cartoons
by Sir John Tenniel.
London: Bradbury, Agnew & Co. [1897] (BM)
Compilation volume from previously published *Punch* illustrations by Tenniel,
R. Doyle, J. Leech, L. Sambourne.
Bound in pictorial wrappers (4to).

Cartoons by Sir John Tenniel. Selected from the pages of *Punch* [1851–1901]
London: Punch Office [1901] (BM)
Tribute volume to mark Tenniel's retirement from *Punch*, 191 pages (4to).

Mr. Punch's Pageant. 1841–1908. With a Foreword by E.V. Lucas.
London: Ernest Brown & Phillips for the Leicester Galleries Jan/Feb 1909
Souvenir catalogue of the artists of *Punch* exhibition, illustrated by works of
Tenniel, Doyle and others (total 36 illustrations), bound in brown buckram,
limited edition 250 copies (sm.4to)

Mr. Punch's Railway Book
The Educational Book Co. Ltd. n.d. [1890s]
Tenniel illustrations among the 160 total, including those by Phil May, G. Du
Maurier, C. Keene, J. Leech, E.T. Reed, J. Partridge, R. Cleaver, etc.

Sir John Tenniel: *Punch Supplement*, 4 March 1914. Memorial tribute with illustrations.

Illustrated London News

Decorative title heading of medieval figures banked by trellis pattern, for *Illustrated London News Supplement*, 29 November 1851, re-used 13 & 27 December 1851.

Full-page colour wood-engraved illustration to "The Unexpected Guest" by M.L, depicting a cloaked bearded figure discovered by an inn-keeper with a lantern, 19 December 1857.

Once a Week

Volume I 1859

2 July issue:	p.4 initial "T"; p.5 half-page illustration of bearded figure, man kneeling to a white bear to accompany "Audun and his White Bear" ("no less typically 'a Tenniel' than his *Punch* work" – cf. White, p.21); p.21 half-page illustration of Italian couple seated talking.
9 July issue:	p.30 half-page drawing of Sir Gawain escorting his wife to "The Song of Courtesy" by George Meredith.
16 July issue:	p.60 initial "M" to "My Friend the Governor" by R.S.W.
30 July issue:	three-fourth page drawing (wood-engraved by the Dalziels) of fairy woodland, of goblins, children rescued, by Echkhart, to "Echkhart the Trusty", translated from Goethe by Theodore Martin
6 August issue:	p.101 initial "T" to "The White Apron" by H.J. (proof in VAM); p.103 one-third page drawing (wood-engraved by Swain) of soldier directing a woman on battlefield.
27 August issue:	p.170 classical inspired drawing of Eros held by angels, to the poem "Lament for Eros" by B. Aikin.
24 Sept. issue:	p.250 half-page drawing (engraved by Swain) of old king throwing a cup into the sea, to "The King of Thule", translated from Goethe by Theodore Martin.
8 Oct. issue:	p.285 half-page to "A Railway Journey" by Anon. (proof in VAM).
19 Nov. issue:	p.435 initial "M" (Negro on a ship), to "My Friend the Doctor" by F.A.N. (proof in VAM).
26 Nov. issue:	p.446 half-page drawing of horseman in snow to "An Incident of Dartmoor" by John F. Collier (2 proofs in VAM).

Volume II 1860 (January–June)

7 Jan. issue:	p.39 three-fourth page drawing (engraved by Swain) of Roman farmer to "Our Own View of Uriconium" by A.W. (proof in VAM).
28 Jan. issue:	p.98 third-page drawing of man and woman prisoners, p.99 Glaucus and Virginia half-page, p.103 third-page death scene, all three to story "The Pythagorean (A Tale of the

	First Century)" by A. Stewart Harrison (proofs in VAM).
12 May issue:	p.444 three-fourth page drawing of oath swearing scene to "Nomenoe" translated from the Breton by Tom Taylor (proof in VAM) reprinted in *Ballads and Songs of Brittany*, 1865. (q.v. Appendix I).

Volume III 1860 (July–December)

7 July issue:	p.52 half-page drawing (engraved by Swain) of Negro struggling with man in boat to "The Negro's Revenge" by Alfred B. Richards (proof in VAM).
10 Nov. issue:	p.533 half-page drawing (engraved by Swain) of man seated in despair, begins series "The Silver Cord" by Shirley Brooks in 97 chapters (proof in VAM).
17 Nov. issue:	p.561 half-page of two men shaking hands, to " The Silver Cord" (proofs in VAM).
24 Nov. issue:	p.589 half-page drawing of domestic scene, to " The Silver Cord" (irresistibly like a 'Wonderland' picture", cf. White p.21) (proofs in VAM).
1 Dec. issue:	p.617 half-page drawing of thwarted lovers, to "The Silver Cord" (proof in VAM).
8 Dec. issue:	p.645 half-page drawing of couple on board ship, to "The Silver Cord" (proof in VAM).
15 Dec. issue:	p.673 half-page drawing of man and woman, to "The Silver Cord" (proof in VAM).
22 Dec. issue:	p.701 half-page drawing of little girl and man boarding a carriage, to Chapter XIV of "The Silver Cord" (proof in VAM).
29 Dec. issue:	p.1 half-page drawing of man at a desk, to "The Silver Cord". (proof in VAM).

Volume IV 1861 (January–June)

5 Jan. issue:	p.29 drawing of two women on settee, to "The Silver Cord" (proof in VAM).
12 Jan. issue:	p.57 drawing of maid and man fighting, to "The Silver Cord" (proof in VAM).
19 Jan. issue:	p.85 drawing of woman pleading with a man, to "The Silver Cord" (proof in VAM).
26 Jan. issue:	p.113 drawing of men fencing a duel, to "The Silver Cord" (proof in VAM).
2 Feb. issue:	p.141 drawing of Devil confronting a man, to "The Silver Cord" (proof in VAM).
9 Feb. issue:	p.169 drawing of man on knees to maid, to "The Silver Cord" (proof in VAM).
16 Feb. issue:	p. 197 drawing of two women and a man, to "The Silver Cord" (proof in VAM).
23 Feb. issue:	p.225 drawing of man and woman, to "The Silver Cord" ("suggests a *Punch* cartoon", cf. White, p.21).
2 March issue:	p.253 drawing of two children kissing, to "The Silver Cord" (proof in VAM).

7 March issue:	p.281 drawing of two men quarrelling, to "The Silver Cord"; p.294 half-page of fairies leading a mounted horseman (engraved by Swain) and p.295 third-page of a roundel of lovers: both to illustrate "Fair Rosamund" by George Meredith (proof in VAM).
16 March issue:	p.309 two men speaking, to "The Silver Cord".
23 March issue:	p.337 drawing of a man showing a woman a book, to "The Silver Cord".
30 March issue:	p.365 drawing of two women, to the "Silver Cord".
6 April issue:	p.393 drawing of two women, one crying, to "The Silver Cord".
13 April issue:	p.421 drawing of two men at a doorway arguing; p.449 man and woman in a tea shop; p.477 man crying and woman comforts him, all to "The Silver Cord".
4 May issue:	p.505 drawing of a woman gasping at a window, to "The Silver Cord".
11 May issue:	p.533 drawing of a man and woman in a forest; (proof in VAM) p.561 drawing of two women, one on knees pleading, both to "The Silver Cord".
25 May issue:	p.589 drawing of three men, to "The Silver Cord".
1 June issue:	p.617 drawing of a man stopping another, to "The Silver Cord".
8 June issue:	p.645 drawing of a woman alone with a letter; p.673 drawing of a man and woman in garden, holding hands, both to "The Silver Cord",
22 June issue:	p. 701 drawing of a man at a window, to "The Silver Cord".

Volume V 1861 (July–December) – issues not fully dated

pp.1, 29, 57, 85,113,141,169,197, 225, 253 all drawings to "The Silver Cord".

p.659 drawing to illustrate "Mark Bozzari" translated from Muller by Theodore Martin.

Volume VI 1862 (January–June)

1 March issue: p.267 half-page drawing (engraved by Swain) to story "At Crutchley Priory" by T. Speight, depicting weary man at a desk (proof in VAM).

p.379 third-page drawing of knight surrounded by sylph-like women to "The Fairies", a verse by Neville Temple from the German of Heinrich Heine ("a very delicate fancy", cf. White p.21).

p.490 half-page drawing of exotic oriental woman and a man picking berries, to "The Adventures of Prince Lulu" by Anon. (proof in VAM)

p.575 half-page drawing of figures searching in a basket of armour, to "Made to Order" by Anon.

Volume IX 1863 (July–December)

1 August issue: p.154 three-fourth page drawing (engraved by Swain) of artist sculptor, chiselling at plaque, to illustrate "Clyte" by Walter Thornbury (cf. Tenniel painting of the subject, "Pygmalion" in VAM).

Volume X 1864 (January–June)

4 June issue: p.658 three-fourth page drawing (engraved by Swain) of Bacchus lashed to a ship's mast, to illustrate "Bacchus and the Water Thieves" by W.T. (proof in VAM).

Volume III New Series, 1867 (January–June)

Frontispiece to volume, "Lord Aythan" printed in green ink, full-page, depicting a series of figures playing croquet, at a flower show, boating, at the opera, on a picnic, all stretched around a border.

Good Words

February 1862:   p.89 three-fourth page drawing (engraved by the Dalziels) of aftermath of battle, to illustrate verse story "The Battle of Gilboa" (by the author of 'Kelavane') (a "typical" Tenniel illustration, cf. White p.48) (proof in VAM).

March 1863:   p.201 full-page drawing of Norse burial scene, to "The Norse Princess" by Alexander Smith (reproduced in White, op. p.49, a subject "that suits him peculiarly well", according to White) (proof in VAM).

May 1863:   p.344 full-page drawing of Queen Dagmar on the shore, to illustrate "The Wooing and Wedding of Queen Dagmar" translated from old Danish ballads by Mary Howitt (a "rude and uncouth" story, cf. White p.48)

July 1864:   p.552 full-page drawing (engraved by Swain) of a woman haunted by a ghost in a forest, to illustrate " The Way in the Wood", by Isa Green (proof in VAM).

Miscellaneous

Happy Families: A new and most diverting game for juveniles.
(44 cards with illustrations and titles after designs by Tenniel, litho-engravings hand-coloured, 3 x 2)
London: John Jacques & Son, 102 Hatton Garden, c1860 (VAM) (for copies and full set of cards see VAM, also UCLA).

Sharp's London Magazine: 7 February 1846, contains Tenniel illustrations to the story "St. Michael's Eve". (not examined)

Appendix III
Work exhibited by Tenniel

Royal Academy

1837 – (No.688): Captain Peppercull interceding for Nigel with Duke Hildebrand, *vide Fortunes of Nigel*.

1838 – (No.635): The Warrior's Return.

1839 – (No.701): Captain Culepepper's visit to Nigel in Alsatia.

1840 – (No.649): Lord Dalgarno's visit to Nigel at the house of John Christie, the ship chandler, *vide Fortunes of Nigel*.

1841 – (No.817): "Lord Soulis he sat in Hermitage Castle, And beside him old Redcap sly . . . ", etc.

1842 – (No.580): A Study.

1843 – (No.1073): "Willie courted Jenny, Jenny she was shy."

1851 – (No.383): Sketch for a large picture in progress, representing allegorically the great Industrial Meeting of all nations, A.D. 1851. "Peace and goodwill to all men . . . ", etc. – Thomson (exhibited Handley–Reade collection, R.A. 1972, No. A48)

1853 – (No.1227): The expulsion from Eden. "The world was all before them, where to choose their place of rest." – Milton (exhibited Glasgow Loan Exhibition 1878, No.443, lent by W. Wallis).

1873 – (No.715): Sir Rupert the Fearless. ". . . Lurline hung her head, turn'd pale and then red, Growing faint at his sudden proposal to wed . . . " (cf. *The Ingoldsby Legends*, 1864).

(No.1215): Study in chalk and charcoal: "Jesus saith unto her, 'Mary'. She turned herself, and saith unto him, 'Rabboni' . . . " – *St. John*, xx,16.

1874 – (No.857): Peace.

1878 – (No.830): Trial by battle. "Bear–crested, broad, the stark mace-wielder towered . . . " – *Punch*, 1877.

1880 – (No.1330): The White elephant turned "Rogue". Finished sketch for *Punch* cartoon.

Royal Institute of Painters in Watercolour (previously New Watercolour Society)

Tenniel was elected a member in 1874, exhibiting 27 watercolours there.

Suffolk Street (Society of British Artists, later Royal – RBA)

1836:   "The Stirrup Cup" (oil painting, sold to Irish actor W. Tyrone Power)
A further 16 works were exhibited when RBA, from 1887 on.

Fine Art Society

March 1895, Exhibition No.132

177 drawings for *Punch* cartoons and books, catalogue preface by E.J. Milliken, "prices on application", "copyrights in all the exhibits are reserved"; items as follows:

1)   "For the Sake of These" – *Punch*, 11 February 1871
2)   "Demand they Life!" – *Punch*, 12 November 1870
3)   "Her Baptism of Fire" – *Punch*, 28 January 1871
4)   The Red "Mokanna":
     "Here – Judge of Hell, with all its powers to Damn,
     Can add one curse to the foul thing I am!"
                     – *Lalla Rookh*
     – *Punch*, 3 June 1871 (cf. Tenniel's illustrated *Lalla Rookh*, 1861)
5)   The Battle of the Amazons:
     Germania: "Terms? Yes, and for security you will give me three fortresses."
     France: "Never!"
     Germania: "So? Then I *shall take them*."
                  – *Punch*, 8 October 1870
6)   Germany's Ally – *Punch*, 10 December 1870

7)   "Vae Victis!" Paris, 1 March 1871 – *Punch*, 11 March 1871
8)   A French Lesson:
     Britannia: "Is *that* the sort of thing you want, you Little Idiot?"
                  – *Punch*, 8 April 1871
9)   Title-page to *Punch*, Volume CV, 1893
10)   "So the Bright Pomp moves on, Jubilant" – Milton, from *Punch's Almanack*, 1876
11)   Punchius Imperator – from *Punch's Almanack*, 1877
12)   The White Elephant turned "Rogue" (with condensed passage from Sir J. Emerson Tennant's work on the White Elephant) – *Punch*, 8 November 1879
13)   A Lesson – *Punch*, 1 March 1879
14)   The Sphynx is Silent – *Punch*, 15 July 1876
15)   "Will He Clear It?" – *Punch*, 15 February 1873

16) Substance and Shadow – *Punch,* 5 November 1881

17) Empress and Earl; or One Good Turn Deserves Another – *Punch*, 26 August 1876

18) "A Cut off the Joint" – *Punch*, April 19 1890

19) The Red–Tape Tangle – *Punch*, 16 June 1888

20) "The Easter Egg – What's to come out of IT?" – *Punch*, 27 April 1878

21) Title-page to *Punch*, Volume C, 1891

22) Punch's Dream of Things Egyptian:

"So of Khedive and Needle, and Canal,

He thought and dreamed!"

– *Punch's Almanack,* 1878

23) Five sketches from *Alice in Wonderland* (cf. Nos. 67, 160, 168 below)

24) The McGladstone! – *Punch*, 25 October 1890

25) Alexander and Diogenes:

Alexander: "Is there anything I can do for you? Castle? Or anything of that sort? "

Diogenes: "No, only leave me to my Tub!"

– *Punch*, 7 October 1893

26) "A Sail! A Sail!" (*The Rime of the Ancient Mariner*) – *Punch*, 19 August 1893

27) "Separatists": "Douglas . . . Mr.Gladstone. Marmion . . . Mr. Parnell"

Douglas: "The hand of Douglas is his own

And never shall in friendly grasp

The hand of such as Marmion clasp."

Marmion, Canto VI

– *Punch*, December 1890

28) "With the Honours of War" – *Punch*, 13 August 1892

29) "As He'd Like It" (William, Touchstone, Audrey) – *Punch,* 3 October 1891

30–31) The Political John Gilpin:

(The Start) – *Punch*, 2 July 1892

(The Finish) – *Punch*, 23 July 1892

32) "The Champion Shaver!":

Mr. G: "You're a bit bristly, Sir, but I think we shall polish you off before closing time!"

– *Punch*, 16 December 1893

33) Title-page to *Punch*, Volume CVII, 1894

34) "Prometheus Unbound; or Science in Olympus" – from *Punch's Almanack,* 1879 (reproduced in *Easter Art Annual,* 1901)

35) Jupiter Pluvius (A Damp Deputation) – *Punch's Almanack,* 1880

36) Family Ties:

John Bull: "Ain't you going to lend a hand?"

Russia: "Well, I don't know; you see, he's a sort of relation of mine!"

– *Punch*, 17 October 1891

37) Nailed to the Mast – *Punch*, 16 March 1889

38) "Innings Closed":

Rt. Hon. Arthur B.: Don't you think it's time to declare this innings closed?" – *Punch*, 11 June 1892

39)   "Under Which Thimble?" – *Punch*, 28 May 1892

40)   April Showers; or a Spoilt Easter Holiday:
  Trio: "Rain, rain, go away, come again another day!"
             – *Punch*, 23 April 1892

41)   "The Minstrel Boy" – Lord S—l—sb—ry (sings) – *Punch*, 27 May 1893

42)   "The Egyptian Pet" – *Punch*, 21 November 1891 (about Lord Salisbury's speech on the art of self-defence)

43)   Putting his foot in it – *Punch*, 18 August 1894

44)   The *Other* "Westminster Stable" – *Punch*, 21 May 1892

45)   "Pluck'd!" – Parish convict's Cockatoo (sadly): "I've had a doose of a time of it!" (unattributed)

46)   The Rival Horses: Abraham (Mr. G.), Sampson (Ld. S–l–sb–ry), Balthasar (Sir W–ll–m H–re–rt) – *Punch*, 24 February 1894

47)   "Not at Home" – Miss Sarah Suffrage and Eight Hours Bill (angrily) – *Punch*, 14 May 1892

48)   "Advance Australia!":
  British Lion: "Bravo Boys! Swing together!"
             – *Punch*, 14 March 1891

49)   The "White Elephant":
  Pres. Proprietor: "See here, Guvnor! He's a likely-looking animal. But I can't manage him! If you won't take him, I must let him go!"
             – *Punch*, 22 October 1892

50)   The Fisherman and the Genius *vide* "Arabian Nights" – *Punch*, 4 February 1893

51)   "Davy Jones' Locker":
  D.J.: "Aha! So long as they stick to them Old Charts, no fear o' my Locker bein' empty!"
             – *Punch*, 10 December 1892

52)   The Black Shadow:
  Nurse Gladstone: "Uganda! Mashonaland!"
             – *Punch*, 4 November 1893

53)   "Through the Lock" – *Punch*, 29 July 1893

54)   Title-page to *Punch*, Volume CIV, 1893

55)   "A Vision of Utopia" – from *Punch's Almanack*, 1881

56)   "The Coming of Force – Mr. Punch's Dream" – from *Punch's Almanack*, 1882

57)   William the Wheelman – *Punch*, 30 July 1892

58)   The "Point to Point Race" – *Punch*, 6 May 1893

59)   Behind the Scenes. Mr. G. and H–re–rt – *Punch*, 1 April 1893

60)   "Over the Hills and Far Away" – *Punch*, 16 September 1893

61)   "Rule Britannia!" (?) Shade of Cobden (quoting from his own speech at Rochdale) – *Punch*, 26 June 1861

62)   Our Giant Causeway (opening of the new Tower Bridge):
  Father Thames: "Well, I'm blowed! This quite gets over *me*!"
             – *Punch*, 30 June 1894

63)   Unarming:
  "Unarm! The long day's task is done!"
  Antony & Cleopatra, Act IV, sc.xii
             – *Punch*, 18 March 1894

64) "A Little too Previous!" – *Punch*, 1 September 1894

65) Pegasus and his Trainer – title-page to *Punch*, Volume CI

66) "To Triumphe!" – March Past of the Old Year – *Punch's Almanack, 1883*

67) Five sketches from *Alice in Wonderland* (cf. no.23 above, also 160, 168)

68) "A Message from the Sea" – Father Neptune – *Punch*, 23 December 1893

69) A Pilgrim's Progress – *Punch*, 15 April 1893

70) "Will they work?" – Lord Rosebery (aside to McHarcourt, the Gillie) – *Punch*, 20 August 1892

71) The "Forlorn Hope" – *Punch*, 30 September 1893

72) "In a Tight Place!" (John Morley) – *Punch*, 17 June 1893

73) Father William: '"You are old," said the youth . . . ' – *Punch*, 15 July 1893

74) A Lullaby – Nurse G. – *Punch*, 25 February 1893

75) "When Greek meets Greek" – *Punch*, 25 June 1892

76) "Ichabod!" (with verse) – *Punch*, 2 November 1892

77) Mr. Punch's Odd Fisheries Exhibition – *Punch's Almanack, 1884*

78) Punchius Claudian! The Benefactor of the Centuries – *Punch's Almanack, 1885*

79) "Mischief!" – *Punch*, 28 January 1893

80) Uncle Toby and Widow Wadman (modern Ulster version after C.R. Leslie, RA's picture) – *Punch*, 22 April 1893

81) "Taking a 'Breather'" – Grand Old Miner – *Punch*, 29 April 1893

82) The Snow Man – *Punch*, 14 January 1893

83) "The Missing Word" (?) (based on agricultural conference) – *Punch*, 17 December 1892

84) The New "Queen of the May" – *Punch*, 30 April 1892

85) "Back!" – *Punch*, 10 September 1892

86) Trying her Strength – Md. La Republique – *Punch*, 2 September 1893

87) The Telephone Cinderella; or, Wanted, a Godmother – *Punch*, 2 April 1892

88) Crossing the Bar (verse by Tennyson) – *Punch*, 15 October 1892

89) The Young Pretender – Md. La Republique – *Punch*, 22 September 1894

90) "Putting on the Hug" – *Punch*, 17 September 1892

91) (no title) – *Punch*, 14 January 1892

92) Reckoning without their Host – *Punch*, 7 May 1892

93) The New Passenger – *Punch*, 5 January 1895

94) Our Own Ambassador (Punch to Columbia) – *Punch*, 20 May 1893

95) "Wigs on the Green!" or, The Friends of United Ireland (?) – *Punch*, 15 September 1894

96) Pan the Poster (figure of Pan chuckling) – *Punch*, 24 September 1892

97) Closed for Alterations and Repairs – *Punch*, 9 July 1892

98) Mr. Punch's Celebration of Queen Victoria's Coming Jubilee – from *Punch's Almanack, 1886*

99) The "Maske" of Momus: A New Year's "Revel" – from *Punch's Almanack, 1888*

100) "Vested Interests" – *Punch*, 20 October 1894

101) The Poor Victim – *Punch*, 26 August 1893

102) "The Light Fantastic!" (The Sagacious Elephant – Sir Bill in his "Thrilling Act") – *Punch*, 16 February 1895

103) Title-page to *Punch*, Volume CIII, 1892

104) The French Wolf and the Siamese Lamb – *Punch*, 5 August 1893

105) "Hymen Hymenaee!" – *Punch*, 8 July 1893

106) "Come Aboard, Sir!" – *Punch*, 6 January 1894

107) "That Con–foundland Dog!" – *Punch*, 4 April 1891

108) "Unrest!" – *Punch*, 13 October 1894

109) "Waiting for Relief" (Turkey) – *Punch*, 27 January 1894

110) Title-page to *Punch*, Volume CII, 1892

111) A Jubilee Pageant (Mr. Punch's design for a wall painting – entrance hall "Imperial Institute") – from *Punch's Almanack,* 1887

112) New London. Mr. Punch's design for a Grand Historical–Allegorical–Almanaical Picture – "The old order changeth, yielding place to new" – Tennyson – from *Punch's Almanack,* 1889

112A) The Modern Medusa – *Punch*, 9 December 1893

113) "L'Union fait La–*Farce!*" – *Punch*, 21 October 1893

114) "A Stiff Job" (Gladstone) – *Punch*, 11 February 1893

115) "Putting Off" (Gladstone) – *Punch*, 25 March 1893

116) In the Paddock (Mr. P. and Lord Rosebery) – *Punch*, 9 June 1894

117) May 10, 1893 (with altered Keats verse) – *Punch*, 13 May 1893

118) Entering the Lists – "From spur to plume a star of Tournament" – Tennyson – *Punch*, 17 March 1894

119) The Knight and the Jester – Sir Rosebery – *Punch*, 24 March 1894

120) "All the Difference" (Rosebery and Harcourt) – *Punch*, 19 May 1894

121) The Handy Boy! (The Missis) – *Punch*, 25 November 1893

122) The Old Woman and her Pig (Home Rule) – *Punch*, February 1893

123) Mr. Punch appears at the Carnival of Nations (with verse – Tennyson's "Ulysses") – from *Punch's Almanack,* 1890

124) Punchius Phoebus, the Great Universal Hypnotiser ("He who must be obeyed!" – A Transformation Scene) – from *Punch's Almanack,* 1891

125) "Squared!" (meeting in Trafalgar Square) – *Punch*, 29 October 1892

126) Bold Robin Hood – *Punch*, 5 May 1894

127) Counting the Catch (Rosebery and Harcourt) – *Punch*, 25 August 1894

128) "A Contented Mind – " (Sir W. Harcourt in scene from *As You Like It*) – *Punch*, 16 June 1894

129) "A Outrance!" (knights jousting):
    "Sir Vernon ye Challenger striketh ye shield of ye Chief Opponent (who blazons on a Field Vert, three beacons flammant tinsel, for Beaconsfield. Crest – a flight of rockets ascendant). Motto – 'Peace with Honour'".
                                    – *Punch*, 18 October 1879

130) Hamlet and the Skull (Sir W. Harcourt) – *Punch*, 12 May 1894

131) Falstaff's Fix – *Punch*, 26 May 1894

132) "Younger than Ever!" – *Punch*, 5 March 1892

133) "All's Well!" (British Lion and Russian Bear) – *Punch*, 1 December 1894

134) "Vive la Republique" – *Punch*, 7 July 1894

135) Turning the Tables – *Punch*, 26 September 1891

136) "What will he do with it?" (a staring Russian peasant) – *Punch*, 10 October 1891

137) Confidences (J. Bull to John Crapaud) – *Punch*, 10 February 1894

138) The Untamed Shrew; or, Wanted a Petruchio (verse from Shakespeare) – *Punch*, 26 January 1895

139) The Road to Ruin – *Punch*, 5 November 1892

140) "Safe Bind, Safe Find!" (Sergeant de Ville) – *Punch*, 19 November 1892

141) Kathleen and Petruchio (Shakespeare Balfourised) – *Punch*, 12 December 1891

142) Between the Rounds – *Punch*, 11 March 1893

143) The Assault!! – *Punch*, 18 March 1893

144) The Attack on the 'Capital' – *Punch*, 6 February 1892

145) A Gift from the Greeks (Rt. Hon. Arthur –) *Punch*, 27 February 1892

146) Springtime in Leap Year (Ld. Salisbury) – *Punch*, 26 March 1892

147) Tuning the Harp – *Punch*, 1 October 1892

148) "A Bicycle Built for Two" (Mr. H. Fowler in Parish Council Bill) – *Punch*, 2 December 1893

149) Mr. Punch's World Fair – from *Punch's Almanack*, 1892

150) Venice–on–Thames ("The baseless fobin of a vision" – Shakespeare) – from *Punch's Almanack*, 1893

151) "Short 'anded" Mrs. Halsby – *Punch*, 30 January 1892

152) "After You!" – *Punch*, 24 October 1891

153) A Very 'Dark Horse' (jockeys) – *Punch*, 4 June 1892

154) The Coming of Arthur (Pan and Disraeli) – *Punch*, 20 February 1892

155) Lying in Wait – *Punch*, 2 June 1894

156) A Friend in Need – *Punch*, 21 July 1894

157) A Fair Exchange:
    Uncle Sam: "See here, Umberto! Give us back your 'minister' and take away that darn'd 'Mafia', and we'll call it a square deal!"
    – *Punch*, 11 April 1891

158) Mr. Punch in Fairyland – A Midsummer Night's Dream ("Weaving spiders, come not here, Beetles black approach not near" – Shakespeare) – from *Punch's Almanack*, 1894 (reproduced *Punch Supplement* 1914, p.13)

159) Mr. Punch's Jubilee Pageant – *Punch*, July 1891

160) Five sketches from *Alice in Wonderland* (see also nos 23,67)

161) "Winding 'em up" – *Punch*, 27 October 1894

162) The Stormy Petrel! – *Punch*, 12 August 1893

163) The Figure Eight (J. Burns) – *Punch*, 20 January 1894

164) The New Monitor – *Punch*, 9 January 1892

165) Little Master Minority (Chamberlain) – *Punch*, 28 October 1893

166) A Touching Appeal – *Punch*, 12 November 1894

167) Punch's "Walpurgis Night" (Faust) – from *Punch's Almanack*, 1895

168) Five sketches from *Alice in Wonderland* (see also nos 23,67,160)

169) Jap the Giant-Killer – *Punch*, 29 September 1894

170) "'E dunno where 'e are" – *Punch*, 3 February 1894

171) An Old Offender – *Punch*, 15 December 1894

172) "Shocking Trade Outrage!" – *Punch*, 21 January 1893

173) The Corean Cock-Fight – *Punch*, 4 August 1894

174)   The Chief Mourner (with Tennyson verse) – *Punch*, 7 April 1894
175)   The Parliamentary "Grand National" – *Punch*, 7 April 1894
176)   "Lying Cow" (Boy Blue) – *Punch*, 22 December 1894
177)   "Nobody Cooking!" (from Wolf) – *Punch*, 24 November 1894

May 1900, Exhibition No.214

Drawings for *Punch* cartoons, books, etc., total 161 items:

1)   The Learned Welsh Goat – *Punch*, 23 February 1895
2)   The Pied Piper of Rhodesia (verse parody of Browning's) *Punch*, 10 May 1899
3)   Title-page for *Punch*, Volume CXIV, 1898
4)   The Elephantine Majority (after A. Balfour) – *Punch*, 13 February 1897
5)   "Hold on, John!" – *Punch*, 2 April 1898
6)   "Just Off!" (railway scene) – *Punch*, 4 January 1896
7)   The Great Political Combination Troupe (Salisbury, Balfour, Duke of Devonshire, J. Chamberlain) – *Punch*, 6 July 1895
8)   "Pinned!" – *Punch*, 16 July 1898
9)   "William! Ahoy!" (on Welsh dis-establishment question) – *Punch*, 29 June 1895
10)   "Keeping Him Going" (Colonel Joe and Chamberlain) – *Punch*, 29 January 1898
11)   The New Conductor (A. Balfour's speech) – *Punch*, 22 April 1895
12)   "Money No Object!" (Vulcan v. Britannia) – *Punch*, 29 February 1896
13)   *Punch* title-page, Volume CXV, 1898
14)   The Junior Partner (German Emperor about the Abyssinians) – *Punch*, 21 March 1896
15)   "Far from the Madding Crowd!" – *Punch*, 29 August 1896
16)   The New Star of India (A. Balfour v. G. Curzon) – *Punch*, 20 August 1898
17)   Hercules and the Farmer (old fable, modern version) – *Punch*, 30 November 1895
18)   "God Save the King!" – *Punch*, 21 May 1898
19)   A Coronation Greeting (Peace to the Czar) – *Punch*, 30 May 1896
20)   The Waning of the Honeymoon (A. Balfour, about Irish Land Bill) – *Punch*, 1 August 1896
21)   Seaside Lodgings (Russian Bear in China) – *Punch*, 19 December 1896
22)   The Empty Cupboard (House of Commons agricultural season) – *Punch*, 7 September 1895
23)   Armenia's Appeal – *Punch*, 21 December 1895
24)   "My Friend – the Enemy!" (Greece and Sultan) – *Punch*, 22 May 1897
25)   The New Lot (A. Balfour) – *Punch*, 12 February 1898
26)   "For Queen and Empire!!" – *Punch* 19 June 1897
27)   Four original sketches for *Ingoldsby Legends*, 1864 (cf. book entry, Appendix I, also no.112)
28)   The Elephant Trap – *Punch*, 10 April 1897
29)   "Rescue!" (Bluebeard scene, Turkey, America, England, Russia, France) – *Punch*, 26 October 1895
30)   The "Tricksy Spirit!" (scene from *The Tempest*, Act I, sc.2, Ld.

74) China in the Bull–Shop – *Punch*, 15 August 1896

75) Unrest 1857–97 (Lord Lawrence) – *Punch*, 17 July 1897

76) Something Large and Round – *Punch*, 2 August 1899

77) The Man for the Job! (Jack Tar – Turk) – *Punch*, 12 September 1896

78) "Doth not a meeting like this make amends?" – *Punch*, 26 November 1898

79) The Greek Moth – *Punch*, 27 March 1897

80) The Free Lance! – *Punch*, 19 April 1899

81) Sentinels – *Punch*, 16 April 1899

82) The Bone of Contention (Dame Europe) – *Punch*, 6 March 1897

83) The Duello – *Punch*, 30 April 1898

84) A Boundary Question (J. Bull) – *Punch*, 11 December 1897

85) "Second Thoughts" (Secretary of State for India) – *Punch*, 16 January 1897

86) Holding the Bridge (quote from Macaulay's *Horatius*) – *Punch*, 31 January 1900

87) Tender Mercies! (Dame Europa) – *Punch*, 13 March 1897

88) Two of a Trade (Herdsmen) – *Punch*, 7 March 1898

89) The Horse and the Loaded Ass (from *Aesop's Fables*) – *Punch*, 2 May 1896

90) The Prize Brand – *Punch*, 14 May 1898

91) "Enough!" – *Punch*, 1 May 1897

92) "Pretty Dick!" (Balfour speech about US and President Monroe) – *Punch*, 8 February 1896

93) A National Question – *Punch*, 9 October 1897

94) Financial Relations – *Punch*, 26 February 1896

95) Plain English (J.B., French explorer) – *Punch*, 5 March 1898

96) The Sooner the Better – *Punch*, 17 August 1895

97) The Crisis!!!! (Salisbury and the East) – *Punch*, 24 April 1897

98) Jonathan's Latest (about Columbus) – *Punch*, 23 May 1896

99) His Strongest Witness – *Punch*, 16 August 1899

100) "A Free Hand!" – *Punch*, 9 August 1899

101) "Ready for Anything!" (J. Bull and Lord Salisbury) – *Punch*, 12 November 1898

102) A Stiff Course – *Punch*, 23 January 1897

103) One Touch of Nature – *Punch*, 4 July 1896

104) The Slave of Duty! (J. Bull about Crete) – *Punch*, 24 September 1898

105) Giving him a lift. – *Punch*, 12 March 1898

106) Warned Off. – *Punch*, 22 February 1899

107) Flora de Cuba (Uncle Sam and Cuba) – *Punch*, 30 July 1898

108) Saved. (Greek freedom) – *Punch*, 19 February 1898

109) On the "Quay Vive"! – *Punch*, 22 January 1898

110) "You go first." – *Punch*, 20 March 1897

111) Our New Knight-Hospitalier – *Punch*, 20 February 1897

112) "The Tragedy" (original sketches for *Ingoldsby Legends*, 1864, see also no.27)

113) "The Pity of It!" (version of *Othello*, about S. Africa) – *Punch*, 16 May 1896

114) After the first Grip (A. Balfour) – *Punch*, 15 February 1899

115) Open at Last (Russian bear) – *Punch*, 23 August 1899

116) "Three's Company, Two's None" – *Punch*, 11 June 1898

117) The New Postillion (Md. La France) – *Punch*, 1 March 1899

118) After the Trial – *Punch*, 20 September 1899

119) "Men were Deceivers ever!" (France, Italy) – *Punch*, 3 December 1898

120) Wanted to Know (King of Siam v. Punch) – *Punch*, 14 August 1897

121) Honour à la Russe (British lion, Russian bear) – *Punch*, 7 May 1898

122) A Gloomy Prospect (Balfour) – *Punch*, 6 November 1897

123) *Punch* title-page, Volume CXVII, 1899

124) No Reasonable Offer Refused – *Punch*, 11 July 1896

125) The New Man (William Harcourt) – *Punch*, 1 February 1899

126) The Sinews of War (J. Bull) – *Punch*, 18 October 1899

127) Diogenes–Morley – *Punch*, 25 January 1899

128) Another "Pin-prick"!! (Lord Salisbury) – *Punch*, 18 January 1899

129) The New Canute – *Punch*, 25 June 1898

130) His first appearance – *Punch*, 31 December 1898

131) At Westminster Hall 1795–1897 – *Punch*, 6 February 1897

132) The Dead-lock – *Punch*, 7 December 1895

133) Harcourt's Pastoral (with Herrick verse) – *Punch*, 8 February 1899

134) Sold! – *Punch*, 15 October 1898

135) Dogs of War – *Punch*, 21 June 1899

136) To Those It May Concern (Jack Tar) – *Punch*, 1 November 1899

137) The War Planet – *Punch*, 6 September 1899

138) Moral Suasion – *Punch*, 31 May 1899

139) Britannia Consolatrix – *Punch*, 8 November 1899

140) A Word to the Un-wise (J. Bull) – *Punch*, 4 October 1899

141) The Smile that Failed – *Punch*, 14 June 1899

142) Advancing – *Punch*, 29 November 1899

143) Standing By – *Punch*, 9 April 1898

144–45) Khartoum! – *Punch*, 26 January 1885; 17 September 1898

146) In the Desert! (Gen. Gordon to J. Bull) – *Punch*, 28 March 1896

147) Jonathan Jingo! – *Punch*, 1 February 1896

148) Reserved Force! (J. Bull & Lord Wolseley) – *Punch*, 15 November 1899

149) Kruger's Vision (from *Macbeth*) – *Punch*, 25 October 1899

150) Home Defence – *Punch*, 14 February 1900

151) The Sullied White Flag (John Bull) – *Punch*, 20 December 1899

152) Hanging Together (Lord Salisbury) – *Punch*, 24 January 1900

153) Plain English (John Bull) – *Punch*, 11 October 1899

154) Full of Resource (President Kruger) – *Punch*, 14 March 1900

155) Bull-baiting – *Punch*, 19 March 1898

156) A Handsome Offer (Boer War) – *Punch*, 21 March 1900

157) Pocket v. Sentiment (French and German Rand Shareholders) – *Punch*, 28 March 1900

158) The Boer at Bay – *Punch*, 5 July 1899

159) "Bravo, bobs!" – *Punch*, 28 February 1900

160) Compliments of the Season (Father Christmas) – *Punch*, 27 December 1899

161) "Who said 'Dead'?" – *Punch*, 7 March 1900

Leicester Galleries, London

"Mr. Punch's Pageant", January–February 1909, a selection of original drawings for *Punch*, 1841–1908. Tenniel exhibited several including his first *Punch* drawing (initial "L" of horse and rider, which was "one of the exhibits . . . that attracted most attention", according to *Punch Supplement* 1914, p.3); for illustrated catalogue see Appendix II.

White City

Tenniel sent some drawings to a *Punch* exhibition here, about August 1911, at the request of the *Punch* publisher Lawrence Bradbury.

Posthumous exhibitions

Tenniel works appeared at various venues including:

Fine Art Society, London, Autumn 1914. Tenniel and Linley Sambourne proofs and drawings for *Punch* cartoons, illustrating "Punch and the Prussian Bully".

Manchester City Art Gallery 1932

Ottawa – National Gallery of Canada 1935

"Tenniel's Alice", Exhibition at Harvard University, Cambridge, Massachusetts, 1978 (illustrated catalogue published, Harvard College Library, Metropolitan Museum, NY, 1978)

"Fantastic Illustration and Design in Britain, 1850–1930", Rhode Island School of Design, 1979 (illustrated catalogue, Tenniel items nos 218–224)

"Graven Images", Arts Council, Scottish Committee, 1979–80 (Tenniel included in survey of art and wood-engraving)

Appendix IV
Portraits of Tenniel

Oil self–portrait dated 1882, in Aberdeen Art Gallery

Pen and ink drawings by Harry Furniss (two) in National Portrait Gallery, London

Pen and ink self–portrait dated 1889 in National Portrait Gallery, London (version wood-engraved by Swain (?) and published in *Magazine of Art*, 1895, Volume 18, p.201)

Oil portrait by Frank Holl (undated, probably 1880s) in National Portrait Gallery (reproduced in *Easter Art Annual*, 1901, p.32), exhibited Manchester Jubilee 1887, (no.409); also Royal Academy 1889 (no.187), owned by William Agnew.

Pencil portrait (dated 1844) by "G.I.R.", in National Portrait Gallery

Published versions:

Critic, 1898, Volume 33, p.316 (photograph); 1901, Volume 38, p.141

Illustrated London News, 1893, Volume 102, p.689 (photo-engraving)

Magazine of Art, 1892, Volume 15, p.44 (Swain engraving); 1895, Volume 18, p.201 (1889 engraved version listed above)

Vanity Fair, 26 October 1878, Volume 10, issue 521, plate 185 (lithographic caricature by "Spy")

Punch Supplement, 4 March 1914 (small version of 1889 engraved ink drawing, cf. above)

Easter Art Annual, 1901, p.30 (full-length oil portrait by Edward Ward)

Appendix V
Paintings by Tenniel

A list of known paintings other than those exhibited and listed in previous appendices, or reworked from *Punch*:

"Pygmalion and the Statue"
(depicts sculptor embracing a nude statue, subject from Ovid's *Metamorphosis*, Book X), signed, dated 1878
    Watercolour, 23 x 14³/8", Victoria and Albert Museum

"Leonardo da Vinci"
(original watercolour sketch intended for mosaic), signed, dated 1866, stamped 1868
    36¹/2 x 26¹/2", Victoria and Albert Museum

"Figures in a Park"
(depicts garden scene, man reading poems (?) to woman with lute)
    Watercolour, 8 x 10", Huntington Art Gallery (from collection of Albert Fleetwood Varley)

"Eve"
(depicts single figure not unlike an early German religious painting) verse accompanying: "And the Woman said, 'The Serpent beguiled me and I did eat.'" – Genesis III, 13), dated 1882
    Watercolour, 16¹/2 x 6¹/4", Private Collection

"How Gil Blas Arrayed Himself in the Blue Velvet"
(depicts single figure dressing at a leaded window), signed, dated 1881
    Watercolour, 15¹/2 x 10³/4", Private Collection (exhibited New Gallery, also Maas Gallery, London 1979; reproduced *Easter Art Annual* 1901)

"Doleful Dumps"
(depicts cavalier slumped in chair attended by Dame Ursley Suddlechop, secret agent. Verse accompanying: "Jim Vin threw himself into Dame Ursley's great leather chair and declared himself the most miserable dog within the sound of Bow Bells" – *The Fortunes of Nigel*), signed, dated 1888
    Watercolour (whereabouts unknown), exhibited RI, (reproduced in *Easter Art Annual* 1901); cf. Tenniel's earlier RA paintings of Nigel story in Appendix III

"St Cecilia"
(oil study, 1846 (TB) for frescoes based on Dryden, Upper Waiting Hall – "Hall

of Poets" – in House of Lords, later retouched by Tenniel in his retirement) (cf.
Punch Supplement 1914, p.15)

"The Entrance of Queen Victoria into the Queenstown Harbour"
(commission by Lloyd brothers to paint figures for eventual engraving) (cf.
Punch Supplement 1914, p.9)

"Griselda being parted from her child"
(watercolour done by Tenniel in retirement 1907) (cf. *Punch Supplement* 1914,
p.15)

"St George and the Dragon"
(one of a series done by Tenniel in retirement) (cf. *Punch Supplement* 1914, p.16)

Scenes from Shakespeare – watercolour series for planned book
(cf. Appendix I, c.1878)

"The Expulsion"
(painting exhibited in Glasgow, 1878 (No. 443) owned by W. Willis)

Index

Page numbers in *italics* refer to illustrations.
The abbreviation JT refers to John Tenniel